Pro SQL Server
Reporting Services

RODNEY LANDRUM, WALTER J. VOYTEK II

Apress®

Pro SQL Server Reporting Services

Copyright © 2004 by Rodney Landrum and Walter J. Voytek II

ISBN (pbk): 1-59059-423-1

Printed and bound in the United States of America 9 8 7 6 5 4 3 2 1

Trademarked names may appear in this book. Rather than use a trademark symbol with every occurrence of a trademarked name, we use the names only in an editorial fashion and to the benefit of the trademark owner, with no intention of infringement of the trademark.

Lead Editor: Tony Davis
Technical Reviewer: Thomas Rizzo
Editorial Board: Steve Anglin, Dan Appleman, Gary Cornell, Tony Davis, Jason Gilmore, Chris Mills,
    Dominic Shakeshaft, Jim Sumser
Project Manager: Laura E. Brown
Copy Manager: Nicole LeClerc
Copy Editors: Suzanne Goraj, Susannah Pfalzer, and Nicole LeClerc
Production Manager: Kari Brooks-Copony
Production Editor: Ellie Fountain
Compositor: Kinetic Publishing Services, LLC
Proofreader: April Eddy
Indexer: Valerie Perry
Artist: Kinetic Publishing Services, LLC
Cover Designer: Kurt Krames
Manufacturing Manager: Tom Debolski

Distributed to the book trade in the United States by Springer-Verlag New York, Inc., 233 Spring Street, 6th Floor, New York, New York 10013 and outside the United States by Springer-Verlag GmbH & Co. KG, Tiergartenstr. 17, 69112 Heidelberg, Germany.

In the United States: phone 1-800-SPRINGER, e-mail orders@springer-ny.com, or visit http://www.springer-ny.com. Outside the United States: fax +49 6221 345229, e-mail orders@springer.de, or visit http://www.springer.de.

For information on translations, please contact Apress directly at 2560 Ninth Street, Suite 219, Berkeley, CA 94710. Phone 510-549-5930, fax 510-549-5939, e-mail info@apress.com, or visit http://www.apress.com.

The information in this book is distributed on an "as is" basis, without warranty. Although every precaution has been taken in the preparation of this work, neither the author(s) nor Apress shall have any liability to any person or entity with respect to any loss or damage caused or alleged to be caused directly or indirectly by the information contained in this work.

The source code for this book is available to readers at http://www.apress.com in the Downloads section.

To all the angels in my life who worked overtime during the writing of this book:
my awe-inspiring (and patient) children Megan, Ethan, and Brendan;
my wonderful parents Faye and Gene Landrum; my encouraging aunt, Brenda Schofield;
and my favorite person (FP)—Karla Kay.

—Rodney

To all those people whose lives touched mine: Kathi, Martin,
Tracie, Walter, Connie, Martha, David, Don, and Mary.

—Walter

Contents at a Glance

Contents

Foreword

With the explosion in information that is created in companies today, many corporations struggle with how to digest and disseminate relevant information to everyone in an organization. For some users, Excel is the best format. Other users just want a simple web browser to slice and dice their data to get at their nuggets of information. Talking to customers about their reporting needs, like the ones cited previously, was the impetus to create Microsoft SQL Server Reporting Services.

However, the road to what you now know as SQL Server Reporting Services was a long one. We started development on the technology around four years ago. A small team started to build a reporting solution that would revolutionize the way corporations build, deploy, and use reporting. We made some big bets along the way, such as building the solution on the new .NET technologies that were just released in beta around the same time that development started. We also made the solution Web services-enabled out of the box. All of these were risky bets when we made them, but in hindsight, they were the right bets, both for Microsoft and our customers. Customers consistently comment about how they like the flexibility that SQL Server Reporting Services provides them by integrating tightly with .NET technologies, while at the same time giving them interoperability through the product's use of Web services. Further, SQL Server Reporting Services is not only a great enterprise reporting solution, but it also shows how you can build rich applications using the latest Microsoft technologies.

SQL Server Reporting Services was originally slated to ship with the Yukon release of SQL Server, which is now called Microsoft SQL Server 2005. However, after showing early versions of the product to a select number of customers and partners, we got overwhelming feedback that the solution was needed and ready to go early. Based on this feedback, we decided to ship SQL Server Reporting Services as an additional component of SQL Server 2000. So far the response to SQL Server Reporting Services has been nothing short of stellar. You can read the case studies on customers building rich reporting solutions with less time and money using our new product. Partners are building additional tools on top of SQL Server Reporting Services that add new capabilities that we didn't even think of when we originally built the product.

With all this said, you need a good guide to SQL Server Reporting Services. This book is that guide. The authors will step you through the overall architecture and components of SQL Server Reporting Services and take you from building your first report to complex and advanced topics. They bring a wealth of experience, both theoretical and real-world, when it comes to SQL Server Reporting Services. Take advantage of the knowledge and wisdom that you read in this book. Some of it was learned the hard way in the authors' day-to-day implementations of the product. As always, for any feedback or comments you have on the product, please do not hesitate to contact me directly.

Enjoy the book!

Tom Rizzo
Director, Microsoft SQL Server
thomriz@microsoft.com

About the Authors

RODNEY LANDRUM is an MCSE working as a systems engineer, DBA, and data analyst for a software development company in Pensacola, Florida that specializes in applications for the healthcare industry. He writes software reviews and feature articles for numerous magazines, including *Windows & .NET Magazine, SQL Server Magazine, Connected Home, T-SQL Solutions, Microsoft Certified Professional Magazine,* and *Electronic House.*

WALTER J. VOYTEK II (Jim) is the CEO and president of HealthWare Corp., a Microsoft Certified Partner, which specializes in information technology solutions for the healthcare industry. He has worked in information technology for more than 30 years and in healthcare IT for nearly 20 years. He has spoken publicly at several national conventions and also speaks for HealthWare in a variety of settings each year. As the founder and chief software architect for HealthWare, Jim has been instrumental in the design and development of HealthWare's award-winning solutions based on Microsoft technologies.

About the Technical Reviewer

TOM RIZZO, a director of product management for SQL Server, has been at Microsoft for nine years. Before joining the SQL Server team, Tom worked with e-business servers, including BizTalk Server and Commerce Server, as well as Microsoft Exchange Server. He's also the author of three Microsoft Press books about programming solutions on Microsoft's collaboration platform. You can reach Tom via e-mail at thomriz@microsoft.com or through his blog at http://sqljunkies.com/WebLog/Tom%20Rizzo/.

Acknowledgments

I would first like to thank my father who, when I was 13, wanted me to be a systems analyst like him. I didn't know what that was exactly, but I knew that there were computers involved. And computers meant games. When he bought my first Atari, with a 300-baud modem and a Microsoft Basic Programming cartridge, I knew his intentions were good. Fifteen years later, when I had become the modern equivalent of a systems analyst, he didn't stop me from getting an Atari tattoo, though he laughed the whole way through. So, I want to thank my dad for his investment in my future and for his continuing encouragement.

I cannot say enough to thank my mother Faye for her support while I was writing this book and for all other times. Knowing that I had three small children, a full-time profession, and a book to write on a tight deadline constantly made her ask, "How do you do it?" I can say now, "Not without you, Mom!"

I would also like to thank Karla, who has been a constant source of inspiration and encouragement, keeping me heads-down at the computer when I would rather have been shooting pool. And for understanding while I worked on Chapter 2 in the train station in Madrid while on vacation.

Jim, thank you for saying yes to coauthor the book. I enjoyed all the book meetings. You did an excellent job.

I also would like to thank Eric Doverspike, who turned me on to the creative uses of ISNULL. Eric is a dedicated .NET programmer with the sort of sound work ethic that I envy. I wish I could get to work as early as he does. Five-thirty a.m. is sleepy time.

Finally, I would like to thank everyone at Apress who had important roles to play in shaping the book. It's immensely better, thanks to all your careful attention. Special thanks go to Tony Davis, editor, and Tom Rizzo, technical editor, whose thoughtful comments not only helped the book, but made me a better writer. Thanks to Laura Brown, who, under a pressured deadline, kept everything moving swiftly forward and brought it all together. Hats off to the copy editors, Suzanne Goraj and Susannah Pfalzer, who leapfrogged over many hurdles to ensure (er, insure?) the text made sense.

You all did a great job!

—Rodney

I would like to thank Rodney, my coauthor, because without him I wouldn't have been involved with this book at all. We've been colleagues for many years and it has been a pleasure working with him. Knowing also that Rodney was an excellent writer made it an easy choice.

I would also like to thank my father, who introduced me to the world of electronics when I was still a young boy. He primarily dealt with power generation and electronics for aircraft, but had an interest in digital electronics too. He brought a book home called *Digital Computers Made Simple*, and I remember reading it and thinking to myself how exciting it was that a machine could be built and programmed to do so many different things. At that point I knew I was hooked.

His interest early on with computer technology started about the time the Intel 8008 became available. We were able to procure one of these early microprocessors, and it became the basis for the first microcomputer that I ever built. My dad's interest in computers eventually faded, but mine continued, and I built and entered several computer systems in science fair projects throughout my high school years. I eventually competed at the international level.

I would like to thank my wife Kathi, who has put up with the long hours that it has taken to write the book. Not only is she a wonderful companion who understood what it would take to do the book, she has also been a great source of encouragement throughout the entire process.

I would also like to thank my mother, who encouraged me all those years in school when I was participating in the science fairs. To my sister, who always tells me she gave up her computer technology genes so I could have them. And to the rest of my family, friends, and colleagues who supported me and Kathi throughout the writing of this book.

A big thank you goes to HealthWare Corp. and all its employees and customers. They've been instrumental in my career and provided inspiration for doing the book.

Thanks also go to Apress and especially to Tony Davis for giving us the opportunity to write this book. I would also like to thank Laura Brown, Suzanne Goraj, Susannah Pfalzer, and others involved for their important roles in getting this book to print.

Special thanks too to Tom Rizzo, SQL Server product manager at Microsoft, for his technical editing and for giving us a glimpse into the future of Microsoft SQL Server 2005.

—*Walter*

Introduction

At its core, the process of designing reports hasn't changed substantially in the past 15 years. The report designer lays out report objects, which contain data from a known data source, in a design application such as Crystal Reports or Microsoft Access. He or she then tests report execution, verifies the accuracy of the results, and distributes the report to the target audience.

Sure, there are enough differences between design applications to mean that the designer must become familiar with each particular environment. However, there's enough crossover functionality to make this learning curve small. For example, the SUM function is the same in Crystal as it is in Access as it is in Structured Query Language (SQL).

With Microsoft SQL Server 2000 Reporting Services (referred to as SRS throughout the book), there is, again, only a marginal difference in the way reports are designed from one graphical report design application to another. So, if you do have previous reporting experience, your learning curve for SRS should be relatively shallow. This is especially true if you come from a .NET environment, because the Report Designer application for SRS is in Visual Studio .NET.

Having said all this, several differences set SRS apart from other reporting solutions:

- It provides a standard reporting platform based on Report Definition Language (RDL), which is the XML schema that dictates the common structure of all SRS reports. This allows for report creation from any third-party application that supports the RDL schema.

- If you already have a SQL Server license, then SRS is essentially free, because it comes as an add-on to SQL Server 2000 and will be an integral part of the SQL Server 2005 release.

- SRS offers features out of the box that in other products would be expensive additions to a basic deployment. These features include subscription services, report caching, report history, and scheduling of report execution.

- SRS, being a web-based solution, can be deployed across a variety of platforms.

This book was written in parallel with a real SRS deployment for a healthcare application, so it covers almost every design and deployment consideration for SRS, always from the standpoint of how to get the job done effectively. You'll find step-by-step guides, practical tips, and best practices, along with code samples that you'll be able to modify and use in your own SRS applications.

What This Book Covers

From designing reports and stored procedures in Chapters 2–4 to deployment, management, and security processes in Chapters 6–9, the book uses a standard real-world theme to show how we chose to work with SRS. Throughout, you'll find tips and tricks that we discovered while working closely with SRS. The book also covers extending SRS functionality with custom code in Chapter 5.

Following is a chapter-by-chapter breakdown to give you a feel for what the book covers:

- **Chapter 1, "Architecture and Overview"**: This chapter introduces SRS and discusses some of the driving forces behind our company's adoption of this technology. We then take a detailed look at the component pieces of the SRS architecture, including Report Manager, Report Designer, and the SRS report server and databases. We describe how these work together to provide an effective reporting solution. We finish with installation and configuration instructions, and a description of the sample application that we use throughout this book.

- **Chapter 2, "Report Authoring: Designing Efficient Queries"**: The foundation of any report is the SQL query that defines the report data. In this chapter, we examine the query development process and show how to build and test high-performance queries for business reports. We also show how to encapsulate such queries in parameterized stored procedures, to benefit from precompilation and reuse.

- **Chapter 3, "The Report Designer"**: This chapter explores the VS.NET Report Designer in detail, demonstrating the use of all the major embedded elements of SRS within that environment. It shows how to create data sources; how to add report parameters, filters, and expressions; and takes an in-depth look at the layout section for report design.

- **Chapter 4, "Building Reports"**: Having covered query and report design basics, we now walk through the process of building a full business report, including interactive features such as document maps, hyperlinks, and bookmarks.

- **Chapter 5, "Using Custom .NET Code with Reports"**: This chapter shows you how to customize your reports using .NET code, either by embedding Visual Basic .NET code directly in your report, or by using a custom .NET assembly. Each technique, and its pros and cons, is discussed and demonstrated.

- **Chapter 6, "Rendering Reports from .NET Applications"**: This chapter shows how to control the rendering of your reports programmatically in a variety of supported formats, either via URL access or by using the Web services API.

- **Chapter 7, "Deploying Reports"**: SRS provides several means of deploying reports: using the Report Manager interface, via VS.NET, using the rs command line utility, or programmatically using the Web services API. This chapter demonstrates and explains each of these techniques.

- **Chapter 8, "Report Management"**: This chapter examines the many facets of SRS report management, including content management, performance testing, report execution auditing and control, and error logging. It shows how to perform each of these tasks effectively, using built-in tools such as Report Manager and command-line utilities, as well as using custom .NET management tools.

- **Chapter 9, "Securing Reports"**: There are several important components of SRS security, namely data encryption, authentication and user access, and report auditing. This chapter shows how to use each of these components in a secure SRS deployment.

- **Chapter 10, "Business Intelligence and SRS"**: In our work, we found that by integrating SRS with many of the other components of the business intelligence (BI) platform, we were able to provide all the necessary information to our employees wherever they were and whenever they needed it, thus dramatically improving our overall business strategy. In this chapter we demonstrate how we set about integrating SRS with BI components such as CRM, SharePoint Portal Server, and Analysis Services.

- **Chapter 11, "Future SRS"**: In this final chapter, we take a brief look at some of the new features coming in SRS 2005, and how they might impact your report design, creation, deployment, and management. We discuss the benefits to be derived from integrating SRS into SQL Server Management Studio and Business Intelligence Development Studio, as well as new end-user reporting tools such as the ActiveViews ad-hoc query tool.

In each chapter, we've tried to touch on every aspect of SRS in enough detail to allow you to translate the concepts into your own applications. Our intention was to provide truly practical, useful information on every page and not to parrot material that's adequately covered in Books Online (BOL). To that end, concepts such as cascading parameters and designing reports with hierarchical data using the LEVEL function aren't covered, because adequate explanations and worked examples can be found in BOL.

We believe that this book will serve as both an introduction and step-by-step guide through many common tasks associated with SRS, while offering concepts and solutions that we've been developing ourselves for our own applications.

Who This Book Is For

We coauthored the book with the intention of demonstrating the use of SRS from multiple vantage points. As a data analyst and engineer, Rodney goes through the report design and deployment processes using standard SRS tools such as Report Designer and Report Manager. As a .NET developer, Jim takes on the role of showing how other developers can extend SRS by creating custom Windows Forms applications, as he explains the SRS programming model.

Source Code

In this book, we use a subset of a real database designed for a healthcare application that we developed. You can find that prepopulated database (which we named Pro_SRS, for the book), along with the data mart database and cube file used in Chapter 10, the completed RDL files, queries, stored procedures, and .NET application projects in the Downloads section on the Apress website (http://www.apress.com).

CHAPTER 1

■ ■ ■

Architecture and Overview

When Microsoft announced in 2003 that it was going to release SQL Server Reporting Services (SRS) as a SQL Server 2000 add-on, there was a frenzy of excitement. The product was originally slated for release with SQL Server 2005, formerly codenamed "Yukon," so the early release was a welcome event for many. Our software development company decided to embrace SRS early on, and was fortunate to work with Microsoft during the beta phases. In January 2004, the month SRS went RTM (Released To Manufacturing), we deployed it immediately. We intended to migrate all our existing reports, which had been developed in as many as five reporting applications and platforms over the past ten years. We can sum up the reason for the seemingly rapid decision in one word: standardization. We needed to provide a standard reporting solution to our customers, just as Microsoft wanted to create an industry standard with the Report Definition Language (RDL), which is the Extensible Markup Language (XML) schema that dictates the common structure of all SRS reports. Even in a version 1 product, SRS delivered almost all the features that we needed from day one. Thanks to its extensibility, we could programmatically add other features that weren't directly supported in version 1. In addition, Microsoft has committed to enhancing SRS over time. For example, Service Pack 1 of SRS is out, and SQL Server 2005 will include a number of SRS enhancements.

Benefits of SRS

As we said, we knew that we would adopt SRS almost from the get-go. There were several key benefits of migrating to SRS that we initially considered for ourselves and for our customers:

- **Standard platform:** In addition to providing a standard realized with the RDL, our development teams had been using Visual Studio .NET as their main development environment. Because SRS reports are currently developed within this platform, we wouldn't need to purchase additional development software. Our clients would only need to purchase a low-cost edition of a designer, VB.NET for example, to gain the benefit of developing custom reports themselves.

- **Cost:** SRS is an add-on to SQL Server 2000 and will be an integral part of the SQL Server 2005 release. So, the entire platform comes with no additional cost to companies that already own a SQL Server license.

- **Web-enabled:** Because SRS is a web-based reporting solution, you can deploy reports across a variety of platforms and make them accessible from many locations.

- **Customizable:** SRS is a .NET Web service, and as such you can access it programmatically to extend the delivery of reports beyond the browser. As .NET programmers, we knew that we would want to build custom applications to render reports where we could control the look and feel of the report viewer. We show one such application in Chapter 6 on report rendering.

- **Subscriptions:** Having the ability to have reports delivered through e-mail or a file share and processed during off-peak hours, which was offered with SRS subscription abilities, was a huge advantage for us and our clients. We show how to set up two different kinds of subscriptions, standard and data-driven, in Chapter 8.

As you'll see, SRS is a full reporting solution that encompasses many professional levels, from report design to database administration. In many organizations, especially small to medium sized ones, information technology (IT) professionals are asked to wear many hats. They write a query and design a report in the morning, perform database backups or restores in the afternoon, and update all the systems before heading home. Fortunately, during our deployment of SRS to our clients and internally for our software development company, I (Rodney) have worn those hats daily. I have been entrenched in every deployment phase. By developing efficient stored procedures, designing reports, testing security, and maintaining deployed reports as a content manager, I have witnessed the day-to-day operation of SRS from many perspectives. In addition to those roles, I have also been responsible for our company's overall strategy for building solutions to transform and analyze the data that's gathered through both our and other third-party applications. To that end, an essential part of my job was rolling SRS into an overall business intelligence (BI) solution that incorporates disparate data sources, front-end applications such as Microsoft Excel, and document management systems such as SharePoint Portal Server. We'll dive into the details of that integration project in Chapter 9, which is devoted entirely to BI.

There's another world to SRS, a world that an administrator who uses standard management tools doesn't typically witness. That is the world of the software developer who can extend and control SRS programmatically, building custom report viewers and deployment applications. In this book, as we work through each step of building a reporting solution for healthcare professionals, we'll demonstrate how an administrator might accomplish the task with built-in tools, as well as how a developer can create an application to provide enhanced functionality.

Green Bar, Anyone?

Before we begin our breakout of the overall SRS platform, I'd like to share a personal experience that I think might illustrate one of the many challenges that SRS addresses. That is creating an environment where the method in which the data is delivered to users is often as crucial as the data itself. Users want easy and fast access to data in an intuitive but powerful interface. SRS overcomes this challenge of changing the way users work by delivering reports in applications that are already familiar to most every user: browsers and e-mail clients.

Jumping back in time a few years—well, ten years—when I started down the path of what is now described correctly as IT, I took a job as an intern in the government sector. I should have known by the banner over the door to my interviewer's office that read Data Processing Center that I wasn't exactly stepping into the modern digital age. I was offered the lowly position of mainframe computer operator, which I took eagerly despite the fact that I knew I would be eating boiled eggs and tomato soup for the foreseeable future. On the first day, I was introduced to two assemblages of technology that my father, who also worked in data processing (DP) introduced me to in the early 1980s: a vault full of reel-to-reel magnetic tapes and box after box of green bar paper. In time I came to both appreciate and loathe the rote task of printing thousands of pages every night of reports that I knew would only be scanned by a few people and then discarded. I say that I appreciated the task because every so often I would be visited by a programmer who wrote the report. We'd talk about the time it took to write the report, why he constantly had to update the reports, and who was asking for the updates (typically a high official). We would also commiserate about the fact that generating such a report each night was a complete waste of valuable resources. I could only hope he meant me.

One day I heard a buzz that my beloved Data Processing Center was being absorbed by another government body. I learned, as many did, that there were to be sweeping changes that would affect my position. New supervisors came in, surveying the inherited archaic technology landscape. What happened was astounding in many regards. The banner over my former boss's door was the first to be altered; with the stroke of a paint brush we were now Information Resources. The new regime didn't feel that "night computer operator" was a good title for me anymore. In less than the time it takes to print 3,000 checks I became a "data specialist," and I could now eat spaghetti with real meat sauce.

I had been biding my time awaiting a new system that I could take the reins on, move into an administrative position, stop hauling the green bar. A new system was purchased and I was elated. Finally, I thought, they'll bring in a modern networked system that will have online report delivery technologies. One day the hardware was delivered and I looked on in awe at my—technically their—new IBM RS6000. Fortunately for everyone except me, the new printer that was delivered with it could hold the exact same green bar paper that we had stockpiled for years to come.

The preceding story demonstrates that often the benefits of new technologies go unrealized because of the habitual nature of the workers who are forced to adopt that new technology. Users at the Data Processing Center were used to receiving their 200-page reports each morning and tossing them by noon. If the reports weren't discarded, they were bound, bundled, and hauled to the basement for future reference. It had been done that way for years. It seemed that only the people who appreciated the work that went into the reports—the programmers and computer operators—understood the ridiculousness of the practice.

In the ensuing years, I held a number of positions, all of which involved delivering data in myriad reporting technologies, using a plethora of data stores. One day it was scrubbing data from Indexed Sequential Access Method (ISAM) files; the next day saw me pulling data from a Unix-based Oracle database. With the blessing of Open Database Connectivity (ODBC), data was accessible in almost any format. Eventually I began work with Microsoft SQL Server in version 6.5, and have remained there through versions 7.0 and 2000. Through the years, I've been fortunate to be able to work with the applications that Microsoft has released to make my job significantly easier while offering much in the way of data delivery. A notable example was the introduction of Online Analytical Processing (OLAP) Services in 7.0, which became Analysis Services in 2000. However, one item that always seemed just out of reach was a client application that could be used to effectively deliver the data contained within these new technologies. Sure, Excel could tap into OLAP cubes and Data Analyzer was a promising addition, but these were expensive applications that required local installations. Surely a web-enabled reporting application would be available soon, right?

This leads us to the present, where SRS has been unveiled as a prime contender in the reporting market space, seeking standardization. SRS is a much anticipated and welcomed release for the SQL Server community for this purpose. More importantly, it provides a cost-effective alternative to other reporting technologies that have heretofore been the standard.

SRS Architecture

You've heard the expression that the devil is in the details. We'll be drilling into those details throughout the book, right down to the very data packets that SRS constructs, as we explore each aspect of SRS from design to security. For now, let's pull back to a broader vantage point—the 10,000 foot view—and look at the three main components that work together to make SRS a true multi-tier application: client, Web service, and SQL Server storage databases. Figure 1-1 shows the conceptual breakdown of the three component pieces. In the illustration, the data source and SRS databases, ReportServer and ReportServerTempDB, are different logical endpoints, but could physically be located on the same SQL Server, assuming the data source were a SQL Server database. The data source could be any supported data provider, such as Lightweight Directory Access Protocol (LDAP), Oracle, or Analysis Services. Though it's possible to configure a single server to be the SRS web and database server as well as the data source server, it isn't recommended unless there's a small user base. We'll test the performance of our SRS configuration and build a small web farm, post installation, in Chapter 8.

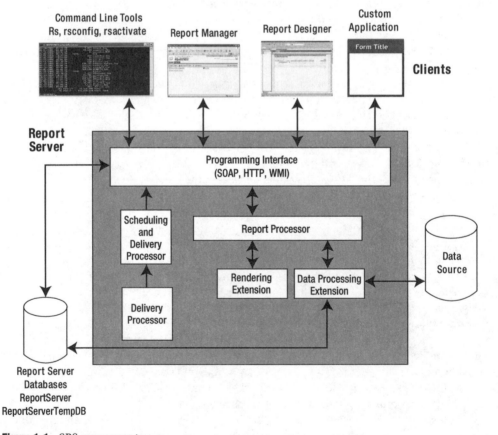

Figure 1-1. *SRS components*

Client Applications

SRS includes a number of client applications that use the SRS programming interface, namely its Web service Application Programming Interfaces (APIs) and URL access methods to provide front-end tools for users to access SRS reports and report objects. These tools provide management, configuration, and report rendering functionality. The tools are as follows:

- **Report Manager:** This browser-based application ships with SRS and provides a graphical interface for users who view or print reports or manage report objects for their workgroups or departments. We cover Report Manager in detail in Chapter 8 on managing SRS.

- **Report Designer:** Report Designer provides embedded report design elements in VS.NET for the release of SRS for SQL Server 2000. We introduce Report Designer in VS.NET in Chapter 3 and step through building reports in this environment in Chapter 4.

- **Command line utilities:** You can use several tools to configure and manage the SRS environment, including rs, rsconfig, rskeymgmt, and rsactivate.

- **Custom applications:** These VB.NET Windows Forms and web applications call the SRS Web service to perform such tasks as report rendering and report object management. SRS includes sample application projects that you can compile and run to extend the functionality provided by the main tools listed earlier. In Chapters 6 and 7 we develop our own custom applications: a report viewer and a report publisher.

When thinking of a web-based application, the natural inclination is to think web browser immediately. Truly, the web browser plays an important role with SRS, providing the graphical interface for users who view or print reports or manage report objects for their workgroups or departments.

Report Manager

Within Report Manager, users may render reports, create report subscriptions, modify the properties of report objects, and configure security, as well as a host of other tasks. Users may access the Report Manager application by simply opening their web browser and navigating to a URL in the form of `http://Servername/Reports`. Another browser-accessible location of SRS is the ReportServer root directory, which is where the true power lies. As you'll see, you can pass many parameters to this base address that the report server processes. Figure 1-2 shows the Report Manager application in action, with a listing of reports in a folder deployed specifically for clinicians.

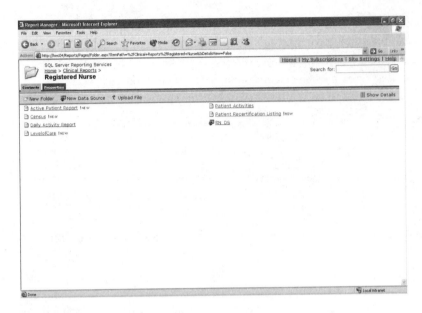

Figure 1-2. *Report Manager web-based application*

The VS.NET Report Designer

The browser is only one of several clients that can use the SRS Web service. In fact, Report Designer, which is embedded in the VS.NET design environment, is a client when it interacts with the web service to deploy reports and data sources. Report Designer offers a graphical design environment that report developers use to produce the RDL files that SRS uses for the deployment and rendering of reports. Because RDL is a defined standard, you can use any design application that supports the creation of RDL files. Other third-party report designers are available, and many more are forthcoming.

By defining the base URL and folder name in a VS.NET report project, you can deploy the RDL files that are created directly to the report server while in design mode. The base URL is of the form `http://Servername/ReportServer`. We'll cover the entire VS.NET design environment in Chapter 3, including most available report objects. We'll also describe the RDL schema that defines every aspect of an SRS report. Figure 1-3 shows the VS.NET design environment, also called an Integrated Development Environment (IDE), with a tabular report loaded in design mode.

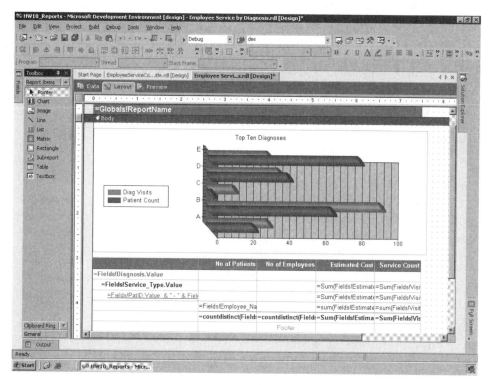

Figure 1-3. *VS.NET design environment*

Command Line Utilities

In addition to graphical applications such as VS.NET and the web browser, SRS provides several command line utilities that are considered Web service clients. The tools have the added benefit of being automated by using built-in task scheduling in Windows. SRS includes four main command line utilities:

- **rs:** Processes report services script files (RSS) that are written with VB.NET code. Because you can access the full SRS API via the code in the script, all SRS Web service methods are available.

- **rsconfig:** Configures the authentication methods and credentials for how SRS connects to the ReportServer database. rsconfig also sets the unattended SRS execution credentials for SRS.

- **rsactivate:** Activates an instance of SRS by creating a unique symmetric key used to encrypt data in the SRS databases. When a server is activated, typically when it joins a web farm as we do in Chapter 8, the SRS Web service is associated to another SRS database.

- **rskeymgmt:** Manages the encryption keys that SRS uses to store sensitive data securely, such as authentication credentials. We use rskeymgmt in Chapter 9.

Custom Clients

The final types of clients are those custom designed to access the SRS Web services. We've built several such applications for our own company, such as a report viewer and report publisher. Third-party commercial applications exist and will be created that provide extended functionality. Microsoft also has plans to extend the current version of SRS to make ad-hoc reporting available through a client application and to provide report controls that you can embed in your Windows and web applications. We'll look at these and many other enhancements in Chapter 11 when we discuss the future of SRS.

SRS Report Server

The SRS report server, where both the SRS Web service and ReportServer Windows service are installed, plays the most important role in the SRS model. Working in the middle, it's responsible for every client request, either to render a report or to perform a management request, such as creating a subscription. The report server itself can be broken down into several subcomponents by their function:

- Programming Interface

- Report processing

- Accessing data sources

- Report rendering

- Report scheduling and delivery

The Programming Interface, exposed as Web service APIs and URL access methods, handles all incoming requests from clients, whether the request is a report request or a management request. Depending on the type of request, the Programming Interface either processes it directly by accessing the ReportServer database, or passes it off to another component for further processing. If the request is for an on-demand report or a snapshot, the Programming Interface passes it to the Report Processor before delivering the completed request back to the client or storing it in the ReportServer database. On-demand reports are ones that are rendered and delivered directly to the client, while snapshots are reports that are processed at a point in time and delivered to the client through e-mail, file shares, or if configured, directly to a printer.

The Report Processor is responsible for all report requests. Like the Programming Interface, it communicates directly with the ReportServer database to receive the report definition information that it then uses to combine with the data returned from the data source.

The current version of SRS supports four data processing extensions to connect to data sources. These are SQL Server, Oracle, OLE DB, and ODBC. When the data processing component receives the request from the Report Processor, it initiates a connection to the data source and passes it the source query. Data is returned and sent back to the Report Processor, which then combines the elements of the report with the data returned from the Data Processor extension.

Finally, the combined report and data is handed off to the rendering extension to be rendered into one of several supported formats based on the rendering type specified by the client (we cover rendering in depth in Chapter 6):

- **HTML:** Default rendering format, supporting HTML versions 4.0 and 3.2.

- **Portable Document Format (PDF):** Format used to produce print-ready reports using Adobe Acrobat Reader. SRS doesn't require that you have an Adobe license to render in PDF, which is a great benefit to customers. All you need is a PDF reader.

- **HTML using the Office Web Components (OWC):** Can be used for rendering reports that are designed to take advantage of the extended features of OWC, such as a pivot table or chart.

- **Excel 2002 and 2003:** Service Pack 1 of SRS supports Excel 97 and later.

- **XML:** Other applications or services can use reports that are exported to XML.

- **Comma Separated Values (CSV):** By rendering to a CSV file, you can further process the report by importing it into other CSV-supported applications such as Microsoft Excel.

- **MHTML:** You can use this format, also known as web archive, to deliver reports directly in e-mail or for storage, because the report contents, including images, are embedded within a single file.

- **Tagged Image File Format (TIFF):** Rendering image files using TIFF guarantees a standard view of the report, as it's processed the same way for all users despite their browser settings or versions.

If the request from the client is one that requires a schedule or delivery extension, such as a snapshot or subscription, the Programming Interface calls the Scheduling and Delivery Processor to handle the request. You can generate and deliver report snapshots based on a user-defined or shared schedule to one of two supported delivery extensions: e-mail or a file share. Note that SRS uses the SQL Server Agent to create the scheduled job. If the SQL Server Agent isn't running, the job won't execute. We'll cover creating subscriptions and snapshots based on shared schedules in Chapter 8.

SRS Databases

Two databases are created as part of the SRS installation: ReportServer and ReportServerTempDB. These databases each serve a distinct purpose, the primary one being ReportServer, which stores all the information related to reports, report objects such as data sources, and report parameters. ReportServer also stores folder hierarchy and report execution log information. ReportServerTempDB's main purpose is to house cached copies of reports that you can use to increase performance for many simultaneous users. By caching reports to a nonvolatile storage mechanism, such as the ReportServerTempDB, cached copies of reports remain available to users even if the report server is restarted. Database administrators can use standard tools to back up and restore these two databases.

An additional database might be added after the initial installation of SRS: the RSExecutionLog database. This database stores more discernable information about report execution, such as the user who ran the report, the time of execution, and performance statistics. We'll cover creating the RSExecutionLog database and discuss report execution logging in detail in Chapter 8.

Installation and Configuration

For the most part, installing SRS is a straightforward procedure. As with most Microsoft applications, you have the ability to install SRS by running Setup or by installing from the command line, passing in installation options. Silent installations, or ones that require no user input, are also supported. When installing SRS from Setup, you can choose which components to install and also make initial configuration settings. You can see the components available when running Setup in Figure 1-4; these include both server and client components.

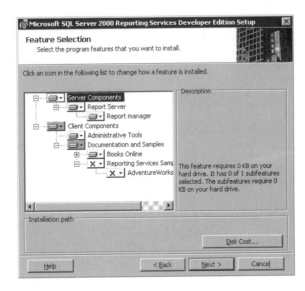

Figure 1-4. *Installation of SRS components*

Server components include the report server and Report Manager. Depending on the edition of SRS that you're installing, you have the option of configuring the installation to connect to an existing SRS database when installing the server components. By choosing this option, the instance of SRS that you're installing joins a web farm of other SRS servers, all using the same ReportServer database. Client components include administrative command-line tools mentioned previously, such as rs and rsconfig, authoring tools that integrate with VS.NET, and documentation and samples.

■**Note** The standard edition of SRS doesn't provide support for setting up web farms. Throughout the book, we'll be using the Developer edition of SRS, which provides support for web farms and for another enterprise feature: data-driven subscriptions.

After you install SRS, you can modify the configuration settings that were chosen during the install in a few ways. For example, you might decide after reviewing performance measures that the report server needs to connect to an existing web farm. You can perform this task using the rsconfig and rsactivate utilities. Another example would be to modify the security settings, forcing the report server to use HyperText Transport Protocol Secure (HTTPS) instead of HTTP to establish secure communications. The final example that's part of the SRS installation is configuring a Simple Mail Transfer Protocol (SMTP) mail server to handle delivery of subscriptions. You can reconfigure these last two examples by altering a value setting directly in a configuration file, RSReportServer.config. We'll cover using these tools, modifying the configuration file settings, and gathering performance measures in Chapters 8 and 9.

Deploying SRS Securely

It needn't be said that security ranks as one of the highest priorities for businesses today. Providing customers and employees with a secure and reliable computing environment is not only good practice, but in many cases like ours, it's a requirement, mandated by stringent federal regulations. In this case, we're speaking of the Health Insurance Portability and Accountability Act' (HIPAA), which requires policies and procedures to be in place to guarantee that confidential patient information is securely transmitted and accessible only by those with authority to view it. To that end, we needed to ensure that the data that we transmit over a network connection, especially the Internet, was encrypted at the source.

SRS is a role-based application that provides access to the objects it stores through the use of defined roles, such as content browsers who may only view reports and report data. The roles that SRS provides are associated with Windows-based login accounts, so SRS relies on Windows as its primary source of authentication.

In this book, we'll cover two deployment scenarios. The first scenario is an intranet deployment using Virtual Private Network (VPN) and firewall technologies to allow access to the SRS report server. The second scenario is an Internet-hosted application that uses Terminal Services to connect securely to an SRS report server. In Chapter 9, we'll step through securing the SRS deployment models with technologies that provide the required encryption levels and user authentication.

Sample Application

Throughout the book, we'll design and deploy a reporting solution and build custom .NET applications for a SQL Server-based healthcare application. It was originally designed as a financial application for home health and hospice facilities that offer clinical care to their patients, typically in their homes. Over the years, more features have been added and the database schema has been altered many times to accommodate the new functionality and capture data that is required. This data is needed not only to perform operational processes such as creating bills and posting payments to the patient's account, but also to provide valuable reports that show how well the company is doing serving its patients. Because these types of healthcare facilities offer long term care, our customers need to know if their patients' conditions are improving over time and an overall cost of the care that was delivered to them.

The database that was ultimately designed for the application consists of more than 200 tables and as many stored procedures. We use a subset of that database here to walk through developing reports that show the cost of care for patients. We use eight main tables for the queries and stored procedures we'll begin developing in the next chapter. These tables are as follows:

- **TRX:** The main transactional data table that stores detailed patient services information. We use the term "services" to refer to items with an associated cost that were provided for patient care.

- **Services:** Stores the names and categories for the detailed line items found in the TRX table. Services could be clinical visits such as a skilled nurse visit, but they could also include billable supplies, such as a gauze bandage or syringes.

- **ServiceLogCtgry:** The main grouping of services that are similar and provide a higher level grouping. For example, all visits can be associated to a "Visits" ServiceLogCtgry for reporting.

- **Employee:** Stores records specific to the employee, which in our case is the clinician or other service personnel such as a chaplain visiting a hospice patient. An employee is assigned to each individual visit that's stored in the TRX table.

- **Patient:** Includes demographic information about the patient receiving the care. This table, like the Employee table, links directly to the TRX table for detailed transactional data.

- **Branch:** Stores the branch name and location of the patient receiving the care. Branches, in our report, are cost centers from where visits and services were delivered.

- **ChargeInfo:** Contains additional information related to the individual TRX records, specific to charges. Charges have an associated charge, unlike payments and adjustments, which are also stored in the TRX table.

- **Diag:** Stores the primary diagnoses of the patient being cared for and is linked to a record in the TRX table.

Figure 1-5 shows a graphical layout of the eight tables and how they're joined.

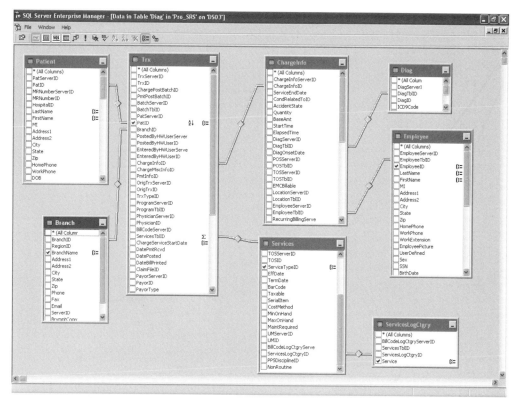

Figure 1-5. *Sample application database tables*

Summary

Chances are that by the time you read this, you'll have already been exposed in some way to SRS, either through online articles, webcasts, newsgroups, or even hands-on use. You might have already deployed SRS and you're at the point of developing and deploying new reports or migrating reports from other systems. This book will serve as both an introduction and a step-by-step guide through many common tasks, while offering concepts and solutions that we've developed ourselves for our own applications.

SRS is a multifaceted, full-featured reporting solution. It spans the professional divide that's typical of a large application that uses multiple services such as Internet Information Services (IIS), SQL Server, Active Directory, e-mail, and security technologies. In the book, we'll approach SRS from each of these professional angles as we build and deploy our healthcare reports and applications. All our technical efforts to learn a technology, design it, test it, deploy it, manage it, and secure it are done for that other important professional: the report consumer. Many of the people who reap the fruits of our labors, the "knowledge workers," are technically savvy themselves, with the ability to drill into and through the data on the reports, export it, e-mail it to colleagues, and ultimately make important strategic business decisions. And for the users who still desire the green bar effect, SRS can handle that too.

CHAPTER 2

■■■

Report Authoring: Designing Efficient Queries

SQL Reporting Services provides a platform for developing and managing reports in an environment that includes multiple data sources of information. Standards such as ODBC, OLE DB, and .NET facilitate obtaining the data from these disparate data stores. Because many systems have one or more of these types of drivers, Reporting Services can access both relational and nonrelational data such Active Directory, LDAP stores, and Exchange Server. In the SRS report design environment that's embedded within Visual Studio .NET, configuring a data set that drives the report content is the first step of the design process.

However, before we introduce the many elements of the report design environment, it's important to begin with the heart of any data-driven report—whether it's Crystal Reports, SRS, or Microsoft Access—and that is the query. With any report design application, the underlying data connection and query to produce the desired data is fundamental. Developing a query that returns the desired data efficiently is the key to a successful report. We'll cover setting up the data source connection required for building an SRS report in Chapter 3. For now, we'll connect directly to our data with Query Analyzer and SQL Enterprise Manager to create real-world reports designed for the healthcare industry. The Online Transactional Processing (OLTP) database that we'll use for demonstration purposes captures billing and clinical information for home health and hospice patients. We'll also create other examples that a wide range of professionals can use. You can easily migrate the core concepts of query design to any Relational Database Management System (RDBMS) that uses SQL.

We'll begin by analyzing the query development process. We'll create queries based on real-world applications—the kind that report writers and database administrators create every day—in addition to other standard data sources, such as Active Directory. The initial query defines the performance and value of the report, so it's important to have an understanding of tools required to create and test the query to ensure that it's both accurate and tuned for high performance. After we design the base query to our satisfaction, we'll make it into a stored procedure that gains the benefit of precompilation for faster performance and is centrally updated and secured on the SQL Server. Later in the book, we'll use the queries and stored procedures produced in this chapter to build reports.

Query Design Basics

Whether you're a seasoned pro at writing SQL queries manually through a text editor, or someone who prefers to design queries graphically, the end result is what matters. Accuracy, versatility, and efficiency of the underlying query are the three goals that designers strive to achieve. Accuracy is critical; however, having a query that's versatile enough to be used in more than one report and performs well makes the subsequent report design task much easier. For scalability and low response times, efficiency is key. Understanding your data source, its data, and the best way to query that data will make your query and the resulting data set responsive and accurate. A great report that takes ten minutes to render will be a report your users never run. Keep the following goals in mind as you begin to develop your report queries:

- **The query must contain accurate data.** As the query logic becomes more complex, the chance of inaccuracy increases with extensive criteria and multiple joins.

- **The query must be scalable.** As the query is developed and tested as we do in this chapter, be aware that its performance might be entirely different as the load increases with more users. We cover performance testing with simulated loads in Chapter 8. However, in this chapter we use tools to test query response times for single execution to improve performance.

- **The query should be versatile.** Often a single query or stored procedure can drive many reports at once, saving on time to maintain, administer, and develop reports. However, delivering too much data to a report at once, to support both detail and summary, can impact performance. It's important to balance versatility with efficiency.

Creating a Simple Query Graphically

Query design typically begins with the request. As the report writer or Database Administrator (DBA), it's common to be tasked with producing data that's otherwise unavailable through standard reports that are often delivered with third-party applications.

Let's begin with a hypothetical scenario. Let's say you receive an e-mail that details a report that needs to be created and deployed for an upcoming meeting. It has already been determined that the data is unavailable from any known reports, yet you can derive the data using a simple custom query.

In the first example, we'll look at the following request for a healthcare organization: deliver a report that shows the 10 most common diagnoses, by service count, for patients admitted in the past 120 days.

Assuming that the database administrator or data analyst who was given the task of delivering this report was familiar with the database, the query design process would begin either in Query Analyzer; a graphical query design application, such as the one included within SQL Enterprise Manager; or in Visual Studio. We'll begin to design the query with the graphical tool from Enterprise Manager to demonstrate how the underlying SQL code is created. You can access the graphical query designer by right-clicking a table that will be used in the query and selecting Open Table ➤ Query (see Figure 2-1).

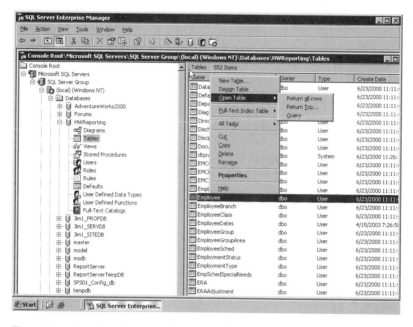

Figure 2-1. *Accessing the graphical query design tool within SQL Enterprise Manager*

Once you open the query designer, you can perform tasks such as adding and joining additional tables, sorting, grouping, and selecting criteria using the task panes (see Figure 2-2).

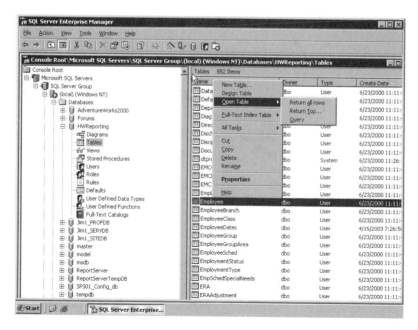

Figure 2-2. *Graphical query designer within Enterprise Manager*

This initial query is a relatively simple one, using four tables joined on relational columns. Through the graphical query designer, we have added basic criteria and sorting and have selected only two fields for the report: a count of the patients with a specific medical diagnosis. You order the count descending so that you can see the trend for the most common diagnoses. You can directly transport the SQL query that was produced to a report, which we'll do in the Chapter 4 (see Listing 2-1).

Listing 2-1. *The SQL Query Produced Using the Graphical Query Designer to Return the Top 10 Patient Diagnoses in the Past 120 Days*

```
SELECT
    TOP 10 COUNT(DISTINCT Patient.PatID) AS [Patient Count], Diag.Dscr AS
    Diagnosis
FROM
    Admissions INNER JOIN
    Patient ON Admissions.PatID = Patient.PatID INNER JOIN
    PatDiag ON Admissions.PatProgramID = PatDiag.PatProgramID INNER JOIN
    Diag ON PatDiag.DiagTblID = Diag.DiagTblID
WHERE
    (Admissions.StartOfCare > GETDATE() - 120)
GROUP BY
    Diag.Dscr
ORDER BY
    COUNT(DISTINCT Patient.PatID) DESC
```

Table 2-1 shows the output produced.

Table 2-1. *Sample Output from the Top Ten Diagnoses Query*

Patient Count	Diagnosis
71	PHYSICAL THERAPY NEC
67	ABNORMALITY OF GAIT
26	HYPERTENSION NOS
21	BENIGN HYP HRT DIS W CHF
20	CONGESTIVE HEART FAILURE
20	DMI UNSPF UNCNTRLD
19	BENIGN HYPERTENSION
19	DMII UNSPF NT ST UNCNTRL
18	CVA
16	URINARY INCONTINENCE NOS

This particular query has a small result set. Even though it's potentially working with tens of thousands of records to produce the resulting ten records, it runs in under a second. This tells us that the query is efficient, at least in a single-user execution scenario.

This type of query is designed to deliver data for quick review by professionals who will make business decisions from the results of the data. In this example, a healthcare administrator will notice that there's a demand for physical therapy and might review the staffing level for physical therapists in the company. Because physical therapists are in high demand, the cost of caring for physical therapy patients might need to be investigated.

Creating an Advanced Query

Next, we're going to design a query that reports on the cost of care for the physical therapy patients. Our goal is to design it in such a way that the query and subsequent report are flexible enough that other types of medical services can be analyzed as well, not only physical therapy. This query requires more data for analysis than the previous query for top ten diagnoses. Because we'll process many thousands of records, the performance impact needs to be assessed.

The design process is the same. We begin by adding the necessary tables to the graphical query designer and selecting the fields we would like to include in the report. The required data output for the report needs to include the following fields of information:

- Patient Name and ID Number

- Employee Name, Specialty, and Branch

- Total Service Count for Patient by Specialty

- Diagnosis of the Patient

- Estimated Cost

- Dates of Services

Listing 2-2 shows the query to produce this desired output from our healthcare application.

Listing 2-2. *The Healthcare Application Query*

```
SELECT
    Trx.PatID,
    RTRIM(RTRIM(Patient.LastName) + ',' + RTRIM(Patient.FirstName)) AS
    [Patient Name],
    Employee.EmployeeID,
    RTRIM(RTRIM(Employee.LastName) + ',' + RTRIM(Employee.FirstName)) AS
    [Employee Name],
    ServicesLogCtgry.Service AS [Service Type],
    SUM(ChargeInfo.Cost) AS [Estimated Cost],
    COUNT(Trx.ServicesTblID) AS Visit_Count,
    Diag.Dscr AS Diagnosis, DATENAME(mm, Trx.ChargeServiceStartDate) AS
    [Month],
    DATEPART(yy, Trx.ChargeServiceStartDate) AS [Year],
    Branch.BranchName AS Branch
FROM
    Trx INNER JOIN
    ChargeInfo ON Trx.ChargeInfoID = ChargeInfo.ChargeInfoID
    INNER JOIN  Patient ON Trx.PatID = Patient.PatID INNER JOIN
    Services ON Trx.ServicesTblID = Services.ServicesTblID JOIN
```

```
      ServicesLogCtgry ON
      Services.ServicesLogCtgryID = ServicesLogCtgry.ServicesLogCtgryID
  INNER JOIN
      Employee ON ChargeInfo.EmployeeTblID = Employee.EmployeeTblID INNER JOIN
      Diag ON ChargeInfo.DiagTblID = Diag.DiagTblID INNER JOIN
      Branch on TRX.BranchID = Branch.BranchID
WHERE
      (Trx.TrxTypeID = 1) AND (Services.ServiceTypeID = 'v')
GROUP BY
      ServicesLogCtgry.Service,
      Diag.Dscr,
      Trx.PatID,
      RTRIM(RTRIM(Patient.LastName) + ',' + RTRIM(Patient.FirstName)),
      RTRIM(RTRIM(Employee.LastName)  + ',' + RTRIM(Employee.FirstName)),
      Employee.EmployeeID,
      DATENAME(mm, Trx.ChargeServiceStartDate),
      DATEPART(yy, Trx.ChargeServiceStartDate),
      Branch.BranchName
ORDER BY
      Trx.PatID
```

The alias names identified with AS in the SELECT clause of the query should serve as pointers to the data that answers the requirements of the report request. Again, knowing the schema of the database that you'll be working with to produce queries is important, but for the sake of the example, the joined tables are typical of a normalized database where detailed transactional data is stored in a separate table from the descriptive information and therefore must be joined together. The Trx table in Listing 2-2 is where the transactional patient service information is stored, while the descriptive information of the specialty services such as "Physical Therapy" is stored in the Services table.

Other tables are also joined to retrieve their respective data elements such as the Patient and Employee tables. You use SQL functions COUNT and SUM to provide aggregated calculations on cost and service information, and RTRIM to remove any trailing spaces in the concatenated patient and employee names. You use the ORDER BY PATID clause for testing the query to ensure that it's returning multiple rows per patient as expected. It isn't necessary to add the additional burden of sorting to the query. As you'll see in the next chapters, sorting is handled within the report.

Testing Performance with Query Analyzer

Now that we have our query developed, let's take a quick look at the output to make sure that it's returning accurate data within acceptable timeframes before we move on to the next phase of development. You can see the results of the output from Query Analyzer along with the time it took to execute the query in Figure 2-3. The output was created by pasting the SQL query into SQL Query Analyzer, another tool for query design that has much more functionality than its graphical counterpart. We can further modify the query directly in Query Analyzer if desired. However, one of the best features of Query Analyzer that we'll be using is the ability to view quickly both the number of records returned and the execution time. Once we do that, the next step is to create the stored procedure.

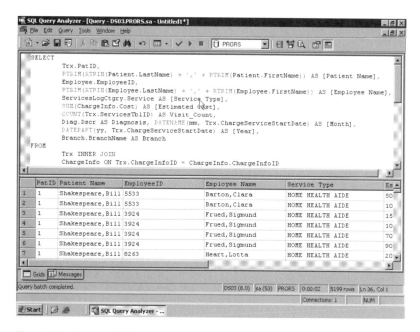

Figure 2-3. *Query Analyzer output*

We now have the data the way we want and the query is executing in an average of three seconds. To verify the execution times, we ran the query 15 times in sequence from two different sessions of Query Analyzer. Execution times varied from two to three seconds for each execution. For 5,199 records, which is what the query is returning, the execution time is acceptable for a single-user execution. However, it needs to be improved before we create the stored procedure and begin building reports. Let's look at the Execution Plan to gain a better understanding of what's happening when we execute the query. In Query Analyzer, select Query on the menu bar and then select Show Execution Plan. When the query is executed, another tab appears in the Results pane called Execution Plan.

The Execution Plan in Query Analyzer shows graphically how the SQL query optimizer chose the most efficient method for executing the report, based on the different elements of the query. For example, a clustered index might have been chosen instead of a table scan. Each execution step has an associated cost. Take a look at Figure 2-4 to see the Execution Plan for our query.

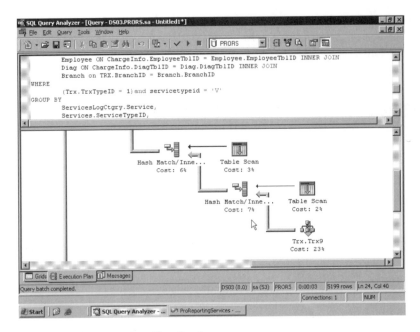

Figure 2-4. *The Execution Plan for the query*

The query took three seconds to execute and, from this execution plan, it's easy to see which section of the query had the highest cost percentage. The WHERE clause in the query had a 23% cost when determining the TrxTypeID and the Service Type. (For reference, the TrxTypeID is an integer field that specifies the type of financial transactions as charges, payments, or adjustments. We're concerned only with the TrxTypeID of 1, representing charges. For Service Type, we're only interested in "V," representing visits, and not other types of billable services, such as medical supplies.) If we could get the cost of the WHERE clause down to a lower number, the query might improve in overall performance.

Dividing the Load

Because SRS and Transact-Structured Query Language (T-SQL) share many data formatting and manipulation functions, you have the option to choose in which process, query, or report these functions should be used. You can choose to have the query handle the bulk of the processing. This limits the number of rows that the report has to work with, making report rendering much faster. Alternatively, you can limit the selectivity of the query, allowing it to return more rows than are possibly required. You can then have the report perform additional filtering, grouping, and calculations, which allows the query or stored procedure to execute faster. With many users accessing the report simultaneously, having the report share the processing load also limits the impact on the data source server; in this case, SQL Server.

In our query, based on initial benchmarking, we've determined that we'll remove the portion of the WHERE clause that specifies that the query should return only Service Types with a value of "V." Instead, we'll let the report filter out any service types that aren't visits. When we remove the Service Type criteria from the query and re-execute it, we see that our overall execution time goes from an average of 3 seconds to 1 second, and the cost of the WHERE clause goes from 23% to 15%. Also, it's important to note in the performance analysis that the record count went up by only 54 records, from 5,199 to 5,253. You can see this in the lower right corner of Figure 2-5 by removing the "V" from the WHERE clause.

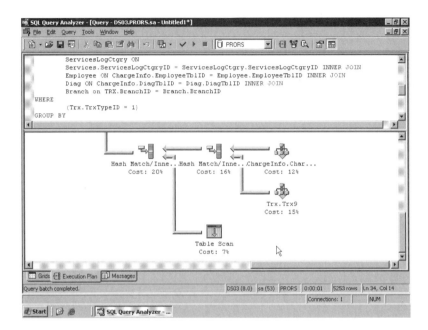

Figure 2-5. *Modified query execution*

To take advantage of a report filter, we need to add an additional field—Services.Service-TypeID—to the SELECT portion of the query, which we'll use as the filter value. Even though we're returning more rows than we might need for a particular report, by proceeding in this fashion we also gain the benefit of using this same stored procedure for other reports, which might include service types other than visits. For example, there might be a need to investigate the cost or quantity of supplies (a Service Type of "S") used by employees. We can use this same query and stored procedure for that report as well.

The query that we have outlined, now including the ServiceTypeID as a value in the SELECT clause and not as criteria, is ready to begin its life as a stored procedure. Queries serve many purposes and are good to develop reports with, as we'll do in Chapter 4. However, encapsulating queries in stored procedures is typically the preferred method of deployment for several reasons. Stored procedures, like ad-hoc queries, execute according to the execution plan generated by the query optimizer. Having the ability to reuse the execution plan saves time and resources. Stored procedures, which are also beneficial because they're precompiled, can reuse an execution plan despite the fact that its parameters, which are passed to it when it's executed, might have changed values. You can centrally maintain stored procedures on the SQL Server, unlike ad-hoc queries that might be embedded in an application or in the RDL file in this case. When the underlying schema of a database changes, you can update the stored procedure in one location, whereas embedded queries all need to be modified separately for each report in which they reside. In the next section, we'll create a stored procedure based on our employee cost query.

Using a Parameterized Stored Procedure

You can use both Query Analyzer and Enterprise Manager to produce the code to create a stored procedure based on the query that we have designed, and also to drop it (if the stored procedure already existed in the database). Enterprise Manager provides the simplest means of creating a stored procedure. In the database where we create the procedure, simply right-click the stored procedures folder and select New Stored Procedure. This opens a window that has a single Create command for the new stored procedure:

```
CREATE PROCEDURE [OWNER].[PROCEDURE NAME] AS
```

To complete our new stored procedure, which we name Emp_Svc_Cost, we simply need to paste in our SELECT statement. However, we do know that we provide optional parameters with the stored procedure. These parameters are used to limit the result set based on the following criteria:

- Service time (year and month)

- The branch where the employee works

- The individual employee

- The type of service

To create parameters for a stored procedure, we add in the variable names preceded by the "@" characters and provide the appropriate data types and initial value; the initial value for all the parameters is NULL, as Listing 2-3 shows.

Listing 2-3. *Code to Create the Emp_Svc_Cost Stored Procedure*

```
CREATE PROCEDURE [dbo].[Emp_Svc_Cost]
@ServiceMonth  Int=NULL,
@ServiceYear Int=NULL,
@BranchID Int=NULL,
@EmployeeTblID Int=NULL,
@ServicesLogCtgryID char(5)=NULL
AS
SELECT
    Trx.PatID,
    RTRIM(RTRIM(Patient.LastName) + ',' + RTRIM(Patient.FirstName)) AS
    [Patient Name],
    Branch.BranchName,
    Employee.EmployeeID,
    RTRIM(RTRIM(Employee.LastName) + ',' + RTRIM(Employee.FirstName)) AS
    [Employee Name],
    Employee.EmployeeClassID,
    ServicesLogCtgry.Service AS [Service Type],
```

```
        SUM(ChargeInfo.Cost) AS [Estimated Cost],
        COUNT(Trx.ServicesTblID) AS Visit_Count,
        Diag.Dscr AS Diagnosis, DATENAME(mm, Trx.ChargeServiceStartDate) AS [Month],
        DATEPART(yy, Trx.ChargeServiceStartDate) AS [Year],
        Services.ServiceTypeID
FROM
        Trx INNER JOIN
        Branch on Trx.Branchid = Branch.BranchID INNER JOIN
        ChargeInfo ON Trx.ChargeInfoID = ChargeInfo.ChargeInfoID
        INNER JOIN  Patient ON Trx.PatID = Patient.PatID INNER JOIN
        Services ON Trx.ServicesTblID = Services.ServicesTblID INNER JOIN
        ServicesLogCtgry ON
        Services.ServicesLogCtgryID = ServicesLogCtgry.ServicesLogCtgryID INNER JOIN
        Employee ON ChargeInfo.EmployeeTblID = Employee.EmployeeTblID INNER JOIN
        Diag ON ChargeInfo.DiagTblID = Diag.DiagTblID
WHERE
        (Trx.TrxTypeID = 1) AND
        (ISNULL(Branch.BranchID,0) = ISNULL(@BranchID,ISNULL(Branch.BranchID,0)))
AND
        (ISNULL(Services.ServicesLogCtgryID,0) = ISNULL(@ServicesLogCtgryID,
          ISNULL(Services.ServicesLogCtgryID,0)))   AND
        (ISNULL(Employee.EmployeeTblID,0) = ISNULL(@EmployeeTblID,
          ISNULL(Employee.EmployeeTblID,0)))  AND


--Case to determine if Year and Month was passed in

        1=Case
            When ( @ServiceYear is  NULL) then 1
            When ( @ServiceYear is  NOT NULL)
            AND @ServiceYear = Cast(DatePart(YY,ChargeServiceStartDate) as int)
Then 1
        ELSE 0
        End
AND
        1=Case
            When (@ServiceMonth is NULL)  then 1
            When (@ServiceMonth is NOT NULL)
            AND @ServiceMonth = Cast(DatePart(MM,ChargeServiceStartDate) as int)
Then 1
        ELSE 0
        END
GROUP BY
        ServicesLogCtgry.Service,
        Diag.Dscr,
        Trx.PatID,
        Branch.BranchName,
        RTRIM(RTRIM(Patient.LastName) + ',' + RTRIM(Patient.FirstName)),
        RTRIM(RTRIM(Employee.LastName)  + ',' + RTRIM(Employee.FirstName)),
```

```
    Employee.EmployeeClassid,
    Employee.EmployeeID,
    DATENAME(mm, Trx.ChargeServiceStartDate),
    DATEPART(yy, Trx.ChargeServiceStartDate),
    Services.ServiceTypeID
ORDER BY
    Trx.PatID
GO
```

Evaluating the Parameters

In the previous query we added several new criteria to the WHERE clause for evaluation of the parameters. We used the ISNULL function and a CASE statement to evaluate the values of the database fields and parameters:

```
    (ISNULL(Branch.BranchID,0) = ISNULL(@BranchID,ISNULL(Branch.BranchID,0)))
    1=Case
AND
    When ( @ServiceYear is  NULL) then 1
    When ( @ServiceYear is  NOT NULL)
    AND @ServiceYear = Cast(DatePart(YY,ChargeServiceStartDate) as int)  then 1
    ELSE 0
    End
```

At first the logic for these evaluations might seem confusing, but remember that as long as the criteria are equal, results are returned. This is true through the entire WHERE clause because it's evaluated with AND. This is easier to understand with a sample statement:

```
SELECT * from Table1 WHERE 1 = 1
```

In this statement all rows are returned because 1 always equals 1. It doesn't matter that you aren't comparing values from the table itself.

For the ISNULL function, you look to see if the value of a database field—BranchID for example—contains a NULL value and if so, ISNULL replaces NULL with zero. The right side of that equation looks to see if the @BranchID parameter was passed in as NULL; if so, then the value for @BranchID is set to the value of BranchID in the database table and equals every row. If the @BranchID parameter is passed to the stored procedure as a value, say 2 for the Branch "Nested Valley," then only BranchID 2 is returned because BranchID = @BranchID = 2. This evaluation is performed when there might be NULL values in the field because NULL values can't be compared with standard operators such as =.

For fields that always have non-NULL values such as service dates, you can evaluate those with a CASE statement in the WHERE clause. For the two time values, Service Year and Month, we're using similar logic as we did with the ISNULL evaluations. If the parameters @ServiceMonth and

@ServiceYear are passed in as NULL to the stored procedure, then the stored procedure returns every record, and the CASE statement sets the equation to 1 = 1. If the parameters contain legitimate values, such as 2004 as the year, the CASE statement is set to 1 = 1 only when the parameter value equals the database value. Otherwise the CASE statement is set to the equation to 1 = 0 and the record is skipped.

Testing the Procedure

The next step is to grant execute privileges for the stored procedure to the appropriate roles or users. In this case, we allow the public role to execute the procedure (we're sure the humor wasn't lost on the developer, who knew someone would grant a public execution).

▮Note The test server on which we're developing the reports is an isolated and secure system. Typically, granting execution privileges to the public role isn't recommended. We'll lock down both the stored procedure and the report in Chapter 9.

We can now test the procedure directly in Query Analyzer with the following command:

```
EXEC Emp_Svc_Cost
```

Because we have allowed NULL values for the parameters, we don't explicitly have to pass them in on the command line. However, to test the functionality of the stored procedure we can pass in the full command line with appropriate parameters; for example, all services rendered in September 2003:

```
EXEC Emp_Svc_Cost 09,2003,NULL,NULL,NULL
```

Executing the procedure in this way returns 321 records and the results verify that indeed, only services in September 2003 were returned (see Figure 2-6).

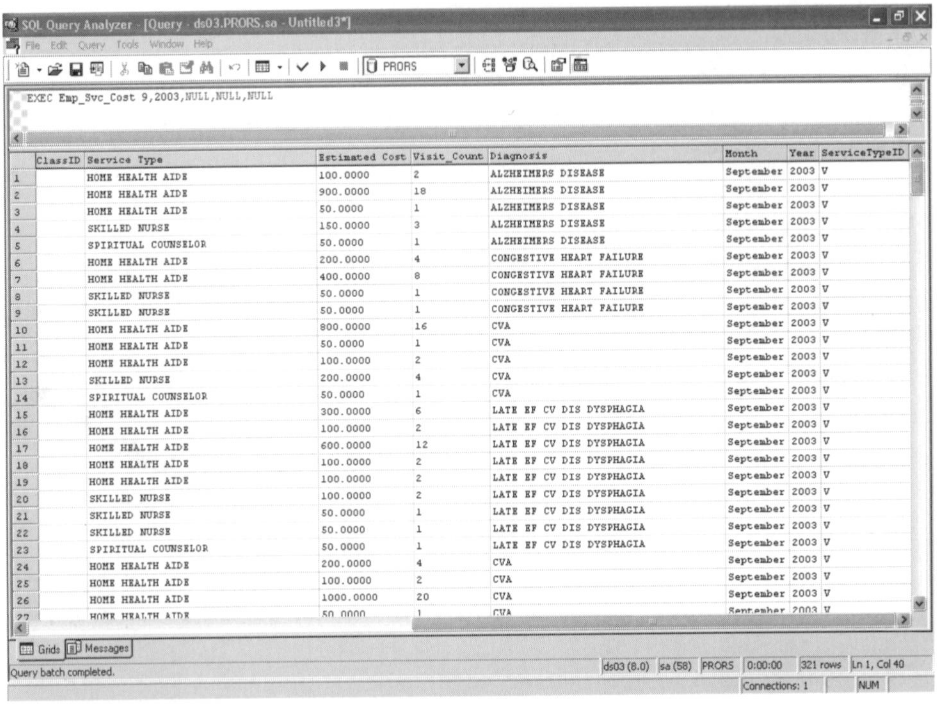

	ClassID	Service Type	Estimated Cost	Visit_Count	Diagnosis	Month	Year	ServiceTypeID
1		HOME HEALTH AIDE	100.0000	2	ALZHEIMERS DISEASE	September	2003	V
2		HOME HEALTH AIDE	900.0000	18	ALZHEIMERS DISEASE	September	2003	V
3		HOME HEALTH AIDE	50.0000	1	ALZHEIMERS DISEASE	September	2003	V
4		SKILLED NURSE	150.0000	3	ALZHEIMERS DISEASE	September	2003	V
5		SPIRITUAL COUNSELOR	50.0000	1	ALZHEIMERS DISEASE	September	2003	V
6		HOME HEALTH AIDE	200.0000	4	CONGESTIVE HEART FAILURE	September	2003	V
7		HOME HEALTH AIDE	400.0000	8	CONGESTIVE HEART FAILURE	September	2003	V
8		SKILLED NURSE	50.0000	1	CONGESTIVE HEART FAILURE	September	2003	V
9		SKILLED NURSE	50.0000	1	CONGESTIVE HEART FAILURE	September	2003	V
10		HOME HEALTH AIDE	800.0000	16	CVA	September	2003	V
11		HOME HEALTH AIDE	50.0000	1	CVA	September	2003	V
12		HOME HEALTH AIDE	100.0000	2	CVA	September	2003	V
13		SKILLED NURSE	200.0000	4	CVA	September	2003	V
14		SPIRITUAL COUNSELOR	50.0000	1	CVA	September	2003	V
15		HOME HEALTH AIDE	300.0000	6	LATE EF CV DIS DYSPHAGIA	September	2003	V
16		HOME HEALTH AIDE	100.0000	2	LATE EF CV DIS DYSPHAGIA	September	2003	V
17		HOME HEALTH AIDE	600.0000	12	LATE EF CV DIS DYSPHAGIA	September	2003	V
18		HOME HEALTH AIDE	100.0000	2	LATE EF CV DIS DYSPHAGIA	September	2003	V
19		HOME HEALTH AIDE	100.0000	2	LATE EF CV DIS DYSPHAGIA	September	2003	V
20		SKILLED NURSE	100.0000	2	LATE EF CV DIS DYSPHAGIA	September	2003	V
21		SKILLED NURSE	50.0000	1	LATE EF CV DIS DYSPHAGIA	September	2003	V
22		SKILLED NURSE	50.0000	1	LATE EF CV DIS DYSPHAGIA	September	2003	V
23		SPIRITUAL COUNSELOR	50.0000	1	LATE EF CV DIS DYSPHAGIA	September	2003	V
24		HOME HEALTH AIDE	200.0000	4	CVA	September	2003	V
25		HOME HEALTH AIDE	100.0000	2	CVA	September	2003	V
26		HOME HEALTH AIDE	1000.0000	20	CVA	September	2003	V
27		HOME HEALTH AIDE	50.0000	1	CVA	September	2003	V

Figure 2-6. *Results of Emp_Svc_Cost with timeframe parameters*

Knowing Your Data: A Quick Trick with a Small Procedure

For every report writer, familiarity with the location of the data in a given database can often come only with time. Of course, having a database diagram or schema provided by a vendor is a useful tool, but this isn't always available. One day, faced with the dilemma of trying to find the right table for a specific piece of missing data, we decided to put together a stored procedure, which we named `sp_FieldInfo`. It returns a list of all the tables in a specific database that contain the same field names, typically the primary or foreign key fields. For example, in the healthcare database, if you wanted a list of fields that contained the `PatID` (Patient's ID number that's used to join several tables), the command would look like this:

```
sp_fieldinfo Patid
```

The output would be similar to that shown in Table 2-2.

Table 2-2. *Output of sp_fieldinfo*

TableName	FieldName
PatMentalStat	PatID
PatMiscNotes	PatID
PatNoteSummary	PatID
PatNurseNotes	PatID
PatNutrition	PatID
PatOccurrence	PatID
PatOrders	PatID
PatPhysician	PatID

Armed with this information, you could at least deduce that, for example, the patient's physician information would be stored in the PatPhysician table. However, often table and field names aren't intuitively named. When we encounter a database such as this from time to time, we run a Profiler trace and perform some routine tasks on the associated application, such as opening a form and searching for an identifiable record to get a starting point with the captured data. The Profiler returns the resulting query with table and field names that we can then use to discern the database structure.

■**Tip** SQL Server Profiler is an excellent tool for capturing not only the actual queries and stored procedures that are executing against the server, but also performance data, such as the duration of the execution time, CPU and I/O measurements, as well as the application that initiated the query. Because you can save this data directly to a SQL table, you can analyze it readily, and it even makes good fodder as a source for a report in SRS.

Here's the simple stored procedure text for sp_fieldinfo:

```
CREATE PROCEDURE sp_FieldInfo
(
@column_name nvarchar(384) = NULL
)
AS
SELECT
    Object_Name(id) as "Table Name",
    rtrim(name) as "Field Name"
FROM
    syscolumns
WHERE
    Name like @column_name
```

Summary

In this chapter, we began the process of designing the essential part of a report: the query and stored procedure. By using stored procedures, you gain the benefits of central administration and security and also gain the ability to execute compiled code to return the data set instead of a standalone query. You can develop queries in conjunction with the report, using the built-in query tools within SRS. However, it's best to deploy the report with a stored procedure.

A report request and target audience are the deciding factors when determining the layout and default rendering of the report. However, even though reports are often designed to answer a specific need, if they're based on the same tried-and-true stored procedures, with similar parameters and groupings, the data will be accurate across all reports. You can then focus the design time on the report itself and not on rewriting queries.

CHAPTER 3

■ ■ ■

The Report Designer

The professional lines between system administrators, DBAs, and developers are blurring. Products are released that carry with them, if not an expectation of custom extensibility through code, then the vast potential to create a product or application that goes well beyond the out-of-the-box offerings. SRS is such an application, as will be SQL Server 2005. The days of the Microsoft Management Console (MMC) are numbered and will be overshadowed by the new interface on the block, the IDE. Actually, the IDE isn't new at all, as any developer will tell you. However, DBAs, system administrators, and even report designers have to become familiar with this new way of working. As you're probably already well aware, you create reports in SRS within VS.NET. This is a boon for developers, because now they can use the same IDE for report creation as they do for application development. For the rest of us, creating reports in VS.NET presents a learning curve. With SQL Server 2005 right around the bend, there's no better time than the present to begin working in the world of the IDE. SQL Server 2005, with the delivery of the Business Intelligence Development Studio and the SQL Server Management Studio, will have essentially the same environment not only for report creation, but also for Data Transformation Services (DTS) packages, query design, database design and management, and almost all tasks currently associated with SQL Server and Analysis Services. So, now that we have our queries and stored procedures developed, we can turn our attention to VS.NET and the tools available to the report designer when SRS is installed. By the way, we'll now work with the queries and stored procedures directly in the IDE.

In this chapter, we'll introduce, set up, and explore the VS.NET IDE using the embedded elements of SRS within that environment. To that end, we'll step through the following tasks to familiarize you with the tools of report design before moving on to creating a full-blown SRS report in the next chapter:

- Introduce the elements of VS.NET.

- Describe the role of RDL in SRS with sample code from the various report objects that it controls.

- Create a data source and data set.

* Define report parameters, filters, and expressions and tell you how you can use them together to control report content and formatting.

- Discuss report pagination.

- Create data region samples: list, table, rectangle, matrix, chart, and image.

- Offer two simple tips for creating report templates and printing labels.

Elements of VS.NET

Installing SRS on a system with VS.NET adds the SRS design elements to the VS.NET IDE. If you aren't familiar with the layout of the VS.NET IDE, begin with this introduction of a few key concepts and procedures that you need to understand as you start designing reports.

Projects and Solutions

In VS.NET, one or more projects contain all reports and shared data sources. In addition to physically and logically grouping reports together, a project also maintains properties that are specific to that project. These properties allow the project to work independently of other projects. All projects that you create are themselves contained within a solution.

We'll now step through the process of creating a project and a solution. Open VS.NET and select File ➤ New ➤ Project on the menu bar. This displays the New Project window. Under Project Types, select Report Project, which is in the Business Intelligence Projects folder. The project name defaults to Report Project1 if this is the first project that you've created. The location of the project can be a local drive or network location. In this case, make it D:\Pro_SRS\Reports.

Click the More button to expand the window to reveal the solution information. By default, the solution is named according to the project name, in this case Report Project1. If you check the box to Create Directory for Solution, you can append a new directory to the base Location, as you can see in Figure 3-1. In this case we choose Solution1.

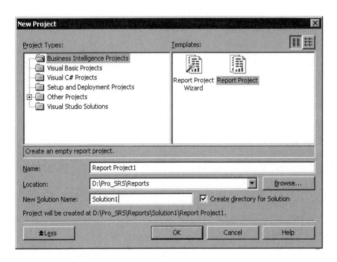

Figure 3-1. *New Project window*

Once you click OK, both the project and solution are created, and you can create report items and data sources within the project.

However, first you should add two important property settings to the project: the target folder in which to deploy the reports on the SRS server, and the SRS server URL itself.

You can set these properties via the Solution Explorer, which displays the solution and the projects it contains, as well as all the reports and other objects that the individual projects might contain. You can access the Solution Explorer by clicking View ➤ Solution Explorer on the menu bar. In the Solution Explorer, highlight the project and select Project ➤ Properties from the menu, or right-click the project and select Properties. The TargetFolder property controls the folder that's created to store the deployed report on the SRS server. The TargetServerURL is the URL to the SRS web server. As you can see in Figure 3-2, the TargetServerURL is in the form `http://servername/ReportServer`. In this case our SRS web server is hwc04.

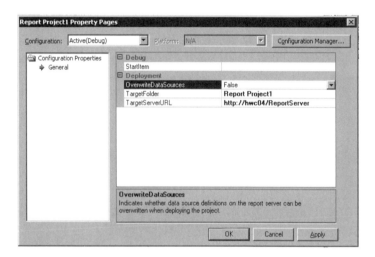

Figure 3-2. *Project properties*

Setting up a Basic IDE

Now that you have a new solution and a new project to contain the reports that you'll build, it's time to get personal. As report designers, we're going to spend many hours gazing at the pixels that are our creations. It's important that we set up the environment exactly the way we want it. The ideal setup for designing reports is a personal choice. Some might prefer high-resolution display settings with every available design toolbar always in view within the environment. Others might prefer undocked toolbars and a dual monitor set up at a lower resolution. Whatever your preference, VS.NET makes it easy to manipulate the design tools within the IDE to personalize your configuration. In addition to the Solution Explorer, which we went over when adding a project to the solution, you can use several common tools within the IDE to design reports:

- Toolbox

- Properties

- Tasks

- Fields

The Toolbox is where you find all the report objects that we cover in this chapter, such as the Matrix and Table data regions. Data regions are the defined report objects within the SRS report design environment that contain the field values from the data source.

In the Properties window, you set the values for the various formatting and grouping properties for report items.

The Tasks window is important when troubleshooting report errors. Mismatched data types and invalid use of functions are common issues that arise when designing reports. The Tasks window is the place to see the details of these errors.

Finally, the Fields window holds the data sets and the field information that we've defined for the report.

Figure 3-3 shows a custom layout for designing reports in SRS. All the toolbars mentioned earlier are dockable anywhere within the IDE, or they can extend beyond the main IDE to their own location on the desktop. Having this setup typically requires a high resolution configuration—1152×864 or higher—to be most effective. In this case, the Solution Explorer is undocked while the Fields and Toolbox toolbars are docked on either side of the report design grid. The toolbars can autohide when not in use, which again is a personal preference.

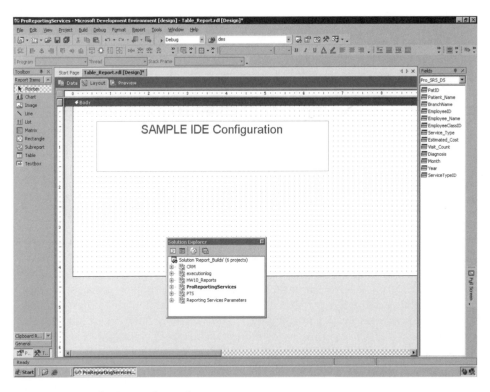

Figure 3-3. *Sample IDE configuration*

Report Basics

In the next sections, we'll focus primarily on how to manipulate objects and their properties, and we'll study the interrelationships between these objects. Our goal is not to build a report to completion. In the next chapter, we'll step through creating an entire report using the concepts covered here.

Note Because SRS has such a broad range of features for reports, you might find tips in this chapter that aren't necessarily included in the reports that we build subsequently in the book. This is because each report has its own unique format and requirements based on the audience need.

To add a new report to your project, right-click the Reports folder in the Solution Explorer, select Add, and then Add New Item. Then click Open. Notice that you have the option of adding an existing item as well. This option is useful if you already have a report to add to a project or if you've built a template report file as a base starting point. We'll show you how to add a template later in the chapter.

Double-clicking the newly added blank report opens it in the design environment. By default the report is named Report##.rdl, where ## is the next available report number in sequence. At this point the report is a blank slate. As with any report that contains data from a data source, the first step is to create one or more data sets. Figure 3-4 shows the IDE, including the Solution Explorer and Toolbox with the report design objects.

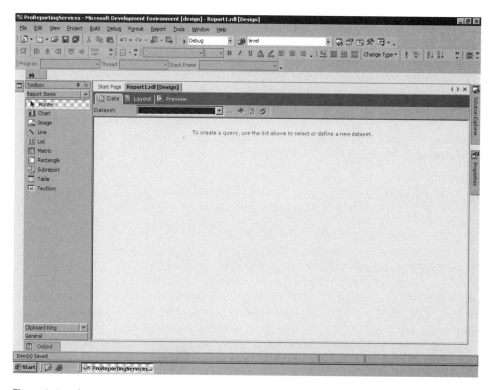

Figure 3-4. *The VS.NET IDE*

Report Definition Language

The RDL is the standard to which all reports created with the embedded SRS tools in VS.NET adhere. SRS uses the RDL file that's stored in the ReportServer database to render the report through the web server. RDL is an XML-based schema that defines each element of a report, such as formatting, data set information, grouping and sorting, and parameters and filters. As you add items to the report, the RDL code is modified to include each new addition.

In the IDE, this is typically invisible to the user as it's done in the background. However, at times you might need to modify the RDL directly to effect global changes, using a find and replace method. I've had to do this several times when a parameter or field name changed in a source stored procedure. Within VS.NET, while working on a report, you can view the RDL code directly at any time by pressing F7.

Because RDL is a standard, you can create it with any report designer that supports it. Currently VS.NET is the main report designer for SRS, but as more and more companies embrace RDL, other report designers will become available.

Throughout this chapter, we'll present the RDL sections of the report objects on which we are working, to show how the RDL is updated while designing a report. The complete RDL schema is located at `http://schemas.microsoft.com/sqlserver/reporting/2003/10/reportdefinition`.

Data Sources and Data Sets

In Chapter 2, we created a stored procedure called `Emp_Svc_Cost` that contains employee and patient visit information. Because it includes detail records that can be aggregated in several different ways, enough information is in this stored procedure to demonstrate how we can use many of the report objects. Therefore, we'll use that procedure as our source data as we work with some of the report objects.

No image field is in our stored procedure, so when demonstrating the use of the `Image` report object, we'll use the visual design tool to create a custom query that returns an image. The visual design tool is one of two query design tools available within VS.NET, the other being the generic query designer. Both designers serve the same purpose. However, the generic query designer allows you to create queries for any supported data provider, such as LDAP or multidimensional expressions (MDX) queries used for Active Directory or OLAP cubes respectively. You use the visual designer to build SQL queries graphically using drag-and-drop capabilities.

Creating a Data Source

Each report can use one or more data sources. Reports that use the same data source—for example, one that connects to a specific SQL Server database—can use what is referred to in SRS as a shared data source. Shared data sources are published along with the report and can be modified on the report server after deployment. In the Report Designer, shared data sources contain several properties that you must define and determine how they're used.

Let's step through the process of creating our shared data source for the stored procedure `Emp_Svc_Cost`. First, right-click Shared Data Sources and select Add New Data Source. In this case, we know that the server that contains our source database and stored procedure is on DS03. The data source property defaults to the OLE DB Provider for SQL Server. We type **DS03** as the server and choose the Pro_SRS database from the database selection. In this case, because the database is configured to use both Windows and SQL authentication, we choose

Windows Authentication. If we chose to use SQL authentication, we could have also chosen to store the password so that while designing the reports we wouldn't be constantly prompted for the password. In addition, storing credentials allows us to create snapshots and subscriptions. Generally, Windows Authentication is the preferred method of authentication because it has a single point of login for users. We'll cover authentication for deployed reports in Chapter 9. Figure 3-5 shows the data source connection properties. If we choose, we can test the connection by clicking the Test Connection button.

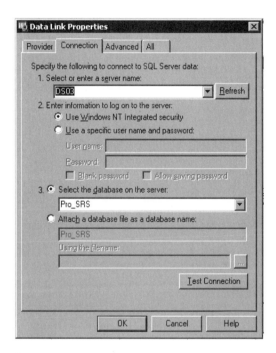

Figure 3-5. *Data source connection properties*

We now have a shared data source. Notice that the name of the shared data source has defaulted to the name of the database, Pro_SRS. You can rename this after creating it by right-clicking it and selecting Rename.

In practice, we've developed all our reports using an identical data source name. However, because each of our online customers had a database that uniquely identified them, we designed an application that reset the database properties in the data source after it was published. In this way, we could use the same reports against the same database schema, but we could deploy the reports to multiple customers on the same report server. We'll cover report deployment and content management in later chapters.

The data source file that we created has an RDS extension, and is stored and published separately from the report. You can open an RDS file in a text editor, because it's an XML file that defines the connection properties that we've just created graphically. Listing 3-1 shows our Pro_SRS RDS file.

Listing 3-1. *Pro_SRS RDS File*

```xml
<?xml version="1.0" encoding="utf-8"?>
<RptDataSource xmlns:xsd=http://www.w3.org/2001/
XMLSchema xmlns:xsi="http://www.w3.org/2001/
XMLSchema-instance">
  <Name>Pro_SRS</Name>
  <DataSourceID>8665c4ac-17ca-436c-be19-334a1fa55274</DataSourceID>
  <ConnectionProperties>
    <Extension>SQL</Extension>
    <ConnectString>data source=ds03;initial catalog=Pro_SRS</ConnectString>
    <IntegratedSecurity>true</IntegratedSecurity>
  </ConnectionProperties>
</RptDataSource>
```

Creating a Data Set

Depending on whether you've developed a query or stored procedure externally to the IDE, or if you're starting to build it here from scratch, you next proceed to the Data tab to create your first data set. In this case, we're using a stored procedure, so half the battle is over.

On the Data tab, we drop down the Data Set list and select <New Data Set>, which opens the Data Set properties window. Next, we add the server name, in this case DS03, and the database name, Pro_SRS. In the query type, we change the default, Text, to Stored Procedure, and in the query box we input the name of our stored procedure, Emp_Svc_Cost, as shown in Figure 3-6.

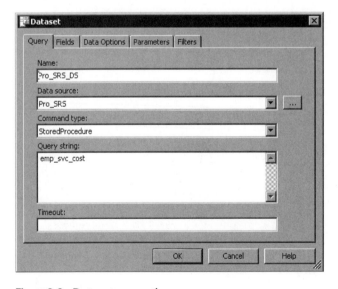

Figure 3-6. *Data set properties*

Next we name the new data set Pro_RS_DS and click OK to complete the data set configuration. This action automatically opens the generic query designer. From here we may execute the query and review the results by clicking the Run button on the Data tab toolbar. When the stored procedure is executed, any parameters that have been defined are created, and before data is returned, you must supply the parameter values. In the case of our stored procedure, we have defined five parameters: @ServiceYear, @ServiceMonth, @BranchID, @EmployeeTblID, and @ServicesLogCtgryID. The available default values for the parameters, when the stored procedure is executed on the Data tab, are either NULL or Blank. A Blank value is different from the NULL value in that it can be an empty string. A NULL value indicates that the value is nothing. NULL values can't be evaluated with non-NULL values. In Chapter 2 we built logic into the stored procedure to handle NULL parameter values so that when the user doesn't supply a value, the query returns all records. If the user selects a specific value, only the records that match that parameter value are returned. We execute the stored procedure with NULL values and make sure that we're getting the results we expect. You can see the results of the stored procedure execution in Figure 3-7.

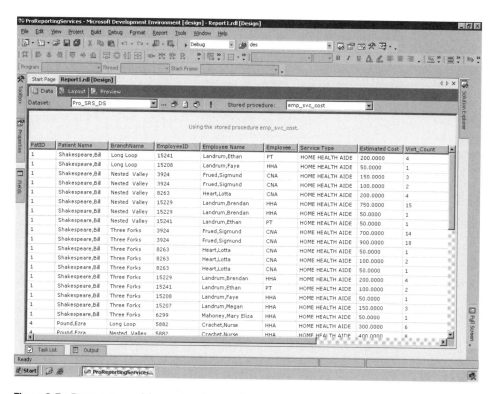

Figure 3-7. *Data returned from stored procedure*

■**Note** When prompted for the parameter values, Blank is the default value. To have the stored procedure execute without a data type error, you must select the value of NULL.

An SRS report can have multiple data sets at one time. This extends the flexibility of our reporting, in that we can provide more data to the user in a single report. Multiple data sets are also useful for populating parameter drop-down lists, which we do in Chapter 4. However, having too many data sets could effect a report's performance, so it's important to make sure that the execution times for each result set are within acceptable ranges.

The RDL file for each report contains a section for each data set defined for the report. Listing 3-2 shows the RDL section for the data set we've defined. Notice that all the field names, the parameters, and the query itself—in this case our stored procedure—are all defined within the schema.

Listing 3-2. *Data Set Section of RDL*

```
<DataSet Name="Pro_SRS_DS">
  <Fields>
    <Field Name="PatID">
      <DataField>PatID</DataField>
      <rd:TypeName>System.Int32</rd:TypeName>
    </Field>
    <Field Name="Patient_Name">
      <DataField>Patient Name</DataField>
      <rd:TypeName>System.String</rd:TypeName>
    </Field>
    <Field Name="BranchName">
      <DataField>BranchName</DataField>
      <rd:TypeName>System.String</rd:TypeName>
    </Field>
    <Field Name="EmployeeID">
      <DataField>EmployeeID</DataField>
      <rd:TypeName>System.String</rd:TypeName>
    </Field>
    <Field Name="Employee_Name">
      <DataField>Employee Name</DataField>
      <rd:TypeName>System.String</rd:TypeName>
    </Field>
    <Field Name="EmployeeClassID">
      <DataField>EmployeeClassID</DataField>
      <rd:TypeName>System.String</rd:TypeName>
    </Field>
    <Field Name="Service_Type">
      <DataField>Service Type</DataField>
      <rd:TypeName>System.String</rd:TypeName>
    </Field>
```

```xml
      <Field Name="Estimated_Cost">
        <DataField>Estimated Cost</DataField>
        <rd:TypeName>System.Decimal</rd:TypeName>
      </Field>
      <Field Name="Visit_Count">
        <DataField>Visit_Count</DataField>
        <rd:TypeName>System.Int32</rd:TypeName>
      </Field>
      <Field Name="Diagnosis">
        <DataField>Diagnosis</DataField>
        <rd:TypeName>System.String</rd:TypeName>
      </Field>
      <Field Name="Month">
        <DataField>Month</DataField>
        <rd:TypeName>System.String</rd:TypeName>
      </Field>
      <Field Name="Year">
        <DataField>Year</DataField>
        <rd:TypeName>System.Int32</rd:TypeName>
      </Field>
      <Field Name="ServiceTypeID">
        <DataField>ServiceTypeID</DataField>
        <rd:TypeName>System.String</rd:TypeName>
      </Field>
    </Fields>
    <Query>
      <DataSourceName>Pro_SRS</DataSourceName>
      <CommandType>StoredProcedure</CommandType>
      <CommandText>Emp_Svc_Cost</CommandText>
      <QueryParameters>
        <QueryParameter Name="@ServiceMonth">
          <Value>=Parameters!ServiceMonth.Value</Value>
        </QueryParameter>
        <QueryParameter Name="@ServiceYear">
          <Value>=Parameters!ServiceYear.Value</Value>
        </QueryParameter>
        <QueryParameter Name="@BranchID">
          <Value>=Parameters!BranchID.Value</Value>
        </QueryParameter>
        <QueryParameter Name="@EmployeeTblID">
          <Value>=Parameters!EmployeeTblID.Value</Value>
        </QueryParameter>
        <QueryParameter Name="@ServicesLogCtgryID">
          <Value>=Parameters!ServicesLogCtgryID.Value</Value>
        </QueryParameter>
      </QueryParameters>
    </Query>
</DataSet>
```

When creating a data set, several additional tabs contain other configuration properties:

- **Fields:** Used to define additional fields such as calculated fields or fields that aren't automatically defined with the data source. You derive calculated fields from an expression.

- **Data Options:** Sets several options specific to the data as it's retrieved from the data provider, such as case sensitivity and collation.

- **Parameters:** Defines the query parameter values for the data set and the order in which they're evaluated. Stored procedures with declared parameters automatically generate the query parameters in SRS.

- **Filters:** Defines filter values for the data set that you can use when the report is executed.

Other Data Sources

One exciting aspect of SRS is its ability to query multiple data source types in addition to SQL Server. Any ODBC or OLE DB provider can be a potential data source for SRS. For a simple example of using a data source other than a SQL Server database, let's look at the OLE DB Provider for Microsoft Directory Services. By using a direct LDAP query, you can generate field information for use in SRS:

```
SELECT cn,sn,objectcategory,department
  FROM 'LDAP://DirectoryServerName/OU=OuName,DC=Company,DC=Com'
```

The query uses a standard SQL dialect that returns the common name, surname, objectcategory (computer or person), and department from the Active Directory. The field names are automatically created and can be used like any other data field for a report.

You must take a couple caveats into consideration when querying Active Directory, as well as other data sources that don't support the graphical query designer in SRS:

- Query Parameters aren't supported directly in the query. However, you can define and use Report Parameters in the query—referred to as a dynamic query—and also to filter data.

- Because a graphical query designer isn't available, you need to develop the query in the generic query designer by typing the query directly and testing. This requires knowledge of Active Directory objects and names.

■**Tip** Several tools are available to assist in managing Active Directory, such as Active Directory Application Mode (ADAM); LDP, an Active Directory tool included with the Windows Support Tools; and ADSIEdit, a graphical Active Directory browser included with the Windows Support Tools.

Parameters

Parameters in SRS come in two flavors, *Query Parameters* and *Report Parameters*, and the two are often tied together closely.

You use a parameter that's based on a SQL query or stored procedure to limit the record set returned to the report, typically in the WHERE clause of a query. In the source query, you define parameters by prefacing the parameter's name with an @ symbol, such as @MyParameter. Within SRS's query design tools, this does two things. First, it forces the query to prompt for the value of the parameter when it's executed. Second, it automatically creates the other parameter: the Report Parameter by the same name. With stored procedures, such as Emp_Svc_Cost, which we created in the previous chapter and use here, any parameters that have been defined are also automatically created for the report.

However, it's possible to have report parameters that are disassociated from a query or stored procedure. For example, you could have a report parameter that controls a report's behavior or layout properties. When you use a report parameter in this way, it's often linked to a report *filter* or is used in an expression that controls a property value of a report item. In Figure 3-8, you can see the Report Parameters property window with the automatically generated parameters from the Emp_Svc_Cost stored procedure that we've already set up for a report. You can use Report Parameters within a report, both for criteria for data sets in the source query and for controlling report design layout elements. Notice that an additional parameter called Branch_URL is also set up. The stored procedure didn't add this particular parameter; we created it manually. It isn't associated with a query parameter. We use the Branch_URL parameter to hyperlink to a website that's specific to an employee's branch location. We step through the process of using this parameter in a report in Chapter 4.

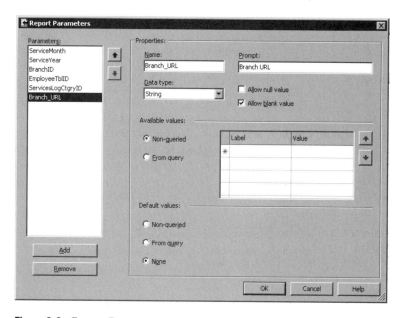

Figure 3-8. *Report Parameters*

Filters

Like parameters, report filters can limit the results of data on a report; however, you don't necessarily have to use them in conjunction with a parameter. In fact, filters, which can be defined at many points in the report, evaluate an expression and filter the results based on that evaluation. Filters take this form:

```
<Filter Expression> <Operator><Filter Value>
```

An example of a filter would be one that limits the data on a report to a specific user, or that's based on user input from a parameter value.

■**Note** In Chapter 9, we demonstrate the use of a filter that limits the report based on a built-in Global collection, which includes the user name of the person executing the report.

Filters are beneficial in that once the report is rendered, you can use them in conjunction with parameters to limit the data in the report without the need to requery the data source. In Figure 3-9, you can see a filter that has been set on a table to limit the data displayed based on a parameter called User. This report is part of an internal deployment for our company, created using the data from a Microsoft business product called CRM. We'll go over the details of this project in Chapter 10, where we discuss BI integration with SRS.

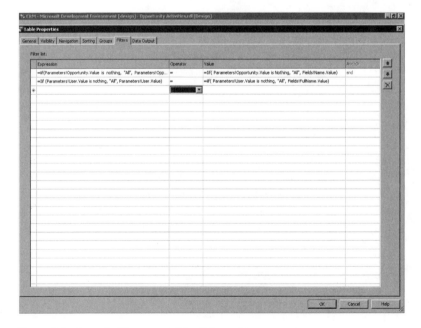

Figure 3-9. *Sample filter on a table data region*

Parameters and filters are also included as elements of an RDL report file. Listing 3-3 shows their sample RDL elements.

Listing 3-3. *Parameter and Filter RDL Elements*

```
<ReportParameter Name="User">
  <DataType>String</DataType>
  <Nullable>true</Nullable>
  <DefaultValue>
    <Values>
      <Value>= nothing</Value>
    </Values>
  </DefaultValue>
  <AllowBlank>true</AllowBlank>
  <Prompt>User</Prompt>
  <ValidValues>
    <DataSetReference>
      <DataSetName>User</DataSetName>
      <ValueField>fullname</ValueField>
      <LabelField>fullname</LabelField>
    </DataSetReference>
  </ValidValues>
</ReportParameter>
<Filter>
  <FilterExpression>=Iif (Parameters!User.Value is nothing, "All",
     Parameters!User.Value)</FilterExpression>
  <Operator>Equal</Operator>
  <FilterValues>
    <FilterValue>=iif( Parameters!User.Value is nothing, "All",
        Fields!FullName.Value)</FilterValue>
  </FilterValues>
</Filter>
```

Expressions

Throughout the next section, we'll use fields from our data set to create sample report segments. Because the values from the fields are derived from *expressions* that are essentially VB.NET code, we cover them now because they play a crucial role in the report design process.

You use expressions to produce a value for any report item that uses them. In SRS, you can assign expressions to almost any report property from formatting, such as color or padding, to the value of a text box. A simple expression such as that of a field assignment is commonly used while designing reports. In fact, every time you add a field to an area of a report, it's automatically converted to an expression:

```
=Fields!FieldName.Value
```

An expression is signified by prefacing its content, typically a VB.NET function, with the equal sign (=). You can also concatenate expressions with other functions and literals. We use several examples of expressions throughout the book. We list several sample expressions here and show how to assign them to report items:

- **=Parameters!ParameterName.Value**: Used to assign the value of a parameter to a report item such as a text box or cell in a table.

- **=IIF(Fields!FieldName.Value > 10, Red, Black)**: You use the IIF function for conditional expressions. In this case, it would set the color for a property, such as text color to red, if the value of FieldName was greater than ten.

- **=Fields!FieldName1.Value & " " & Fields!FieldName2 .Value**: Used to concatenate the value of two fields.

- **=Avg(Fields!FieldName.Value)**: Aggregate functions such as Sum, Avg, Min, and Max that returns the average value of the fields.

- **=RowNumber(Nothing)**: Used to maintain a running total for the row numbers in a report. Nothing in this case is a scope parameter passed to the function indicating a grouping or data set. The scope parameter could be a group name or data set, in which case a new row count would begin at the end of each group or data set.

Finally, let's look at how you add expressions to a report. Typically, you key them in or select them in the Expression window, as seen in Figure 3-10. In this case, the IIF function is used with the RowNumber function so that every other row, defined by the MOD operator, is assigned a different background color. This produces the green bar effect that we mentioned in Chapter 1. However, in this case, we're using a jazzier color in light steel blue.

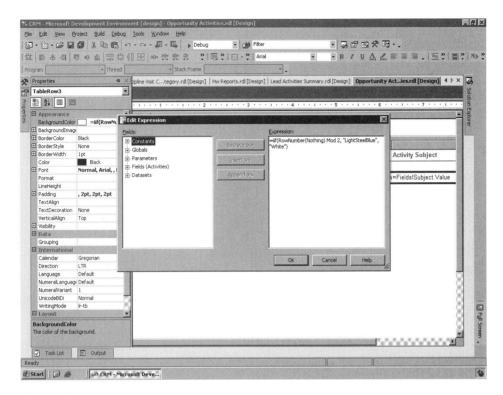

Figure 3-10. *Assigning an expression*

Report Layout

Now that you've created a data set, you can move on to the area in the IDE in which you'll probably spend the most time: the Layout tab. The real creative magic begins here, and we don't mean because there might be a wizard or two involved.

Based on the report request and target audience, the look and feel of each report might be entirely different. One user might expect drill-down functionality and other users might need full detailed listings of data for printing. Whatever the case, SRS provides many tools in the Toolbox for building high-quality reports quickly and efficiently that can be immediately deployed from within the Report Designer. Now, let's take our sample data and put it to use as we explore the functionality of each of the available tools and data regions.

For each object that we demonstrate, we'll give the graphical representation of the design environment as well as its RDL counterpart. Note that defined sections of the RDL file contain every aspect of a report, from the general layout to pagination. This is important because often it's easier to work directly within the RDL file to make alterations to a report. As we go through adding functionality to the sample report projects here, we'll point out sections of the RDL files where our graphical report design is converted to code.

Pagination Settings

To begin with, we look at the general report properties for our new report. While on the layout tab, select Report and then Report Properties from the drop-down menu on the toolbar.

Five tabs are in the Report Properties window; for now we're concerned with the Layout tab. As you can see in Figure 3-11, the Layout tab contains property settings for pagination, such as number of columns, page width, and margins. Because a number of our reports will be printed in landscape format, we set the page width to 11 inches and the page height to 8.5 inches. We leave all the margins at 1 inch.

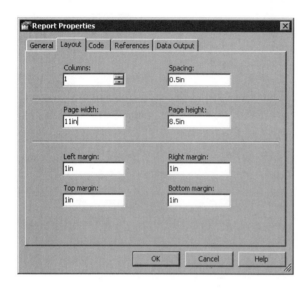

Figure 3-11. *Report Properties Layout tab*

The margins play an important role in printing. I (Rodney) can say with some embarrassment that I had some initial issues with configuring reports to print out on a single sheet, even though I'd thought I had set the margins and the page width and height correctly. The issue turned out to be a combination of these settings and the size of the design grid. The general formula for calculating the correct pagination settings would be as follows: the right side of the design grid needs to be equal to or less than the page width, minus both the right and left margin sizes. So, in our case, for a width of 11 inches with margins of 1 inch each for right and left, the design grid would need to be no wider than 9 inches. If you ever have any issues with printing blank pages, or with data going to a second page, the issue is most likely caused by the design area. Because the design area expands automatically as you add report objects such as data regions, you might exceed the width without realizing it until you go to print the report.

The Layout tab also contains a Columns setting, where you can specify the number of columns. We use multicolumn reports frequently in our industry, primarily for printing labels. Later in the chapter we'll create a multicolumn report to do just that.

List

The List data region is one of the two free-form container objects that allow a single grouping of data. The other free-form data region is the Rectangle, and the two are similar in that they can contain other report objects and data regions. Free-form data regions don't constrain the layout of fields to a fixed format; the person creating the report is responsible for aligning the objects.

Because it contains a grouping level, you can only use the List data region with a single data set. Note that the List data region displays one record at a time from the data set based on this grouping. By default, no grouping is assigned to a list. To demonstrate how we can use the List data region with our Emp_Svc_Cost stored procedure, which returns detail records for the number of visits for patients, we add a list to our design area and drag fields from the data set into it. We use Employee_Name, Patient_Name, Visit_Count, and Estimated_Cost to show total visits and cost for each patient/employee combination.

To begin, on the report Layout tab single-click the List object in the Toolbox. The mouse icon changes to show that the List can be sized on the grid. We click in the upper left area of the grid and drag the List until it's approximately three inches by two inches. Next, we drag several fields to the design area and place them into the List data region:

- Patient_Name

- Employee_Name

- Service_Type

- Estimated_Cost

- Visit_Count

We size the fields so that when we're finished, the report looks like Figure 3-12. Notice that the two fields, Estimated_Cost and Visit_Count, have the aggregate Sum applied to them. We use this expression to apply a special value to the fields. Also, as is obvious, we aren't concerned with beauty at this point but functionality.

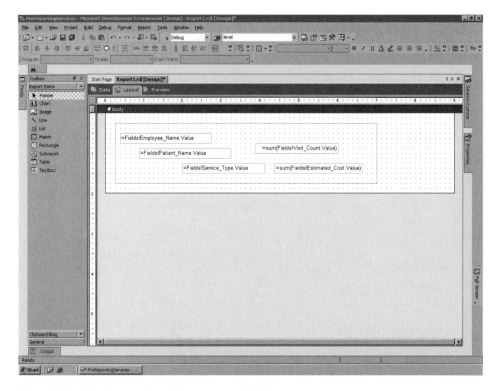

Figure 3-12. *List data region with ungrouped fields*

When you preview the report, you can see that the default List properties, without specifically assigned group expressions, force the List to repeat after each row (see Figure 3-13). Also notice that the sum of the fields is the same, which is reflective of the values for the entire record set. In other words, the stored procedure returned 34 total visits for all the patients at a total cost of $1,700. Each sum amount is the same for all patients and employees. To show where the List repeats, we've added a simple object to the report—the Line from the Toolbox—by simply dragging it and sizing it in the List data region below the fields. Because the Line object is self-explanatory and is used primarily for formatting, we won't cover it in its own section.

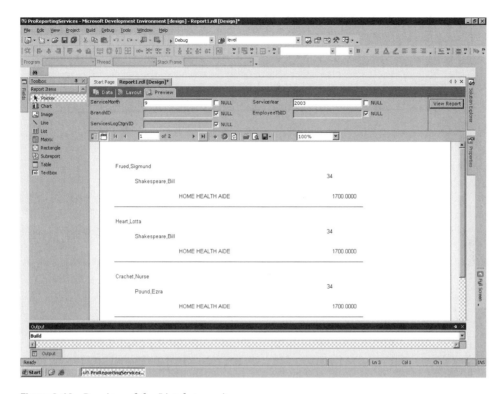

Figure 3-13. *Preview of the List data region*

Now we add a grouping to the List data region so that the Visit_Count and Estimated_Cost aggregated sums are calculated correctly. Back on the Layout tab, we right-click inside the List data region and select Properties. This opens the List Properties window. Next, we select the Edit Details Group button and we add two fields in the Group On area—Patient_Name and Employee_Name—as group expressions. We can also swap the location of the patient and employee fields on the report. This makes it easier to see the number of visits for each patient when we group by the Patient_Name field. The preview of the new list with grouping levels now shows the correct number of visits for each patient and employee combination. However, notice that in Figure 3-14 our now familiar Bill Shakespeare is showing up twice with 18 visits for employee Sigmund Frued and 1 visit for employee Lotta Heart. We could remove the grouping for the employee, but that would cause the report to group all 19 of the patient's visits under a single employee and reflect the data inaccurately. In this case, we need to use a nested list that contains its own grouping level for employees. We do this by adding another List data region to the existing data region. This should force each detail record for the employee to show, yet still be contained within the individual patient group. To accomplish this, we need to rearrange our layout somewhat.

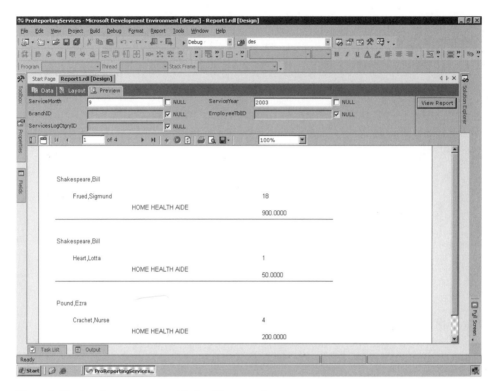

Figure 3-14. *Previewed report with duplicate patient*

The first step is to add another list to our initial list by clicking the List data region in the Toolbox as we did previously, and sizing the new list into our existing list, which we refer to as list1. Next we move all the fields from list1, except for the Patient_Name field, into the new nested list, which we call list2. The report layout looks like Figure 3-15. Finally, we go to the properties of the new list2, assign the same data set, and add the grouping for Employee_Name. We can't forget to remove the Employee_Name grouping from list1.

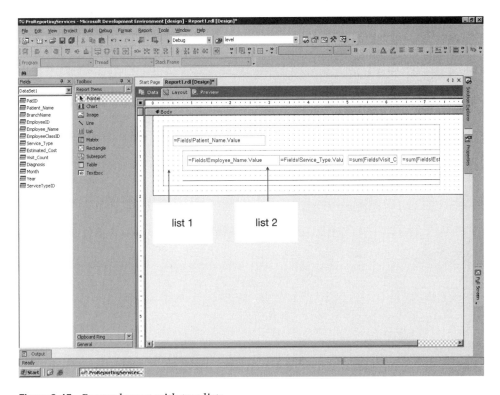

Figure 3-15. *Report layout with two lists*

Now, when we preview the report with the two lists—list1 grouped by patient and the nested list2 grouped by employee—we can see that multiple employees are associated with a single patient, with each employee displaying the correct total number of visits and estimated cost (see Figure 3-16). Our line still separates the grouped results, showing where our main List data region is repeating.

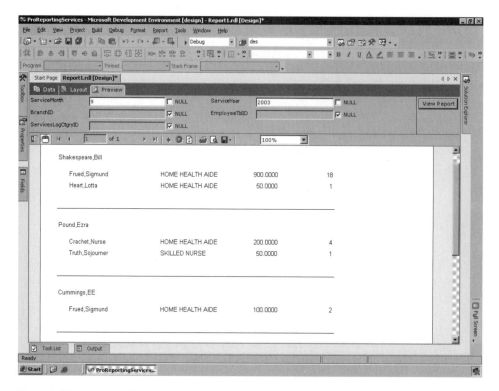

Figure 3-16. *Previewed report with two lists*

You can see the section of the RDL file that shows a sampling of the List data region we just created in Listing 3-4. Notice in the XML schema that the <List> element encapsulates everything that has been graphically added to the List data region, including all formatting, grouping, and the nested list.

■**Note** To access the full RDL file from within VS.NET you can press F7. To return to the design view, press Shift+F7.

Listing 3-4. *RDL List Section*

```
<List Name="list1">
        <Style>
          <BorderStyle>
            <Bottom>None</Bottom>
          </BorderStyle>
        </Style>
```

```
<Height>1.625in</Height>
<Top>0.25in</Top>
<Grouping Name="list1_Details_Group">
  <GroupExpressions>
    <GroupExpression>=Fields!Patient_Name.Value</GroupExpression>
  </GroupExpressions>
</Grouping>
<Width>6.875in</Width>
<DataSetName>Pro_SRS_DS</DataSetName>
<ReportItems>
  <List Name="list2">
```

Table

The Table data region provides a means of organizing data into tabular rows and columns with possible multiple grouping levels. Every table data region has, by default, a row that contains detail records as well as table headers and footers. You can group tables on individual fields from a single data set or with expressions that might combine multiple fields. Tables make it easy to make a report uniform because of the structured nature of the table itself. Fields from the data set are simply added to a cell within the table, and when the report is rendered it's automatically formatted. This is in contrast to the List data region that provides much of the same functionality as tables, but requires manually positioning and aligning fields. As you'll see in our example, it's often useful to combine data regions such as a Table, Rectangle, or List to get both free-form control and structure simultaneously.

In the report that we used for the List data region previously, we go back to the Layout tab and delete the List data region. Because all the objects were contained inside of the list, notice that they were all deleted when the list was deleted. We should now have a blank Layout tab again.

Next, single-click the Table in the Toolbox and then single-click in the design area. This adds a table that's the exact width of the design area, with each of the three columns equally divided in width. We could have sized the table by dragging it into position in the design area if we didn't want the table to encompass the entire design area.

Next, we drag the same fields that we used for the List example to the detail row of the table. In the List example, we used the fields Employee_Name, Service_Type, Estimated_Cost, and Visit_Count for the detail row and Patient_Name for the grouping value. To add four fields to the detail row, we need to add a fourth column to our table. We accomplish this by right-clicking the bar at the top of the middle column and selecting Insert Column to the Right. We now have four equally sized columns to which we can add our four fields, so that the report appears as it does in Figure 3-17. We wait to add the Patient_Name field until we configure the grouping. Notice that the column headings for each of the fields were added automatically when the fields were dropped into the individual cells.

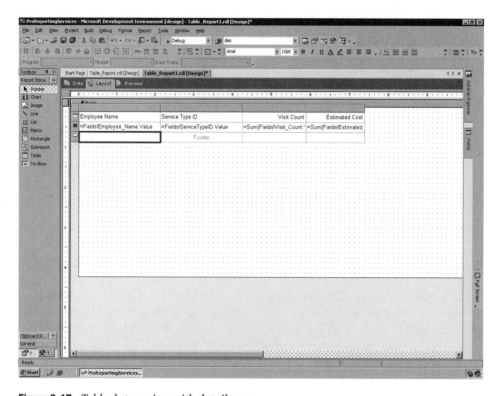

Figure 3-17. *Table data region with detail rows*

To add the Patient_Name field to the table, so that the report has the same functionality as the List we created previously, we need to insert a group in the table. To do this, we right-click the Detail button to the left of the detail row and select Insert Group. This brings up the Grouping and Sorting Properties window (see Figure 3-18). In the Group On section of the General tab, we drop down and select "=Fields!Patient_Name.Value," which forces the grouping on the patient. Because we also would like the report sorted by patient, we next go to the Sorting tab in the same window, select the same field expression for the patient as we did for the grouping, and leave the default order of ascending.

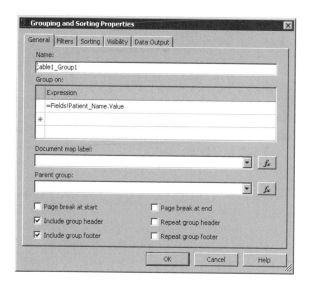

Figure 3-18. *Grouping and Sorting Properties window*

■**Tip** Though we don't use it here, notice in Figure 3-17 that the group can contain a parent group. Parent groups are based on hierarchical data, such as an organizational chart. By assigning a parent group, you can use the Level function to create an expression that automatically recognizes the data's hierarchical relationships. The Level function is useful for formatting a report, for example by indenting the lower levels, to display that relationship correctly.

After we click OK in the Grouping and Sorting Properties window, we need to add the Patient_Name field to the new grouping row that was created in the previous steps. To do this, drag the Patient_Name field to the header cell in the group, directly above the Employee_Name field. To distinguish the patient from the employee, we make the Patient_Name cell bold. For clarity, we delete each of the headers that were originally added when we added the detail row fields. Also, we need to size the columns so that the data is closer together. We can accomplish this by either dragging the right edge of each column to the left, or by selecting the entire column and keying in the desired width in inches in the Properties window. When the report is rendered, it performs similarly to the list that we created previously, as you can see in Figure 3-19.

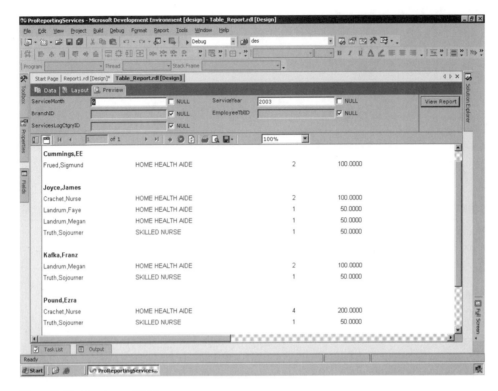

Figure 3-19. *Preview of table*

We could add more grouping levels to the table at this point if we needed to, but for now, let's combine the table with the free-form Rectangle to show how it's possible to extend beyond the structured nature of the table while maintaining multiple grouping levels.

The RDL listing for the table that we've created would span many pages, so we have chosen, where appropriate, to include a section of the RDL output for each of the data regions. In Listing 3-5, you can see a complete <Table Cell> section that would be a child node to the <Table Cells>, <TableRows>, and ultimately the <Table> element itself. The particular cell from the table that the RDL is referencing is the Patient_Name field that we added to its own grouping in the table. Notice also that the Patient_Name has a section of RDL that defines CanGrow. By assigning the CanGrow property to a cell within the table data region, it automatically expands to fit the length of the data that it contains. The opposite is true as well by assigning the CanShrink property.

Listing 3-5. *RDL Section for Table Data Region*

```
<TableCell>
  <ReportItems>
    <Textbox Name="Patient_Name">
      <Style>
        <PaddingLeft>2pt</PaddingLeft>
        <PaddingBottom>2pt</PaddingBottom>
        <PaddingTop>2pt</PaddingTop>
```

```
        <PaddingRight>2pt</PaddingRight>
        <FontWeight>700</FontWeight>
      </Style>
      <ZIndex>15</ZIndex>
      <rd:DefaultName>Patient_Name</rd:DefaultName>
      <CanGrow>true</CanGrow>
      <Value>=Fields!Patient_Name.Value</Value>
    </Textbox>
  </ReportItems>
</TableCell>
```

Rectangle

The Rectangle data region, as discussed earlier, is similar to the List data region in that it's a free-form container object for report items. Like the List, it encapsulates all the objects into one defined area. So, when it's repositioned or deleted, the objects inside are also repositioned or deleted. Also, like all the other report objects and data regions that we'll cover, you can position and scope the Rectangle inside other data regions.

The Rectangle is more limited than the List data region, as it contains no grouping levels. You can group the objects or data regions that are placed inside of a rectangle. You can use Rectangles in several creative ways in an SRS report. We pick up where we left off on the previous sample, using the Table data region, and add a Rectangle as a placeholder inside the table. This way, we can add a level of free-form design to the report while maintaining the structure afforded by the Table data region. In this example, we also introduce the Textbox report object. A text box can contain literal string values such as a report title; it might also contain an expression. We use a text box to add titles to our free-form objects that we place inside the rectangle.

We're going to add a rectangle to the entire detail row. To accomplish this, we return to our table that we created in the previous section.

1. We highlight all the fields in the detail row and press the Delete key. We can highlight every row at once by clicking the detail icon to the left of the detail row. Once we remove the detail row items, we also delete every column except the first one that contains the Patient_Name field. We can do this by selecting multiple columns, holding down the Control key, and clicking the bar at the top of each column we intend to delete. We then right-click and select Delete Columns, or again press the Delete key.

2. Next we drag a Rectangle data region into the one remaining column in the detail row. Notice that when the rectangle is added, it appears inside the table as a grid. We need to resize the table to accommodate the data we add to the rectangle.

3. We drag the bottom of the detail row down approximately one and a half inches and drag the right-most edge of the table over approximately two inches.

4. We drag the two fields, Visit_Count and Estimated_Cost, into the detail area. We place them vertically so that the Visit_Count field is above the Estimated_Cost field. Notice that the fields are automatically assigned the Sum aggregate function by SRS.

5. Next, we drag two text boxes from the Toolbox into the rectangle to the left of the two fields we just added. The text boxes, which can contain expressions or literal strings, serve as labels. Inside of the text boxes we type **Visit Count** and **Estimated Cost**, respectively.

6. Next, we select each text box using the Shift key and add formatting to the font. We set the color property to Firebrick and the font size to 12 point.

7. Finally, we highlight the two fields and set their properties to bold so that the report layout looks like it does in Figure 3-20.

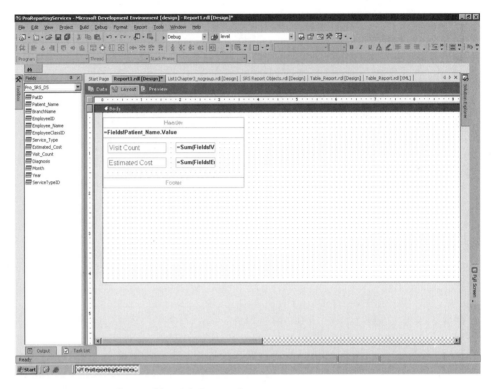

Figure 3-20. *Rectangle in table with formatting*

When we preview the report, the Estimated_Cost field doesn't appear to be in the correct format. The format should be currency. Each text box contains formatting properties that you can set in several different ways. While on the Layout tab, we right-click the text box that contains the sum of the Estimated_Cost data field and select Properties. As you can see in Figure 3-21, a Format section is in the Textbox Properties window and Currency is an available selection. The default currency format contains two decimal places. If we chose to, we could override this by choosing Custom and entering **C0** or **C1**, which would give us no decimal places or one decimal place, respectively. We leave the default two decimal places for this sample.

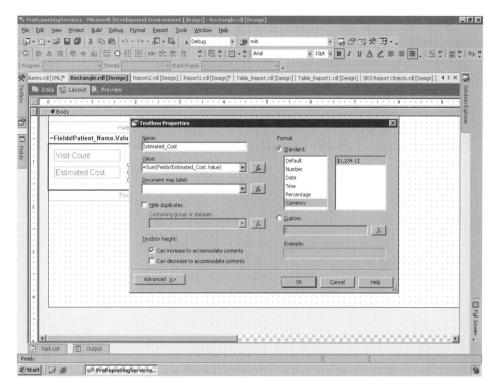

Figure 3-21. *Textbox Properties window*

When we click OK and preview the report, we can see that we now have a single detail row that's formatted with vertically aligned text boxes with appropriate formatting. Figure 3-22 shows the formatted report. Using a Rectangle in this manner allows more flexibility when adding several free-form elements to a report, while still providing the multiple grouping levels of the table.

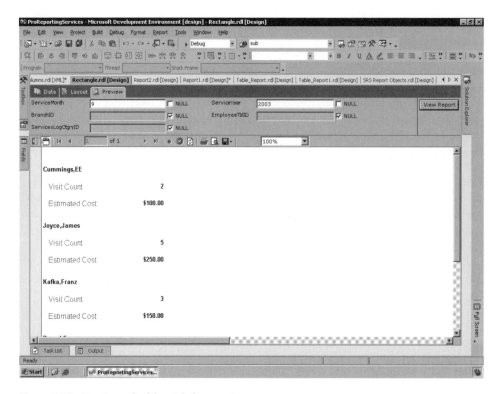

Figure 3-22. *Preview of table with formatting*

You can see the RDL output of the Rectangle that we added to the table in Listing 3-6.

Listing 3-6. *RDL Output for Rectangle*

```
<Rectangle Name="rectangle1">
  <ReportItems>
    <Textbox Name="textbox2">
      <Style>
        <PaddingLeft>2pt</PaddingLeft>
        <FontSize>12pt</FontSize>
        <Color>Firebrick</Color>
        <PaddingBottom>2pt</PaddingBottom>
        <PaddingTop>2pt</PaddingTop>
        <PaddingRight>2pt</PaddingRight>
      </Style>
```

Matrix

You can use the Matrix data region to produce output formatted in rows and columns around aggregated measures. A matrix in SRS is similar to a pivot table or a crosstab report. You can group data fields in a matrix together with other fields, producing a natural summary and detail relationship. Simple single-level matrices with one column and one row provide valuable BI that you can deploy for quick analysis. However, to tap into the true benefit of a matrix, SRS provides the ability to render the output in the interactive OWC format so that users can manipulate the matrix report for in-depth analysis. This is true for data derived from standard SQL queries or from data derived from an MDX query used with Analysis Services (we do this in detail in Chapter 10 on business intelligence). For now, let's introduce some of the properties of the Matrix data region and use our stored procedure, Emp_Svc_Cost, to populate it with the Estimated_Cost value for each patient over a period of time. We concatenate the field values for Year and Month to use for the column grouping section of the matrix and Patient_Name for the row grouping

On a blank report that has the Pro_SRS_DS data set defined, we click the Matrix data region in the Toolbox and then place it in the design area. By default, only three cells are in a matrix data region that defines Columns, Rows, and Data cells, as seen in Figure 3-23. You can use the fourth blank cell at the top left for a label or for an expression-and-parameter combination that can control the layout of the matrix itself. We discuss how to change the default static grouping of a matrix report by using a parameter value in Chapter 9, where we use a matrix report to analyze SRS execution statistics.

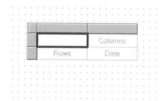

Figure 3-23. *Matrix data region*

Next we drag two fields onto the matrix, Estimated_Cost and Patient_Name, which go in the Rows and Data areas respectively. For the Columns area, we define an expression that concatenates the Service_Year and Service_Month fields. The expression is as follows:

```
=Fields!Year.Value & " - " & Fields!Month.Value
```

We also use this expression to create a custom grouping with the combined fields. To group the Columns area on the expression, we right-click the column, select Edit Group, and place the expression in the Group On section. Next, we left align the Estimated_Cost field and set the formatting to Currency, as we have already demonstrated. When we preview the report and change the default parameter values to include all months and all years by selecting NULL, we can see in Figure 3-24 that the matrix shows the estimated cost of care for our familiar patients for each month that they had service.

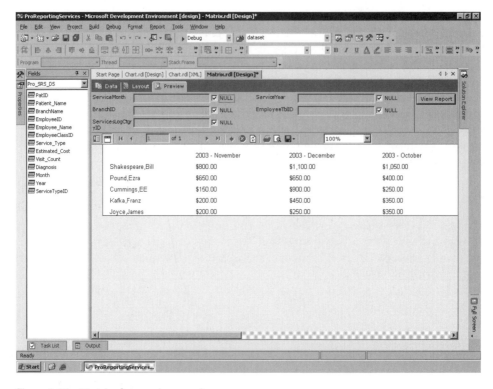

Figure 3-24. *Matrix data region preview*

You can see the RDL output of our matrix in Listing 3-7.

Listing 3-7. *Matrix RDL Listing*

```
<Matrix Name="matrix1">
  <Corner>
    <ReportItems>
      <Textbox Name="textbox1">
        <Style>
          <PaddingLeft>2pt</PaddingLeft>
          <PaddingBottom>2pt</PaddingBottom>
          <PaddingTop>2pt</PaddingTop>
          <PaddingRight>2pt</PaddingRight>
        </Style>
        <ZIndex>3</ZIndex>
        <rd:DefaultName>textbox1</rd:DefaultName>
        <CanGrow>true</CanGrow>
```

Chart

The Chart data region of SRS, like the Matrix, allows multiple grouping levels from a single
data set. Instead of the column and row level groupings that the Matrix provides, the Chart

data region uses Series, Categories, and Values. You can set many properties for a chart, and as with all other data regions, a chart can use expressions to define its properties. Also, like other data regions, you can place charts by themselves, or scope them within another region such as a List or Table data region. For example, we could use a simple chart to show the overall visits by type of clinician, which in our stored procedure is determined by the Service_Type field. We could also add the chart to a cell in a table that's grouped by patient and time frame, such as Month and Year. The chart would show for each grouping a visit count for that patient over time. Let's add a chart to our report that uses our stored procedure. In this case, we add in three familiar fields to the chart, one for each chart area: Series, Categories and Values, Patient_Name, Employee_Name, and Visit_Count, respectively.

1. To begin, we click the Chart tool in the Toolbox and then click the blank design area of a report that already has the Pro_SRS_DS data set defined. After the chart is added, we can see each of the three areas of the chart that hold the fields we add.

2. We drag the Visit_Count field to the area labeled Drop Data Fields Here.

3. Next, we drag the Patient_Name field to the Series area labeled Drop Series Fields Here.

4. Finally, we drag the Employee_Name to the Category area labeled Drag Category Fields Here. We resize the chart so that it's approximately five inches by five inches (see Figure 3-25).

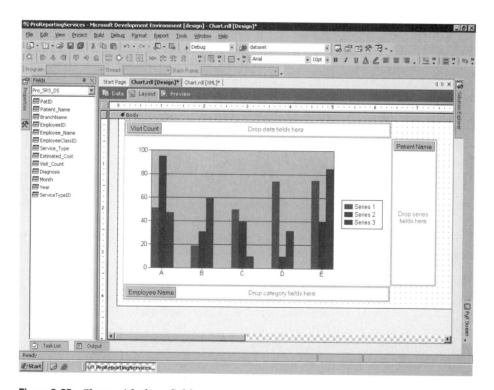

Figure 3-25. *Chart with three fields*

Before we preview the chart, let's look at its properties. By default, the chart is a column type. We'll modify several properties of the chart to add functionality and visual appeal. First we right-click in the chart area on the Layout tab and select Properties. On the General tab we change the Chart Type to Bar and set the Chart Sub-Type to Stacked. Next we change the Palette to Light. Now the properties should look like Figure 3-26.

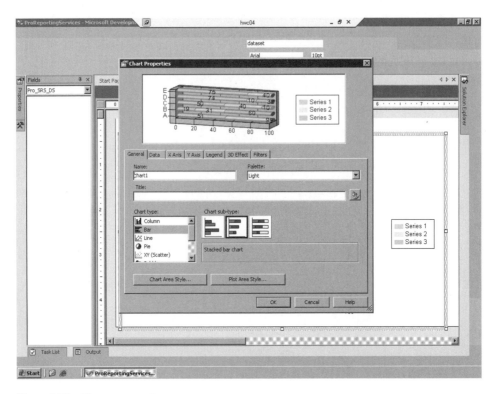

Figure 3-26. *Chart properties*

You might notice in Figure 3-26 that black numbers are in the chart. These don't appear by default. These are called Point Labels and can be set from the second tab of the chart properties window, the Data tab. On the Data tab we select the Edit button for the Values section of the chart. From the property window that displays, we click the Point Labels tab and set the label expression to be the same as the data itself, as follows:

```
=Sum(Fields!Visit_Count.Calue)
```

Adding this expression adds data labels or pointers to the report so that users can easily discern what values are set for the data series. Finally, we click the 3D tab and check the box to Display Chart with 3D Visual Effect. We also choose Cylinder on the same tab and set the Horizontal Rotation to 20 degrees. We can now click OK and preview the chart, as displayed in Figure 3-27.

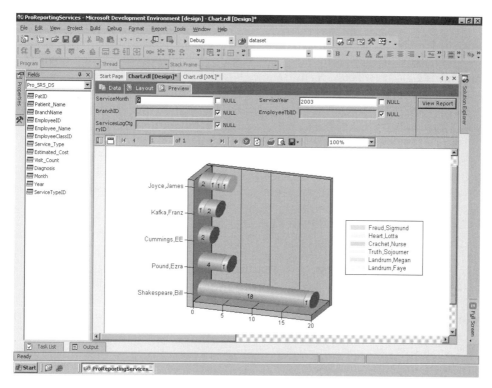

Figure 3-27. *Chart with custom properties*

You can see the RDL output for the chart we just created in Listing 3-8.

Listing 3-8. *Chart RDL Sample*

```
<Chart Name="chart1">
  <ThreeDProperties>
    <Enabled>true</Enabled>
    <Rotation>30</Rotation>
    <Inclination>20</Inclination>
    <Shading>Simple</Shading>
    <WallThickness>50</WallThickness>
    <DrawingStyle>Cylinder</DrawingStyle>
  </ThreeDProperties>
  <Style>
    <BackgroundColor>White</BackgroundColor>
  </Style>
```

Image

Having images in a report can give it a polished and professional appeal while extending its value as a resource. Fortunately, SRS includes an image tool that can add images from a variety of different locations and supports many standard image formats. Our healthcare application stores many images in a SQL server database as Binary Large Objects (BLOBs), as part of a patient Electronic Medical Record (EMR). We can load any type of image into the database and associate it with the patient using a front-end image retrieval application. Once the image is in the database and tagged to a patient's identification number, which is a field in the database, we can use SRS to display that image in a report. For this sample, we continue with our theme of famous author patients and add their images to a simple report. The report is a list with text boxes and some patient demographic information returned from a single query. We'll add the image into the list.

While on the Layout tab, we select the Image tool from the Toolbox and click into the List data region. As you can see in Figure 3-28, we're presented with the Image Wizard when we add the Image tool to the list. We can choose several ways to retrieve images. For example, we could use an image that we've added to the project, or we could embed the image directly into the report. This option would serve us well if the report contained a single image that wouldn't be used again and was intended to be distributed to a variety of sources that might not have access to the image at any other location. We choose Database for our source image and click Next.

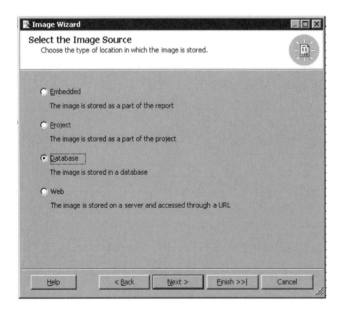

Figure 3-28. *Image Wizard source selection*

The next step of the Image Wizard is to select the data set where the image will be returned from. We've created a data set called Get_Image that's the query to return the images that are associated with each patient. It contains limited fields for the sample, and we're retrieving only a patient photo to add to the list. However, if this were a real report, we could use other images that would be standard to a patient record, such as X-ray images or photos of a patient's wounds. Even scanned images of paper documentation or faxes could be stored in the database and effectively added to a full report. Figure 3-29 shows the selection of the image field and MIME type, such as BMP or JPEG. The images we'll be using are stored in JPEG format.

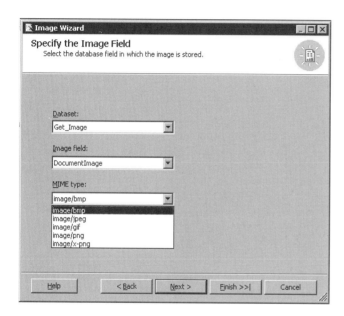

Figure 3-29. *Image field selection*

Finally, we click Next and then Finish in the wizard and preview the report. As you can see in Figure 3-30, the three photo images are correctly associated to the patient.

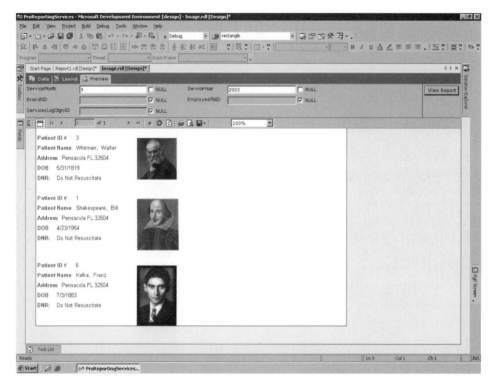

Figure 3-30. *Preview of report with images*

Listing 3-9 shows sample RDL elements for images.

Listing 3-9. *RDL Output for Image*

```
<Image Name="image1">
  <ZIndex>10</ZIndex>
  <Top>0.375in</Top>
  <MIMEType>image/jpeg</MIMEType>
  <Height>0.75in</Height>
  <Width>0.75in</Width>
  <Source>Database</Source>
  <Style />
  <Value>=Fields!DocumentImage.Value</Value>
  <Left>2.875in</Left>
  <Sizing>AutoSize</Sizing>
</Image>
```

Two Simple Tips

For a version 1 product, SRS provides invaluable tools that cover most of the bases when designing distinctive, interactive, and flexible reports. There are a few, we'll call them "desirable," features that aren't included with the version delivered for SQL Server 2000. In this case, we're referring to the lack of support for report styles or templates. Though SRS does include some templates in the Report Wizard, which we cover in the next chapter, there's no way to select a template for a blank report. In other words, you need to create every report from scratch from a blank design, and you need to apply the styles as the report is built. For reports that have a similar look and feel, this can be time consuming. You can use the tips included in this section to add some level of the desired functionality.

Using a Report Template

To address this lack of support, we've created our own template reports. These reports are built to the point of having predefined parameters—which are standard across all the reports—as well as predefined groupings. Also, you can add any formatting such as standard color patterns and report titles, defined by a global collection value ReportName, to the template file or files. Once you create the template files, you can copy or paste them into the project as starting points for new reports. Or, if you place them in the correct folder, they're available when the designer opts to add a new report. Simply by placing the template RDL file into the location Drive:\Program Files\Microsoft SQL Server\80\Tools\Report Designer\ProjectItems\ReportProject when you add a new report to the project, the template file is available like any other report or wizard. You can see this in Figure 3-31, where the template file is called HWTemplate.

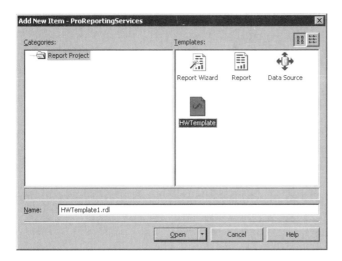

Figure 3-31. *Report template file selection*

Creating a Multicolumn Report for Printing Labels

The second tip deals with a need that's similar to styles and templates. Our company has many reports that produce labels using standard label forms. We noticed that when we began looking at SRS to deliver this functionality, we happened upon the best way to produce data driven labels: using multiple columns. We discussed multiple columns previously when looking at the Report Properties windows. Setting multiple columns for a report forces the data to be placed on a single multicolumn page. This "snaking" effect is perfect for labels. Figure 3-32 shows the output of a report that we created using four columns with a single list data region that contains patient address labels. The list was sized to be two inches by one inch, with appropriate spacing set between the columns. The data shows our familiar author patients with other patients FirstName and LastName. We've modified these name field values in the database for security reasons; however, these are legitimate individual database fields.

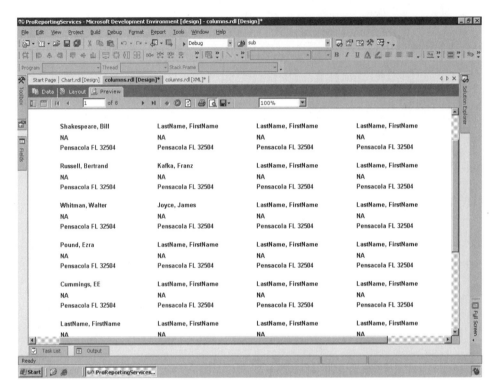

Figure 3-32. *Multicolumn output for labels*

Summary

In this chapter, we've covered a big chunk of the VS.NET IDE and the tools we'll use to build a reporting solution. You learned that each report consists of defined elements that are based on a defined schema in the RDL, which gives SRS the advantage of standardization. We covered the report objects that make up reports, and viewed their properties and functionality. You also saw for each object how the graphical design components are directly translated to RDL through the design process. Now that you're more comfortable with the design environment, let's move on to using it to design and deploy some real reports. In the next chapter, we'll take a step-by-step approach to adding these report items to a report that was designed as part of an SRS migration for our healthcare application.

CHAPTER 4

■■■

Building Reports

We have laid the foundation for our first report with the creation of the query and subsequent stored procedure. We also have seen the fundamental elements that are used to build reports and are familiar with the design environment. Now it is time to put all of the pieces together and begin to build reports. The concepts can easily be applied to any company that uses SQL Server and relational database systems. This chapter will focus primarily on creating a reporting solution based on data from a SQL Server healthcare database using many of the available report elements in SRS.

The report that we will be creating in this chapter is called the Employee Service Cost report. This report will utilize the same query and stored procedure, `Emp_Svc_Cost`, that we have been working with since Chapter 2 to provide the report data. As a reminder, the query returns detail records that represent services, such as a skilled nurse or home health aide visit, performed for patients. Each type of service has an associated cost for the healthcare company. This report, when complete, will show important cost points based on associated data provided by the query, such as the patient's diagnosis, the employees who performed the services, the date of each service, and the branch location of the patient. By grouping and sorting the report at these cost points, the user will be able to see the cost of services from the individual patient all the way up to the branch location, which might serve hundreds of patients. The cost amount will be grouped and totaled at each level.

In the following sections, we will create the Employee Service Cost report, initially with this Report Wizard, which produces a report based on predefined selections, and then we will build the same report ourselves from scratch. We go through the process of using the wizard for demonstration purposes only and therefore will not continue with the report that it produces. We will add all of the features that the Report Wizard can add plus much more to the report that we build on our own. The following list highlights our design goals for the Employee Service Cost report:

- Step through adding a base report that uses the table data region based on the data set we have defined for the Emp_Svc_Cost query.

- Add several basic formatting elements to the report.

- Add interactivity to the report with document mapping, visibility, and hyperlink actions. Both document mapping and hyperlink actions allow the user to navigate to defined locations either within the report or external to the report, such as a website. We will use visibility properties within our report to expand and collapse report items from summary to detail.

- Add parameters to the report automatically by changing the data set from a query to the parameterized stored procedure. We will also add additional data sets to populate the parameters defined by the stored procedure.

- Add a filter to the table data region to only show service types that are visits.

- Add a chart for Top Ten Diagnoses to the report.

- Add the final touches to the report, such as a page header and footer, title, and page numbers.

In the preceding chapters we have covered steps to create a solution, a project, and a data source that will be used within our report, so we will not cover these again here in detailed steps. We will, however, use the same data source properties to connect to the healthcare database where the data for our report resides. The same database also contains the stored procedure that we created in Chapter 2, Emp_Svc_Cost, that we will use later in the chapter.

Creating a Report with the Report Wizard

In many scenarios, the Report Wizard is a fast method for creating a basic report that can be further enhanced before deployment. The Report Wizard is suitable for reports that are primarily listings of data that do not require much special formatting. We will step through the Report Wizard to create the Employee Service Cost report before we design the same report ourselves manually.

To begin the Report Wizard in our report project, right-click the Reports folder in the Solution Explorer and select Add New Report. The first wizard screen defines the data source. For this example, we will check New Data Source; however, we also have the choice to use a shared data source that has already been defined as part of the project. We will supply the same data source information as we did in the previous chapter to connect to the healthcare database.

The next screen in the wizard defines the query. We will paste the query that we created in Chapter 2 into the Query String window (see Figure 4-1). The Edit button launches a limited query designer.

■Note The query designer in the Report Wizard does not support stored procedures or other nonstandard SQL queries, such as LDAP, which we will use later.

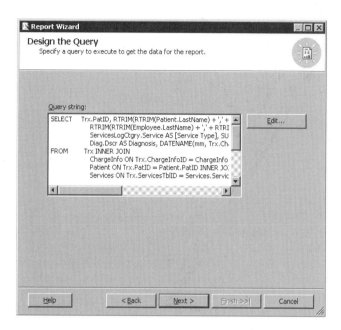

Figure 4-1. *Pasting the query in the Query String window*

The next screen of the Report Wizard asks whether the report should be in tabular or matrix form. Selecting Tabular will trigger the Wizard to provide grouping information on the next screen, while selecting Matrix will provide a similar screen for rows and columns instead of groups. For our example we will select Tabular and choose the grouping and detail layout to show Year as the primary group, with Month, Employee ClassID, and Employee_Name next. For details we would like to see the patient-specific information—Diagnosis, Visit_Count, Estimated_Cost, and Service_Type—as shown in Figure 4-2.

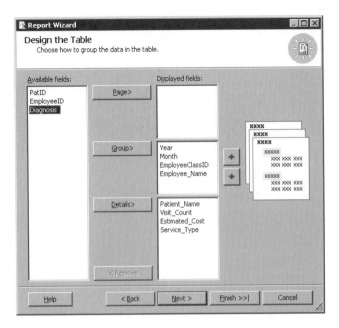

Figure 4-2. *Report Wizard Group and Details selections*

Once we have completed the grouping of the data that will be in the report, the next two screens are primarily for formatting. Here we can specify whether we want the report to have a Stepped or Block layout, as well as whether or not the report will include subtotals and provide drilldown functionality. You can also choose a custom style for the report.

■**Tip** You might notice that the wizard is very similar in appearance to that provided for Microsoft Access. Access and SRS share many of the same features, and the Access report format is currently the only supported format that can be automatically converted to RDL. There is a big caveat, though, when converting: any Visual BASIC for Applications (VBA) code you have written in Access will not migrate over to SRS. You will have to rewrite that functionality.

We will choose Stepped with no drilldown functionality for now, and apply the Corporate style to the report and finish the wizard. After a few moments the resultant report appears. Though at first glance it does appear to need many cosmetic changes, such as extending the size of the column for the service type and formatting the Estimated_Cost field for currency, the report is functional, as you can see in Figure 4-3.

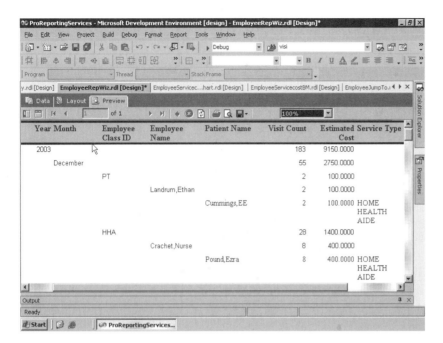

Figure 4-3. *Report generated from the Report Wizard*

To fully take advantage of the flexibility of SRS and the report design environment of Visual Studio .NET, let's move on to creating the same report from scratch.

Building Reports from Scratch

When working with a blank report, the first decision will be which data regions to use in the body of the report. This decision is driven mostly by the type of data you are working with and by the report audience. For example, a CEO might not be concerned with details, preferring to see summary information about the status of his or her business products and services, and therefore would be more inclined to view a matrix report with column and row totals. However, in our initial report we will be working with the table data region because we want to see the interrelationships between patients and employees with multiple groupings in tabular rows, not columns.

In this section, we will follow steps to get our report to a basic starting point by adding a table data region and then continue to add formatting and functionality. When we are finished, the report will contain many SRS features including interactive drilldown and navigation links, custom formatting, populated drop-down parameters, and a chart that displays the Top Ten Diagnoses by cost. We will finish the report by adding several final design touches, such as dynamically changing the report title, page numbers, and execution times.

In our report project, add a new report from Solution Explorer and create a data set that uses the same query from the previous section of this chapter. You can use the shared data source, Pro_RS, that we created in Chapter 3. We will begin by using just the basic query and not the stored procedure. Later in the chapter, we will modify the data set to use the stored procedure and see how the parameters defined in the stored procedure will automatically create the report parameters.

After the data source and data set have been defined for the blank report, we can move to the Layout tab. The following steps were used to get us to our starting point in the report, where we will begin to apply more advanced formatting and logic.

1. Drag the table report element to a blank section of the design grid.

2. Right-click the center table column and select Insert Column to the Right.

3. Drag the four fields EmployeeID, Employee_Name, Estimated_Cost, and Visit_Count to the last three columns on the detail row.

4. Edit the Visit_Count and Estimated_Cost field expressions to be sums, as in =sum(Fields!Estimated_Cost.Value).

5. Right-click the detail row and select Insert Group.

6. In the Group On ➤ Expression drop-down list, select =Fields!Diagnosis.Value. Leave the Include Group Footer checked for the Diagnosis group. For subsequent groupings we will uncheck this box.

7. Perform steps 5 and 6 for ServiceType and PatientName, replacing the Group On expression with their respective field values for step 6, =Fields!Service_Type.Value and =Fields!Patient_Name.Value.

8. Right-click the PatientName group and select Insert Row Below.

9. Add column headers "Employee," "Estimated Cost," and "Service Count" to the row created in step 8.

10. Right-click the detail row and select Edit Group. In the GroupOn drop-down list, select =Fields!Employee_Name.Value.

After these ten steps, the report is starting to take form, as can be seen in the preview. Though not yet aesthetically appealing, it displays the data in the appropriate, hard-fixed groupings and is tabulated so that it is easy to discern the detailed service information, such as the cost and counts of services for each patient (see Figure 4-4).

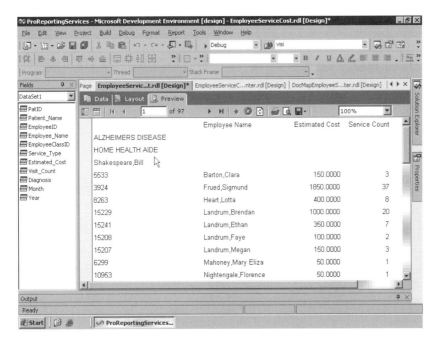

Figure 4-4. *Employee Service Cost report details and groups*

Formatting the Output

There are several quick and easy report properties we can modify to add a more professional look and feel to the report:

- Border Style

- Format

- Padding

By using the Shift or Control key, or clicking and dragging the mouse, it is easy to apply report properties to many cells simultaneously. For the Employee Name, Estimated Cost, and Service Count header cells, we would like to add a border to the bottom, separating the record header from the actual data. The Properties window contains a Border Style property for each area of the selected cells—top, bottom, left, and right. We will select Solid for the bottom border.

Selecting the detail column, Estimated Cost, we can format the cell in the Properties window to be currency by adding the formatting command C0 for the Format property.

Two of the groups inside the report, Service Type and Patient, would be more distinguishable if they were indented. We can select each group cell individually and in the Properties window modify the Padding property from the default of 2 points to 10 points for Service Type and 15 points for Patient.

After we have applied the formatting, we can immediately see how these changes affect the output by clicking back on the Preview tab (see Figure 4-5).

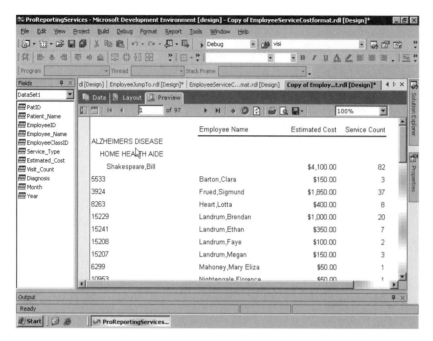

Figure 4-5. *Report output with formatting*

Adding Subtotals

Having subtotals at each grouping level makes the report much easier to read for the user. This is especially true if the report will have interactive drilldown features, as ours will have. Adding subtotals to the groups is as easy as dragging the fields that will be summed to the appropriate position in the table. When fields are dragged into a grouped row, the SUM function is automatically applied to the field expression, as in =Sum(Fields!Diagnosis.Value). The same applies to the detail row if any detail grouping is defined. For our report, we have defined a group for the Employee_Name field in the detail row. This forces the report to roll up the sums of the Estimated_Cost and Visit_Count fields for each employee. For this report, this is all that is required, but for many other reports that we will be creating, the detail records will need to be included for a more granular analysis.

In preparation for adding interactivity to the report, we will sum the Estimated_Cost and Visit_Count fields at all grouping levels by dragging the two fields to the Estimated Cost and Visit Count locations in each group heading row—in our case, for Diagnosis, Service Type, and Patient Name. We will also make the fields bold by holding down the Control key and clicking to highlight each cell, then clicking the Bold button on the toolbar. With the bold formatting applied, the summed values at the group level will be distinguished from the detail row values.

The output of the report, which we can see by selecting the Preview tab, has much more valuable information now for each grouping. For Alzheimer's disease, for example, we can now see that there were 1249 services for a total estimated cost of $62,350, and the bold format does help to separate the values. Our patient, Bill Shakespeare (whose name is indented because of the padding we applied to the Patient group) is an Alzheimer's patient and has had 82 of the 1036 Home Health Aide visits. We can further see each employee's visit count and cost for this patient in the detail rows (see Figure 4-6).

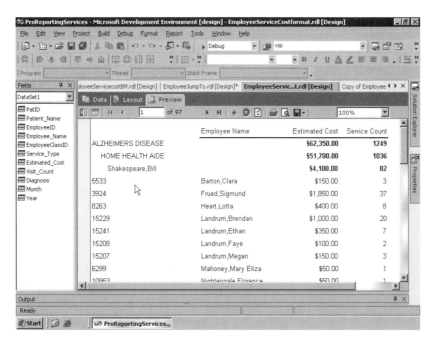

Figure 4-6. *Report with grouping level subtotals*

Adding Interactivity

Regardless of the audience for a particular report—whether it is a decision maker interested in onscreen summarized data or a knowledge worker who needs the ability to print reports—interactivity within the report makes navigating to specific information easier and more efficient. There are several ways to provide interactivity within an SRS report. We will be working with three basic types of interactivity in this section:

- **Document mapping**: Provides a navigation pane within the report with values based on a field or grouping

- **Visibility**: Adds interactivity to a report by means of hiding and showing report items based on user input

- **Hyperlink actions**: Allows the user to click a report item that is linked to a location within the same report or external to the report

The different rendering formats provided with SRS, which we will cover in detail in a later chapter, were designed to accommodate viewing and printing reports to meet the needs of different types of workers. This does produce one limitation in that some of the functionality of one rendering format is not available in other formats. This is most evident when working with interactivity, as you will see.

Document Mapping

Creating a document map in an SRS report will present users with an integrated navigation pane when the report is rendered. The user can select an item in the navigation pane, which will cause the report to jump to the position where that item is located. In our report, for example, a user might be interested in viewing information about Alzheimer's patients. We can create a document map for the Diagnosis group in the report so that when the user selects Alzheimer's from the navigation pane, the report will automatically skip to that section; the user will not have to manually search through the report to find desired information. Document maps can also be added at multiple levels, creating a hierarchical selection in the navigation pane. Keeping with the example, we can add a document map to the Service Type group in addition to the Diagnosis group; the user can then expand Alzheimer's in the navigation pane and see all the types of services—Home Health Aide, for example—that have been performed for each Diagnosis.

Document maps are created by adding an expression to the Document Map Label property available for individual report items or for groups. We will add a Document Map label at the Service Type and Diagnosis grouping levels and then preview the report to see the document map that is automatically generated.

1. On the Layout tab, right-click the entire row for the second-level grouping, which is the Service_Type group, and select Edit Group.

2. On the General tab of the Grouping And Sorting Properties box, drop down and select =Fields!Service_Type.Value in the Document Map label drop-down list and click OK.

3. Complete steps 1 and 2 for the Diagnosis grouping, which is the first-level grouping above Service_Type.

Now when the report is previewed, the navigation pane will automatically be displayed on the left-hand side of the report. The preview, which is HTML by default, is one of the rendering formats that supports document mapping, as does PDF and Office Web Components (see Figure 4-7).

■**Note** Adobe Acrobat views document mapping as bookmarks when the report is rendered in PDF. Bookmarks in SRS, which we demonstrate in the following section, perform a different function altogether. They are embedded within the report, and report items are assigned bookmark links.

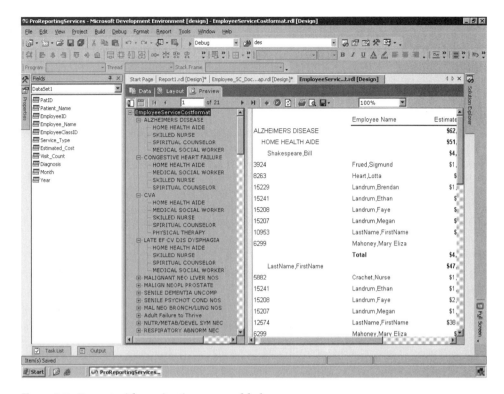

Figure 4-7. *Report with navigation pane added*

Visibility

Another feature of SRS is the ability to show or hide areas of the rendered report based on user input. Often users want to see only summary information on a report but be able to drill into the summary data to see the detail information. Report designers might make two reports, a summary and a detail report, which have to be updated and maintained separately. The reports are often based on the same query. Fortunately, SRS's ability to show or hide report data does away with the need to create separate reports. Showing or hiding report items is controlled by the visibility properties settings for report items.

Let's assume that we have distributed our report to our intended audience and they have come back with "suggestions" for how to improve the report; this is real-world reporting, after all. They indicate that they would like to see the following:

- Summary totals for visit count and estimated cost of each diagnosis when the report is first rendered, but with the ability to drill to the detail of the patient and employee if they want to

- The number of patients that have a specific diagnosis

- The number of individual employees that have provided care for these patients

With SRS this is fairly straightforward, and we can knock out an improved report quickly.

The visibility state of report items, hidden or visible, is controlled by setting visibility property values. Report items can be hidden at any level in the report and their visibility property values toggled when a user clicks on the "+" or "–" icon to show or hide them. The toggle point of the hidden items is another report level, such as a group. In our example, we would like to hide every level except the Diagnosis and Service Type fields but give the user the ability to show or hide the details. To begin, we will hide every group except the Diagnosis and the Service Type. We will also remove the Totals row for the Patient group footer, as it will no longer be necessary. The steps to accomplish this are as follows:

1. Right-click the detail row icon and select Edit Group.

2. On the Visibility tab, select Hidden.

3. Check Visibility Can Be Toggled By Another Report Item.

4. In the Report Item drop-down list, select Patient_Name.

5. Perform steps 1 through 4 for the Patient group, selecting Service_Type as the toggle report item.

6. Highlight the group footer row for Patient and press the Delete key.

The other two requests were to be able to see the patient and employee totals for each diagnosis. We can add an expression, CountDistinct, to the report that will count each unique patient and employee and roll up the amounts at the diagnosis level. The syntax used for the patient count is as follows:

```
=CountDistinct(Fields!FieldName.Value)
```

By adding the CountDistinct expression for the field PatID (which we know to be unique per patient) as well as for the EmployeeID, it will be much easier to see at a glance how many patients with a specific diagnosis have been cared for.

Though it might not have been requested, let's go one step further and sort the report by diagnosis in descending order based on the sum of the estimated cost. In this way, we can see what the costliest diagnosis is and compare the visit counts and number of patients. To do this, we will simply right-click the Diagnosis group icon, select Edit Group, and then select the Sorting tab. We will add a sum of the estimated cost expression and select Descending (see Figure 4-8).

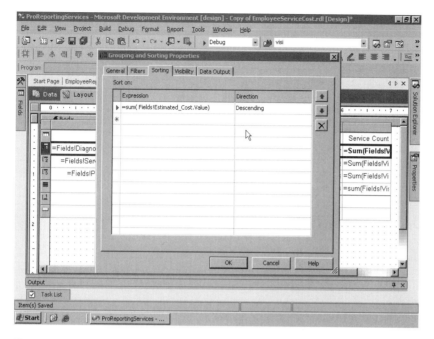

Figure 4-8. *Expression used to sort the Diagnosis group*

Though the report is very similar to the noninteractive report, with the drilldown additions it will look much different when previewed (see Figure 4-9).

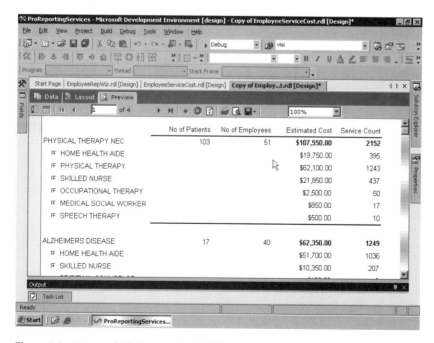

Figure 4-9. *Report with interactive drilldown*

Hyperlink Actions

Having the ability to link one report item, such as the contents of a text box, to another report or URL adds another valuable level of interactivity in SRS. By adding hyperlinks to an SRS report, users can work with the report as they would an application or web page, making their tasks more efficient. In this section, we add several links or actions to our reports to aid users in linking to other reports and locations, such as a company intranet site.

There are three basic actions that can be associated with values in a report:

- Jump to bookmark

- Jump to URL

- Jump to report

These can be seen on the Navigation tab of the report items that support these actions, such as text boxes and images.

To demonstrate each of these hyperlink actions, we will use a report that is more suited to hyperlink actions than the one we have been designing thus far, which already contains one level of interactivity in the drilldown functionality. The next report, EmployeeListing.rdl, will provide a simple list of employees, grouped according to their clinical specialty. We will add the three interactive hyperlink actions to the report to deliver the following features:

- **Bookmark**: When the employee name is selected, the report will jump to a bookmarked location within the report that contains more details about the employee, such as the number of patients they have seen.

- **URL**: We will also set up a link to the employee's department website, based on the employee's discipline or clinical specialty. We will also use a report parameter that we will set up specifically for the purpose of selecting the employee's branch location. When a user selects a branch location from a drop-down list provided with the report parameter, they will be taken to their own department's intranet site.

- **Report**: We will add a link to our Employee Service Cost report that will pass an EmployeeID parameter to limit the results of the linked report.

We will begin by creating a data set to deliver employee information to be displayed in the Employee Listing report. The Employee Listing report will contain two table data regions, one for summary information and one for detailed information about the employee's visits. We will add the hyperlink actions to the summary portion of the report, which will be the first page that the user sees. The query to deliver the employee information is in Listing 4-1.

Listing 4-1. *Employee Listing Query*

```
SELECT
    Employee.EmployeeID AS EmployeeID, Employee.LastName AS LastName,
    Employee.FirstName AS FirstName,
    Employee.EmployeeTblID AS EmpTblID, Employee.EmploymentTypeID AS
    EmploymentType, Employee.HireDate AS HireDate,
                Discipline.Dscr AS Discipline, Patient.LastName AS
    patLastname, Patient.FirstName AS patFirstname,
    Trx.ChargeServiceStartDate,Discipline.DisciplineID
```

```
FROM
    Employee INNER JOIN
    Trx INNER JOIN
    ChargeInfo ON Trx.ChargeInfoID = ChargeInfo.ChargeInfoID ON
    Employee.EmployeeTblID = ChargeInfo.EmployeeTblID INNER JOIN
    Discipline ON Employee.DisciplineTblID =
    Discipline.DisciplineTblID INNER JOIN
    Patient ON Trx.PatID = Patient.PatID
```

The steps to produce the initial basic report as seen in Figure 4-10 are straightforward, with only a few pointers. We will be using a table data region again, so we will simply drag the table to the report area on the Layout tab. We will want to add an additional column to the default three columns of the table. Next we will drag our five fields onto the detail columns: EmployeeID, FirstName, LastName, HireDate, and DisciplineID. The employee DisciplineID references employee's clinical specialty, such as Home Health Aide or Skilled Nurse. For the employee name, because the fields have been padded with spaces, we will want to use the rtrim function and concatenate the LastName and the FirstName fields:

```
=rtrim(Fields!LastName.Value) & ", " & rtrim( Fields!FirstName.Value)
```

Additionally, when using dates the default format is to include the date and time values, even if there is no time associated with the date. The hire date might look like this, for example: 10/20/2003 12:00:00 AM. By selecting the properties of the Hire Date cell, we can change the format from the default to a more standard format, MM/DD/YYYY, excluding any time value.

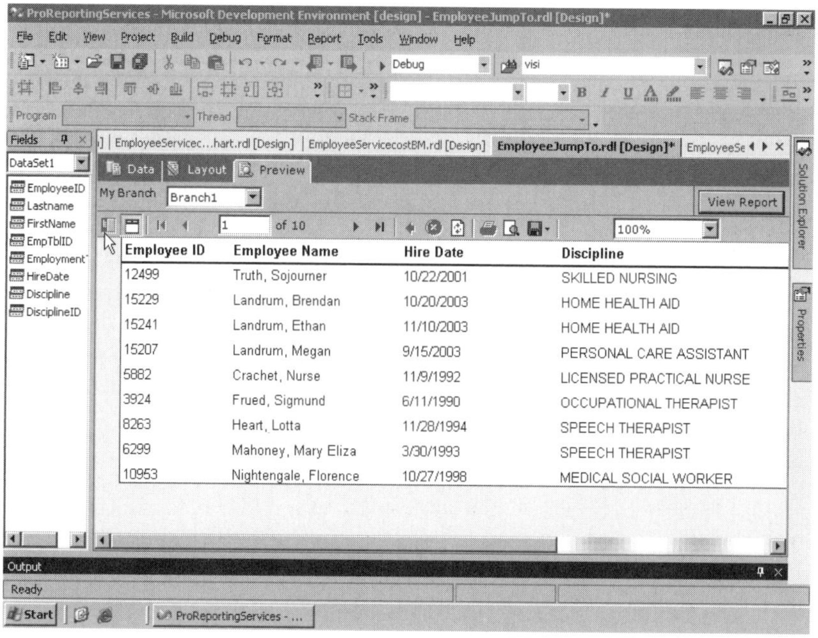

Figure 4-10. *Employee Listing Report with hyperlink actions*

Next, because we are returning detail records, more than one per employee, we need to group the detail row itself using the value of the Employee Name field. We can do this by right-clicking the detail row and selecting Edit Group. In the Group On expression field, we will add the same trimmed employee name as shown in the previous code line. Now when we preview the report we have our list of employees to which we can add hyperlink actions. Finally, we will force a page break after this table so we can add an additional, detailed table that will be used as a bookmark link. To add a page break, simply right-click to get to the table properties in the uppermost left of the table. On the General tab, select Insert A Page Break After This Table.

Adding a Bookmark Link

In this section, we will add a bookmark link to the Employee Name field in the Employee Listing report that, when clicked, will jump to a defined location within the report. In our case we are going to add another table data region to the report that will contain detail information about employee visits. Bookmarks ease the navigation burden on large reports when users are looking for specific information. As we discussed in the section on visibility, summary and detail information can exist within the same report; in the case of adding a bookmark, we are not hiding the data so much as moving it to another location within the same report. The net effect for the user is the same, however, in that they control when they see the detail information.

To add a bookmark to the Employee Listing report, first we will follow the procedure to drag a new table element to the layout tab. Next, we will add the patient name and the trimmed employee name. For this table we will want to group by the employee name, so we will right-click our detail row and select Insert Group. We will use the same trimmed expression

```
=rtrim(Fields!LastName.Value) & ", " & rtrim( Fields!FirstName.Value)
```

as the group value expression. On the General tab for the grouping, we will select Page Break At End, which will force the detail line for each employee to start on a new page. Next, we will add the date field that represents when the service was performed, `=Fields!ChargeServiceStartDate.Value`, to the third column and format the date as we did earlier.

Now when we preview the report, the summary employee listing will appear on the first page and the detail records that show the employee visits will appear on each subsequent page.

Next, we will add a BookmarkID to the Employee Name field in the detail row in the table. By right-clicking the field and selecting Properties and then Advanced, we can view the Navigation tab that controls all three hyperlink actions. In the BookmarkID field we will again add our trimmed employee name expression. This will serve as the pointer record for the bookmark link we will now create.

To create the bookmark link, we will perform the same steps to get to the Navigation tab for the Employee Name field in the first table. In the Hyperlink Action section of the tab, we will select Jump To Bookmark and paste in the trimmed employee name expression that we used for the BookmarkID.

Tip Hyperlink actions do not automatically change the formatting of the field to indicate that there is an associated hyperlink. You can manually change the color and add underline formatting so that the user knows to click the link.

When the report is previewed in Figure 4-11, we see the detailed information for the selected employee, in this case Sojourner Truth, presented on page 2; the first page of the report is the Employee Listing table, where we clicked on the bookmark link in the Employee Name field.

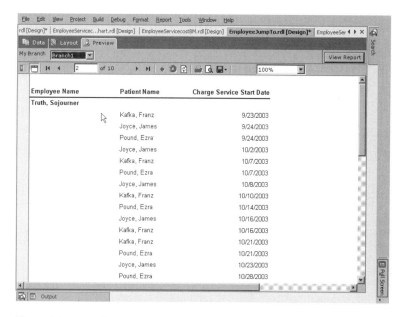

Figure 4-11. *Employee visit detail report called from a bookmark link*

Adding a URL Link

URL links connect a report to information stored in other locations, such as a Microsoft SharePoint site or the Internet. Like bookmark links, URL links are defined on the Navigation tab and can be applied to many report items. As we discussed in Chapter 3, in almost every value field that is used in reporting services, expressions are used to define the contents. In the case of the URL, we will build an expression that will define the HTTP location, using a combination of the literal URL and a field value from the data set.

For example, let's assume that for each employee discipline there is a home page on our intranet site designed specifically for that discipline. An employee who is a home health aide would have a DisciplineID of HHA, and our website designed for home health aides would be at http://webserver1/hha. Assuming that the same is true for each discipline, it would be easy to add a URL link for each discipline on our report.

Just as we did for the bookmark link for Employee Name, let's open the Navigation tab for the DisciplineID field. We will select Jump To URL and add the following expression:

```
="http://webserver1/" & Fields!DisciplineID.Value
```

When the DisciplineID field is selected within the report, the browser will open and connect to the site of the specific employee's discipline—for example, HHA for the home health aides site or RN for the registered nurses site.

Building the URL Link with a Report Parameter

Taking the concept one step further, if we had multiple web servers at different locations or branches we would not want to hard-fix the web server name in the URL string. By using a report parameter to select the server name based on the branch location, it would be possible to control the web server portion of the URL string that we created in the previous example. Let's step through this procedure. Figure 4-12 shows what the Report Parameters Properties page should look like.

■**Note** The report parameter that we are using for this example is different from a query parameter. There are examples of different types of parameters in the sections on using parameters and filters in this chapter.

---

1. While on the Layout tab, select Report ➤ Report Parameters from the menu bar.

2. Click Add and name the parameter Branch_URL.

3. Name the Prompt My Branch.

4. In the Available Values section, add the following Labels/Values: Branch1/Webserver1, Branch2/Webserver2, Branch3/Webserver3.

5. Set the Default value to be Webserver1.

6. Return to the Navigation tab for the Discipline field and apply the new expression ="http://" & Parameters!Branch_URL.Value & "/" & Fields!DisciplineID.Value.

7. Preview the report. Notice that we have a new parameter drop-down list called My Branch that was set to Branch1 based on the default value of Webserver1.

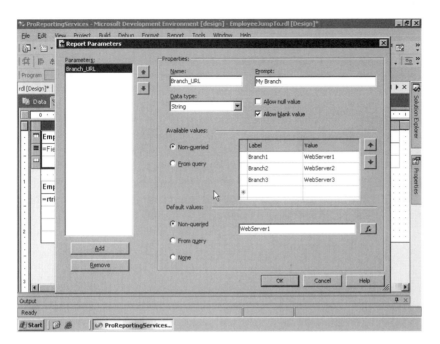

Figure 4-12. *Report Parameters Properties page*

■**Note** Many expressions and report items are case sensitive inside the Visual Studio environment. Often if you receive an error indicating that a value is not valid, it will turn out to be that the case was incorrect.

With the URL location assigned to be that of the parameter Branch_URL, whenever a different branch is selected from the drop-down list the appropriate server for that branch will be selected.

Jumping to a Report

Quite possibly the most useful hyperlink action in SRS is the ability to link to another report, called a drillthrough report, from a specified location within the current report. We have been working on two reports in this chapter, demonstrating many of the elements available. Now, let's tie the two reports, Employee Listing and Employee Service Cost, together by creating a hyperlink from one to another. We will also pass a parameter value along with the hyperlink to narrow down the results of the Employee Service Cost report when it is called from the Employee Listing report. The parameter value will be the EmployeeID.

To add the hyperlink action that links to the Employee Service Cost report, we will go back to the Navigation tab, this time from the EmployeeID text box within the Employee Listing report. After selecting the Jump To Report button, a drop-down list appears with all of the reports that are available in the current solution. If the report has already been deployed to the report server and is not in the current solution, you can use the relative path based on the target server that is defined in the project. In our example, our target server is `http://hwc04/reportserver`. We could add the relative path to any report on the report server. In this case, we will select the EmployeeServiceCost.rdl report and then click the Parameters button. Choose the parameters that are populated when the report is selected; later in this chapter, we will show how these parameters were added to the report. We will choose `EmployeeTblID` as the parameter and assign its value `=Fields!EmpTblID.Value`, which is a field in the Employee Listing report that has a corresponding value to the `EmployeeTblID` parameter. After applying the new action, if the EmployeeID field is clicked when previewing the Employee Listing report, the Employee Service Cost report will be called and the parameter passed, thus narrowing down the data set for that report to only that selected employee.

Adding Hyperlink Formatting and ToolTips

Before we save the new Employee Listing report, let's add two formatting properties that will make the link more obvious as well as provide feedback on what will happen when the link is selected. The first task is to simply make the EmployeeID field resemble a hyperlink. We will select the field and apply an underline and color format of Blue (see Figure 4-13).

Next we will add a ToolTip to the same field. ToolTips are displayed whenever a user hovers the cursor over the field and will provide additional information. In this case, we use it simply to show which report will be called when the EmployeeID field is clicked —the Employee Service Cost report. The ToolTip property is located in the Misc section of the Properties window. After selecting the field, open the Properties box and enter "Employee Service Cost" as the ToolTip. Notice that the ToolTip, like most other values, can be an expression as well as a literal string.

■**Note** ToolTips will not display in preview mode and the report must be deployed before they can be viewed in the browser.

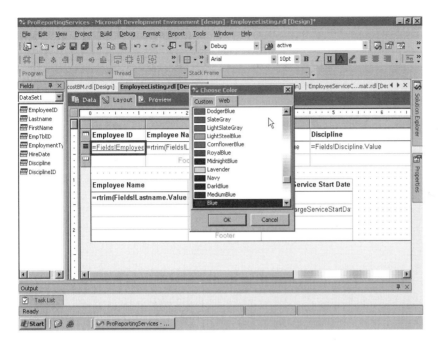

Figure 4-13. *Employee Listing report with visible hyperlinks*

It is possible to assign multiple parameter selections as input for the drillthrough report. Now that we are linking to the Employee Service Cost report, which will have multiple parameters, let's take a closer look at how parameters and filters work together to deliver data to a report.

Report Parameters with Stored Procedures

In Chapter 3, we introduced report parameters and explained how they could be used within reports and queries to limit the results returned from the data source. To this point we have been working with a query instead of a stored procedure to demonstrate how to build reports, but we have only touched the surface of how parameters can be used within SRS. Parameters get their values primarily from user input and are most often associated with a data set; they are used to limit the amount of data returned. When a parameter is used in this way, it is called a query parameter. Query parameters that are part of a data set, such as a SQL query or stored procedure, automatically generate report parameters within SRS.

In this section, we will modify the data set of our Employee Service Cost report to use a parameterized stored procedure instead of a query. By default, report parameters generated from stored procedures do not have populated drop-down lists of data for users to select, so in this section we will also populate the report parameter lists with valid data for user-selectable input. Finally, we will show how SRS works with NULL parameter values and how to generate a NULL value for the parameter. This will become especially important when retrieving data for our SRS report, as we will explain.

We will return to the stored procedure that we have already created, called Emp_Svc_Cost, that, as you might recall, will deliver the same data set as the SQL query we have been using. The stored procedure has the added benefit of accepting all of the parameters that we wish to use in the report. SRS will automatically create the report parameters from the stored procedure. Let's quickly review the parameters that will be passed into the report from the stored procedure:

- BranchID

- EmployeeTblID

- Service Month

- Service Year

- ServiceLogCtgryID

To create the parameters automatically for our Employee Service Cost report, which is currently using a nonparameterized query, we will simply change the data set for our report to be the stored procedure.

On the Data tab that lists DataSet1, we can select the ellipsis button (...) next to the Dataset field to open the Properties window. In the Command Type drop-down list, we will change the value from Text to Stored Procedure. Next we will type in the name of the stored procedure, Emp_Svc_Cost, in the Query String window. When we select OK and then execute the query in the generic query designer, we are prompted to input parameters (see Figure 4-14). Since the stored procedure is designed to accept NULL values, we will change the default input value in the Define Query Parameters dialog box from Blank to NULL and click OK to complete the execution.

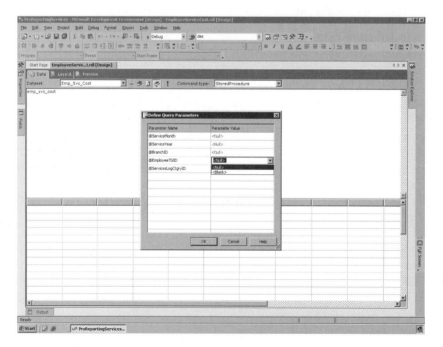

Figure 4-14. *Parameters required for the stored procedure Emp_Svc_Cost*

In the Report Parameters Properties box, we can see that the report parameters were automatically created from the stored procedure. Though SRS did correctly assign the data type for each parameter, integer, and string, it did not automatically set the field to allow NULL values (see Figure 4-15). For the purpose of this report, which expects NULL values as possible parameters, it is important that the Allow Null Value check box is selected.

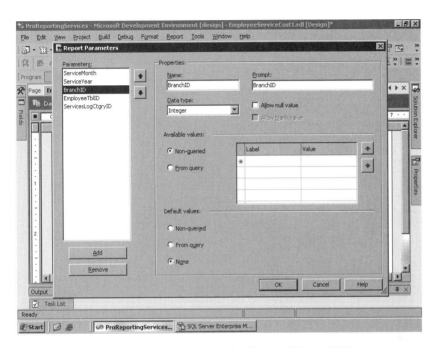

Figure 4-15. *Parameter Properties box with Allow Null Value field*

Default parameter values will also need to be manually configured. If no default parameter value is assigned to an available parameter, the report, when rendered or previewed, will not process the incoming data until a value is supplied by the user. Previewing the report without modifying the parameter selection reveals that the user would need to enter a value for each parameter that has no default value assigned. The user would not be able to choose from a list of values but would have to type them in manually. This is unacceptable because the user will not always have knowledge of the correct values; good examples of this are the EmployeeTblID field that is used to select a specific employee and the BranchID used to retrieve the Branch Name.

The first step is to provide valid query-assigned values for the parameter drop-down lists and give them a more lucid label than the generic ones derived from the stored procedure. It would be beneficial to provide a view of the report in preview mode prior to adding the values from a new data set (see Figure 4-16).

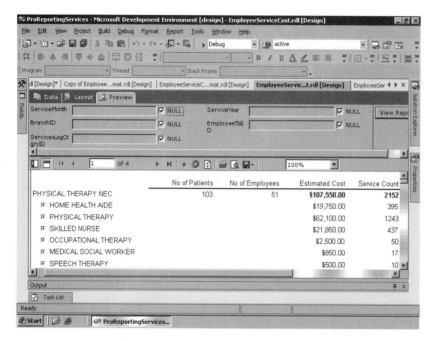

Figure 4-16. *Nondescriptive parameter values*

The following list of procedures will add two data sets to populate the Branch and Employee drop-down lists for the parameters:

1. On the Data tab we will create two new data sets and add a simple query to each that will return the ID and Name values for the Branch and Employee. The data sets will be named Branch_DS and Employee_DS.

```
--Query for Employee Parameter
SELECT
    EmployeeTblID,rtrim(rtrim(employee.lastname) + ',' +
    rtrim(employee.firstname)) as Employee_Name
FROM
    Employee
--Query for Branch Parameter
SELECT
    BranchID, BranchName
FROM
    Branch
```

2. On the Properties pages for the Report parameters, select the BranchID parameter and rename the Prompt from BranchID to Branch for clarity, as we will be selecting the Branch Name in the drop-down list. We will do the same for the Employee parameter.

3. In the Available values for the Branch parameters, select From Query and select the Branch_DS data set. The Value field will be BranchID and the Label field will be BranchName.

4. We will follow the same steps to modify the Employee parameters, assigning the Employee_DS and choosing the Value and Label fields as EmployeeTblID and Employee_Name, respectively.

5. Finally, on the Layout tab we will add an additional grouping for Branch Name to the table in the report so that as the parameters are selected, we can see that the report is specific to a branch. We will also make the field bold and resize the font to 12 points.

The report will now have populated drop-down lists for the available parameter values, as you can see in Figure 4-17.

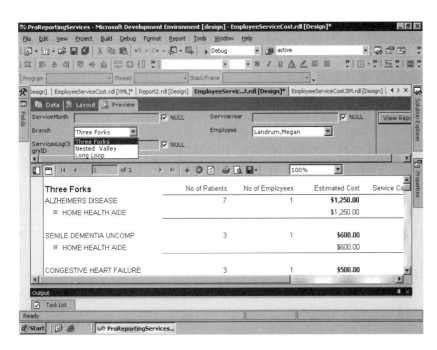

Figure 4-17. *Report with populated parameter selections*

We could perform the same steps for the ServiceLog CtgryID parameter and provide a valid drop-down list from table values. However, since we will also be viewing the report in a custom report viewer that will also accept parameter values, we will leave this parameter as is for now.

It would be beneficial to modify the time-based parameters (Service Year and Service Month) for this report. Time-based values are often tricky to deal with because of the special formatting needs of the datetime data type, which can store years, months, and days as well as hours, minutes, and seconds. The procedures for setting up the Service Year and Service Month parameters with valid values is almost identical to the Branch and Employee procedures covered earlier, with the exception that the Service Year needs to default to the current year and not NULL.

The first step would be to create a data set for the Service Year and Month based on the service date, which is the field ChargeServiceStartDate in the stored procedure. We will use the DatePart and DateName functions in the two queries to derive valid values. The valid values for the dates are contingent upon their existence in the table, so, for example, if our data contained values for 2003 and 2004, only those two years would show up in the drop-down list. Populating the date values in this way precludes the user from having to type in a date and also prevents the report designer from having to hard-code year and month values into the report itself.

In Listing 4-2, let's take a look at the two queries that drive the parameter values, paying special notice to the UNION operator.

Listing 4-2. *Parameter Value Queries*

```
SELECT
    DISTINCT DatePart(yy,ChargeServiceStartDate) as Year
FROM
    TRX
UNION
SELECT
    Null as Year
ORDER BY YEAR

--Query to Derive Month
SELECT
    DISTINCT  DatePart(mm,ChargeServiceStartDate) as DateNum,
    DateName(mm,ChargeServiceStartDate) as Month
FROM
TRX
Union
Select Null as DateNum,Null as Month
ORDER BY
DatePart(mm,chargeservicestartdate)
```

There is one major caveat currently when working with stored procedures that allow NULL values: if a report parameter has available values, the Allow Null Values parameter is overridden and the report expects the value to come from the data set used to drive the parameter selection. By using the UNION clause in the data set to return a NULL value in addition to the valid values, we can overcome this current limitation, as the report still allows NULL values as a "valid value." We will apply the same UNION to the Branch and Employee data sets as well as in Listing 4-3.

Listing 4-3. *Employee and Branch Queries*

```
SELECT
EmployeeTblID,rtrim(rtrim(employee.lastname) + ',' +
    rtrim(employee.firstname)) as Employee_Name
FROM
Employee
UNION
SELECT    Null as EmployeeTblID,Null as Employee_Name
```

The output of each of the data sets with the UNION clause will have NULL values as well as valid ones, as Table 4-1 shows.

Table 4-1. *Output of Employees Including NULL Value*

EmployeeTblID	Employee_Name
NULL	NULL
15	Crachet,Nurse
26	Nightengale,Florence
32	Frued,Sigmund
34	Heart,Lotta
44	Truth,Sojourner
129	Mahoney,Mary Eliza
146	Landrum,Megan
155	Landrum,Brendan
159	Landrum,Ethan

To finish the report, we will add the Service Year field to the report, formatting it with a distinct color (in this case, Dark Salmon), and then resize the field to 12 points. Before we preview the report, it is important to set the default value for the year so that a valid Service Month selection is not based on the default Service Year of NULL. This could potentially have undesired results; in other words, the user might select January and assume that it means January for the current year, when in fact it would be all occurrences of January.

To make the Service Year parameter default to the current year, we will go to the Report Parameters Properties box and set the Default Value to the following expression, which will convert the results of the DatePart function to an integer value compatible with the data type of the parameter:

```
=cint(DatePart("yyyy",Now()))
```

We can preview the report and provide values, which now include NULL, to the parameters (see Figure 4-18).

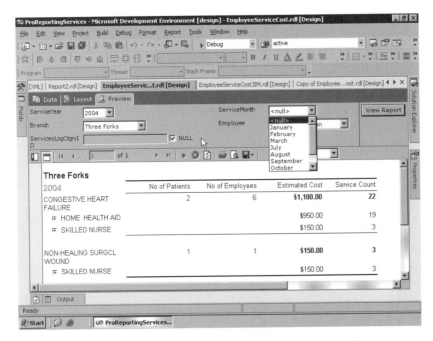

Figure 4-18. *Report with valid Year and Month as well as NULL values*

Applying a Filter

You might recall from Chapter 2 that we made a decision to enhance the performance of our stored procedure Emp_Svc_Cost by removing the criteria that only looked at visits. We will now apply a filter to the report to take the place of the original query criteria so that only visits will be displayed.

Filters can be used to exclude values from a report after the results have been returned by the query. Filters, in that sense, will prevent a requery; however, the full data set will be returned to the report. In our example in Chapter 2, we knew that a limited number of excess rows would be returned. Filters should be used when a query parameter is not supported by the data provider, or with report snapshots. Filters should also be used in reports that address a specific request or solution and are based on the same stored procedure as other reports, because filters can be used without modifying an existing stored procedure. Here is a simple filter expression applied to the table region of our report that will exclude any rows that are not visits:

```
=Fields!ServiceTypeID.Value != "V"
```

Adding a Chart

SRS provides a chart data region that has a style very similar to Microsoft Excel. Charts can be scoped within the current data set or use their own data set. For our example, we are going to add a stacked bar chart to the beginning of the report that will show the top ten diagnoses and a count of the number of services and the number of patients for each diagnosis. This will essentially mirror the data provided in the report thus far, but because we only want to see the top ten diagnoses by number of services rendered, we will use a new data set and use the T-SQL function TOP. The standard list of functions with SRS itself does not support the TOP function. This query is similar to the one we wrote in Chapter 2; however, it looks at the overall diagnoses history, not just the past 120 days. The query to deliver the top ten diagnoses is in Listing 4-4.

Listing 4-4. *Top Ten Diagnoses Query*

```
SELECT
    TOP 10 Count(Diag.Dscr) as [DiagVisits], Count(distinct Patid) as
    [Patient_Count],Diag.Dscr as [Diagnosis]
FROM TRX
    INNER JOIN Chargeinfo on TRX.chargeinfoid = chargeinfo.chargeinfoid
    INNER JOIN Diag on Chargeinfo.Diagtblid = Diag.diagtblid
    INNER JOIN Services ON Trx.ServicesTblID = Services.ServicesTblID
    INNER JOIN Employee ON ChargeInfo.EmployeeTblID =
    Employee.EmployeeTblID
WHERE
    (Trx.TrxTypeID = 1) AND (Services.ServiceTypeID = 'v')
GROUP BY
    Diag.Dscr
ORDER BY
    DiagVisits DESC
```

When we run this query in Query Analyzer, we can see that because the diagnoses are in descending order based on the service count, the results match the first ten diagnoses on our report. This is shown in Table 4-2.

Table 4-2. *Top Ten Diagnoses by Patient Count*

Services	PatCount	Diagnosis
2152	103	PHYSICAL THERAPY NEC
1249	17	ALZHEIMERS DISEASE
1034	15	SENILE DEMENTIA UNCOMP
753	43	DECUBITUS ULCER
545	22	CONGESTIVE HEART FAILURE
513	19	CVA
462	28	DMI UNSPF UNCNTRLD
331	22	CHR AIRWAY OBSTRUCT NEC
283	20	ABNRML COAGULTION PRFILE
275	19	BENIGN HYPERTENSION

Someone perusing this report might find it interesting that there are only 17 patients for Alzheimer's disease, yet these patients have accumulated 1249 total visits. Contrasting these statistics with those of congestive heart failure, where for 22 patients only 545 services were rendered, provides a starting point for further investigation.

To begin, let's walk through the steps to get the new data set and chart added to the report.

1. On the Data tab for the report Employee Service Cost, drop down the Dataset and select New Dataset. Name the dataset Top10Diag.

2. Paste in the TOP query that we have created to show the Top Ten Diagnoses.

3. On the Layout tab, click and drag the table we have already defined to make room for the chart.

4. Click and drag the Chart data region to an area above the table.

5. Right-click anywhere on the chart and select Chart Type ➤ Bar ➤ Stacked Bar.

6. In the Fields box, drop down the data set and select Top10Diag.

7. Drag the Diag Visits and Patient_Count fields to the Data area of the chart.

8. Drag the Diagnosis field to the Category area of the chart.

9. Resize the chart so that it aligns with the table below it. You can select both report elements, and on the toolbar select the Make Same Width icon.

When previewed, the report should look like Figure 4-19.

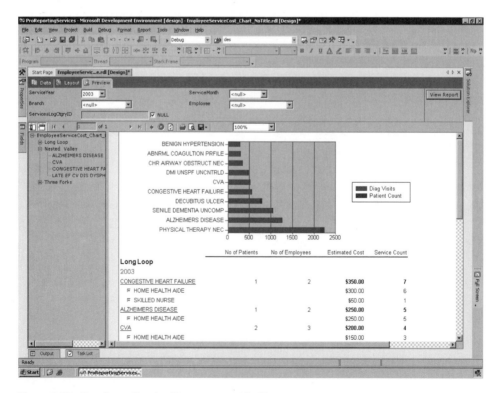

Figure 4-19. *Employee Service Cost report with Chart*

The Chart data region has many properties that can be applied, as we covered in Chapter 3; however, the appearance of the stacked bar is suitable for our report and can be deployed as is.

Adding the Final Touches

In many projects, the final touches can be quite time consuming. We have the Employee Service Cost report to the point where it is functioning the way we expect and has had formatting applied to some extent during development. There are only a few final elements to apply before we call the report complete and ready to deploy to our SRS web server for production:

- Add a page header and footer
- Add a report title
- Add page numbers
- Add report execution time

To add a page header and footer to the report, we will select Report on the menu bar and then click Page Header and Page Footer. This will add the two new sections to the report where we will add our additional values that will print on every page.

In the toolbox, there are two report items, text box and line, that we will use in the page header and footer sections. We will first drag the two text boxes to the header and one to the footer. We will align one of the header text boxes to be the same width as the table and then enter our report title, "Employee Service Cost by Diagnosis," change the font size to 16 points, and apply bold formatting. Then we will drag a line into the header section and position it between the chart and the report title text box that we just created.

In the second text box in the header section, we are going to add an expression based on global parameters as defined in the Edit Expression window:

```
= "Page" & "   " & Globals!PageNumber & " of  " & Globals!TotalPages
```

Finally, in the text box in the footer, we will add another expression for report execution time:

```
=Globals!ExecutionTime
```

We are now ready to preview our report one last time before we deploy it to our users. This time, let's take a look at the final version in the browser (see Figure 4-20). This is what the report will look like when it has been deployed to the web server. We will discuss methods for deploying reports in Chapter 6.

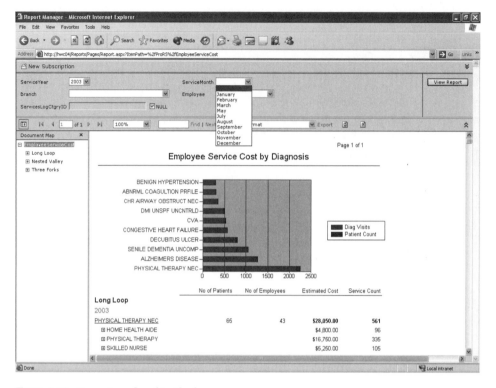

Figure 4-20. *Report rendered in the browser*

Summary

It seems as if we have covered much ground in the actual design of a reporting solution with SRS. However, at the same time we have only scratched the surface of getting to the raw power and flexibility of SRS. We have yet to interweave custom assemblies to perform specific functions that go beyond basic expressions. There are also other data regions that we will be working with in other parts of the book that we have not touched on here, such as the matrix. Additionally, we have only been working with a small number of reports in this chapter; often in a business, especially when faced with migrating existing reports to SRS, you will be working with many reports simultaneously. Deploying, administering, and securing these reports are going to become critical next steps.

Luckily, a robust and flexible design environment is only one component of SRS. In the upcoming chapters, we will deploy, secure, and analyze the performance of the reports we are designing here, using a variety of methods.

CHAPTER 5

■■■

Using Custom .NET Code with Reports

SRS offers the software developer a variety of options when it comes to customizing reports through the use of code. These options give the software developer the ability to write custom functions using .NET code that can interact with report fields, parameters, and filters in much the same way as any of the functions that come "built in." To give just two examples, you can create a custom function that

- Implements a business rule and returns `true` or `false` based on the logic. Such a function can be used as part of an expression to change the value or style of a field based on the fields or parameters passed to the function.

- Reads data from sources not otherwise available to SRS directly.

In short, the use of custom .NET code gives the developer the ability to extend the capabilities of SRS far beyond those that are available out of the box.

This chapter will cover the following:

- Custom code for use within your report using code embedded in the report. This method is the simplest way to add custom code to your report, and it deploys along with your report since it is contained in the RDL. However, it limits what you can do, must be written in VB.NET, and offers limited debugging support.

- Custom code for use within your report using a custom assembly called by the report. This method is more involved to implement and more difficult to deploy, but it offers you nearly unlimited flexibility. Your custom code has the full power of the .NET Framework at its disposal and has the added benefit that the custom assembly can be used across multiple reports. You can also use the full debugging capabilities of Visual Studio while developing your custom assembly.

Generally, you will add custom code to your report when you need to perform complex functions and you need the capabilities of a full programming language to accomplish them. However, before you embark on writing custom .NET code, you should first evaluate whether using the built-in expression functionality can meet your needs.

Embedded Code in Your Report

Use of embedded code is by far the easiest way to implement custom .NET code in your reports, for two main reasons. First, you simply add the code directly into the report using Report Designer's user interface (UI). Second, this code becomes a segment within the report's RDL file, making its deployment simple because it is a part of your report and will be deployed with it.

Although it is easier to use, embedded code does have a few considerations that must be taken into account:

- Embedded code must be written in VB.NET. If you are a C# programmer or use some other .NET-compatible language as your primary development language, this may make you consider using the custom assembly for all but the simplest of functions.

- All methods must be instance based. This means that the methods will belong to an instantiated instance of the Code object and that you cannot have static members.

- Only basic operations are available because, by default, code access security will prevent your embedded code from calling external assemblies and protected resources. Changing this can be done through SRS security policies but would require granting FullTrust to the report expression host, which would grant full access to the Common Language Runtime (CLR) and is definitely not recommended. If you need these capabilities, use custom assemblies so you can use security policies to grant each assembly only the security it needs. We will look at custom assemblies and setting security for them later in this chapter.

The ExceedMaxVisits Function

Listing 5-1 is the full listing of the custom code that we are going to add to our Employee Service Cost report. It is a simple function, called ExceedMaxVisits, that will determine if a patient has exceeded a certain number of visits over some period of time. This will allow us to identify cases for review to determine why they have such a high utilization of services.

Listing 5-1. *The ExceedMaxVisits Function*

```
Function ExceedMaxVisits(ByVal visitCount As Integer,
    ByVal visitMonth As Integer,
    ByVal visitYear As Integer) As Boolean

    ' Our businesses logic dictates that we need to know if
    ' we exceed 240 visits per patient per visitYear
    ' or 20 visits per patient per visitMonth
    If (visitMonth = Nothing And visitYear <> Nothing) Then
        If visitCount > 240 Then
            Return True
        End If
    ElseIf (visitMonth <> Nothing) Then
            If visitCount > 20 Then
                Return True
```

```
        End If
    End If

    Return False

End Function
```

To add this code to our Employee Service Cost report, select Report Properties from the Visual Studio Report menu or right-click within the report design area and select Properties. On the Code tab in the Custom Code text box, add the code from Listing 5-1, as shown in Figure 5-1.

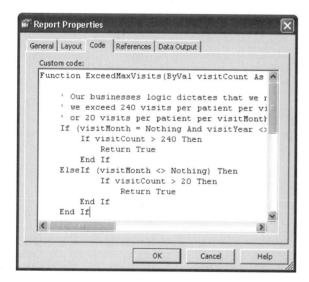

Figure 5-1. *Entering embedded code in the code editor*

Now that we have our custom code defined, we want to use it to highlight the patients who have exceeded the maximum visit count. To do this we will need to access the ExceedMaxVisits method as part of an expression.

Methods in embedded code are available through a globally defined *Code* member. When a report's RDL file is compiled into a .NET assembly (at publish time), SRS creates a global member of the class called "Code" that you can access in any expression by referring to the Code member and method name, such as Code.ExceedMaxVisits.

Listing 5-2 shows the use of a conditional expression in the Color property of a text box to set the color of the text depending on the return value of our function call.

Listing 5-2. *Using a Conditional Expression*

```
=iif(Code.ExceedMaxVisits(Sum(Fields!Visit_Count.Value),➡
Parameters!ServiceMonth.Value,Parameters!ServiceYear.Value), "Red", "Black")
```

The method `ExceedMaxVisits` determines if the patient has had more visits in the time span than allowed and returns `true` if so, `false` if not. Using a Boolean return value makes it very easy to use in formatting expressions, because the return value can be tested directly instead of comparing the returned value to another value.

When a patient exceeds the maximum visits allowed, `ExceedMaxVisits` returns `true`, which sets the value of the text box color property to `Red`, which in turn will cause the report to display the text in red. If the patient has not exceeded the allowable number of visits, then `ExceedMaxVisits` returns `false` and the color property is set to `Black`.

Using the ExceedMaxVisits Function in a Report

Now let's walk through how to actually add this expression to our report. First select the field in the report to which you want to apply the expression. In this case, we are going to select the patient name text box, as shown in Figure 5-2.

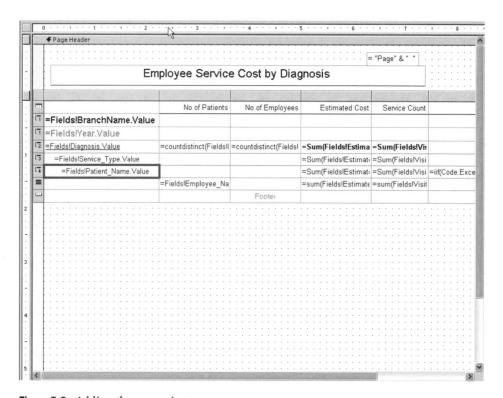

Figure 5-2. *Adding the expression to our report*

With the text box selected, go to the Properties dialog box and select the Color property (see Figure 5-3).

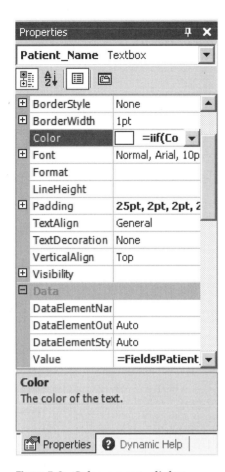

Figure 5-3. *Color property dialog*

Next, click the down arrow and from the color selection list select Expression (see Figure 5-4).

Figure 5-4. *Color selection list*

Now you will see the Expression dialog box, shown in Figure 5-5. Enter the expression using your custom code here. You can just type the expression in or you can use the features of the Expression Editor to help by using it to insert the parameters that you need into your expression.

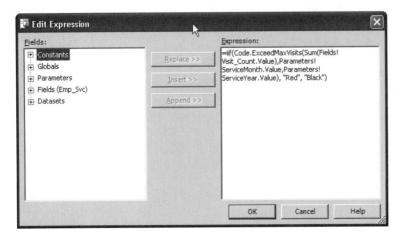

Figure 5-5. *Entering an expression in Expression Editor*

You can now run your report and the Patient Name field will be displayed using Red or Black according to our business logic in the Code element of the report.

Accessing .NET Assemblies from Embedded Code

Referencing many of the standard .NET assemblies in your embedded custom code requires that you create a reference in the report. To do this, go to the References tab of the Report Properties, click on the ellipsis by the References: Assembly Name grid, and then select the appropriate assembly that you want to reference. Note that, by default, these referenced assemblies will only have Execution permission.

The Code element of the report was primarily designed for basic use of the .NET framework and the VB.NET language syntax itself. Access to many of the framework namespaces is not included by default in the Code element.

While it is possible to use other .NET Framework and other assemblies directly within the Code element of the report, as just described, it is highly recommended that you consider using a custom assembly instead. One of the primary reasons for this is security. By default the Code element runs with Execute permission only, which means that it can run but cannot access protected resources. If you need to perform certain protected operations, such as reading data from a file, you'll have to set the security policy for the code group named Report_Expressions_Default_Permissions to FullTrust. This code group controls permissions for the report expression host assembly, which is an assembly that is created from all of the expressions found within a report and is stored as a part of the compiled report.

But making this change to the security policy is not recommended. When you change the permissions for the code that runs in the Code element, it is changed for all reports that run on that report server. By changing permissions to FullTrust, you enable all expressions used in reports to make protected system calls. This will essentially allow anyone who can upload a report to your report server complete access to your system.

If you need to use features outside of the VB.NET language syntax, have more complicated logic, need to use more of the .NET Framework, or want to use the same functionality within multiple reports, you should move your code into a custom assembly. You can then reference that assembly in your report and use the code through methods and properties of your custom class. Not only does a custom assembly allow you a lot more flexibility in the code itself; it also allows you to control security at a much more granular level. With a custom assembly, you can add a permission set and code group for your custom code without having to modify the permissions for all code that runs in the Code element.

There's another reason for using custom assemblies. With embedded code, you do not have the benefit of developing the Code section of your report using the full Visual Studio IDE with features such as IntelliSense and debugging at your disposal. Writing code in the Code section of your report is not much different than working in Notepad.

However, there is a way around this. If the code you do choose to place in the Code element is more than just a few simple lines of code, it can be easier to create a separate project within your report solution to write and test your code. A quick VB.NET Windows Form or Console project can provide the ideal way to write code you intend to embed in your report. You get the full features of the IDE, and once you have the method or methods working the way you want you can just paste them into the code window of the report. Remember to use a VB.NET project, since the Code element only works with code written in VB.NET.

Using Custom Assemblies

Custom assemblies are harder to implement but offer you greater flexibility than embedded code. Their creation is a bit more involved because they are not part of the report's RDL and must be created outside of Report Designer. This also makes them more difficult to deploy because, unlike the embedded code, which becomes a part of the report's RDL, the custom assembly is a separate file.

However, your hard work is repaid in many ways:

- Custom code can be used across multiple reports without the need to copy and paste code into each report. This allows you to centralize all of the custom logic into a single location, making code maintenance much simpler.

- It allows you to more easily separate the tasks of writing a report from the creation of the custom code. This is somewhat similar in concept to writing an ASP.NET application using the code-behind feature. This allows ASP.NET developers to separate the page markup, layout, and graphics from the code that will interact with it. If you have several people involved, you can let those who specialize in report writing handle the layout and creation of the report while others who may have more coding skills write the custom code.

- You can use the .NET language of your choice. Choose from C#, VB, J# or any third-party language that is compatible with the .NET Framework.

- If you use Visual Studio.NET to develop your custom assemblies, you get the full power of its editing and debugging features.

- You can exercise very fine-grained control over what your assembly can do using security policies.

To use a custom assembly from within our report, we will need to create a class library to hold our code, add the methods and properties we want to use from our report to our class, and then compile it into an assembly. To use it from within Report Designer, we can add a class library project to our Solution in Visual Studio, allowing us easy access to both the report and code we will use in it.

Adding a Class Library Project to Your Reporting Solution

First, you will need to write your custom code in the form of a .NET class. You can do this by adding a Class Library Project to our existing SRS project solution so that you can work on the report and the custom code at the same time.

In this example, we want to display the amount an employee is paid for a visit to a patient. Our class will get this information from an XML file that is periodically exported from the human resources system.

■**Note** If possible, you would want to get this information directly from the HR system, possibly through a Web service.

Using the XML file EmployeeCost.xml (supplied as part of the code download for this chapter) in our example allows us not only to write a custom assembly but also to see the steps necessary to access a protected resource such as a local file. In order to get the information from the XML file and make it available to our report, we will create a class with a method that takes EmployeeID as a parameter and that will read the employee pay per visit rates from the XML file and then return the pay rate. If no pay rate is found in the file we will return $25, which is our default rate of pay.

We could then reference the assembly from an expression in our report, and use it to calculate the total visiting costs per patient.

To start, select File ➤ Add Project ➤ New Project from the menu. Pick Visual Basic Projects or Visual C# Projects, depending on your preference. Select Class Library, and enter "Employee" for the name of the Project. In our example, we are using a Visual C# Class Library Project, as shown in Figure 5-6.

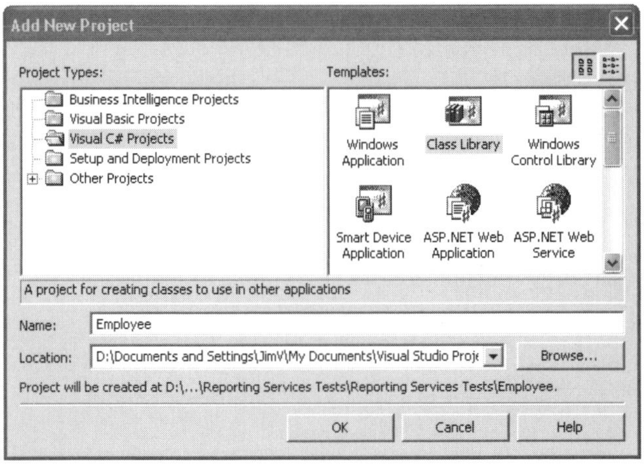

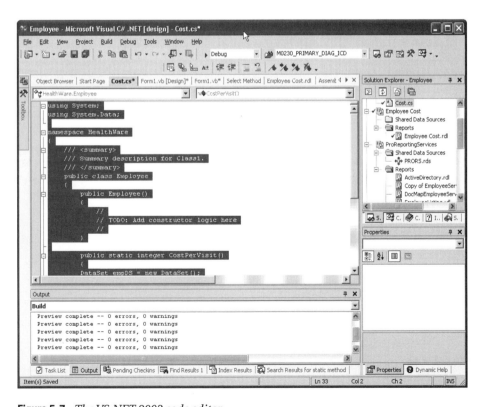

Figure 5-6. *Add New Project dialog*

Select the Class1.cs and let's rename it to something a bit more descriptive, such as Cost, because we are going to use this class to calculate the cost of a visit provided by our employees. Open the Cost.cs file in the VS.NET IDE and you will see the code editor in Figure 5-7.

Figure 5-7. *The VS.NET 2003 code editor*

In our example, we are going to select the System.Data and System.Xml assemblies so we can reference the DataSet and LoadXml methods of the data set in our Employee assembly, as shown in Listing 5-3. We will use them to load the XML into a data set. Having the employee pay information stored in memory allows us to access it quickly.

The System.Data and System.Xml assemblies must be available on both the computer being used to design the report as well as the SQL Reporting Server itself. Since we are just using common .NET Framework assemblies, this should not be a problem because the .NET Framework is installed on our local computer as well as on the SRS server. If you reference other custom or third-party assemblies in your custom assembly, you will need to make sure that they are available on the SRS server where you will be running your report.

Listing 5-3. *The Code for the Employee Assembly*

```
using System;
using System.Data;
using System.Xml;

namespace HealthWare
{
    /// <summary>
    /// Summary description for Employee.
    /// </summary>
    public class Employee
    {
        public Employee()
        {
        }
        public static integer CostPerVisit()
        {
            DataSet empDS = new DataSet();
            empDS.ReadXml(@"D:\Temp\EmployeeCost.xml");
            DataRow[] empRows = empDS.Tables["Employee"].
                Select("EmployeeID = " & empID);
            Decimal empAmt;
            if (empRows.Length > 0)
            {
                empAmt =  Convert.ToDecimal(empRows(0)("EmployeePayPerVisit"));
                return empAmt;
            }
            else
                return 25;
        }
    }
}
```

Adding an Assembly Reference to a Report

On the Report menu, click Report Properties or click within the report design area. Then do the following:

1. In References, click the Add button and select or browse to the assembly from the Add References dialog box.

2. In Classes, type the name of the class, and for instance-based members provide an instance name to use within the report. If you use static members, you will not need to specify them in the instance list, since they are accessed through the globally available Code member, as shown in Figure 5-8.

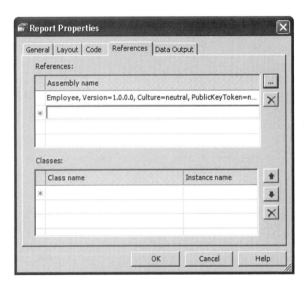

Figure 5-8. *References dialog*

To use the custom code in your assembly in a report expression, you must call a member of a class within the assembly. This will be done differently depending on how the method was declared.

If the method is defined as static, it is available globally within the report. You access it in an expression by namespace, class, and method name. The following example calls the static CostPerVisit method, in the Employee class, which is in the Healthware namespace, passing in an EmployeeID value. The method will return the cost per visit for the specified employee:

```
=HealthWare.Employee.CostPerVisit(empID)
```

If the custom assembly contains instance methods, you must add the class and instance name information to the report references. You do not need to add this information for static methods.

Instance-based methods are available through the globally defined Code member. You access these methods by referring to the Code member, and then the instance and method name. This is how we would call the `CostPerVisit` method if it had been declared as a instance method instead of a static method:

```
=Code.rptHealthWare.Employee.CostPerVisit(empID)
```

■**Tip** Use static methods whenever possible because they offer higher performance than instance methods. However, be careful if you use static fields and properties, because they expose their data to all instances of the same report, making it possible that the data used by one user running a report is exposed to another user running the same report.

Debugging Custom Assemblies

For ease of debugging, the recommended way to design, develop, and test custom assemblies is to create a solution that contains both your test reports and your custom assembly. This will allow you easy access to both the report and the code you will use in it at the time from within Visual Studio.

What we will do now is set up Visual Studio to allow us to debug the Employee assembly we have just written.

1. In the Solution Explorer, right-click on the Solution and select Configuration Manager. This will allow us to set the build and deploy options for debugging.

2. Select DebugLocal as the Active Solution Configuration.

3. Make sure that the report project in your solution is set to DebugLocal and that Deploy is unchecked. DebugLocal is used to debug reports on your local system, rendering the report in the preview pane within Visual Studio. If Deploy is checked, it will publish the reports to the report server instead of running them locally and you will not be able to debug them.

4. Right-click on the project containing your reports.

5. Set the Report project as the startup project. This will make the report run first when you start debugging. We will set the specific report that will call our custom assembly in a subsequent step.

6. Right-click again and select Project Dependencies.

7. In the Project Dependencies dialog, select the Employee project as the dependent project, as shown in Figure 5-9. This will tell Visual Studio that our report is dependent on the custom assembly we have written.

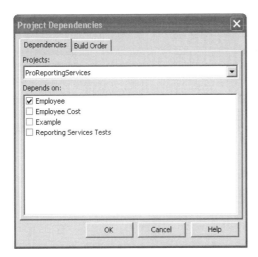

Figure 5-9. *Project Dependencies dialog*

8. Click OK to save the changes, and close the Property Pages dialog.

9. Right-click again on the report project and select Project Properties.

10. Select StartItem and set it to the report you want to debug. The StartItem tells Visual Studio specifically which report to run when you run with debugging.

11. In Solution Explorer, select the Employee custom assembly project.

12. Right-click and select Properties.

13. Expand Configuration Properties and click Build.

14. On the Build page, enter the path to the Report Designer folder (by default, C:\Program Files\Microsoft SQL Server\80\Tools\Report Designer) in the Output Path text box.

■Tip You could leave the default output path, but changing it saves you some work. With the default path, you'd have to build and then manually copy your custom assembly in order for Report Designer running within VS.NET to find it and run it.

---

15. Now set breakpoints in your custom assembly code.

16. Make sure to set the Report as the startup project and then press F5 to start the solution in debug mode. When the report uses the custom code in your expression, the debugger will stop at any breakpoints that you have set when they are executed. Now you can use the all the powerful debugging features of VS.NET to debug your code.

■Note It is also possible to use multiple copies of VS.NET to debug your custom assembly. See SRS Books Online (BOL) for details.

Deploying a Custom Assembly

Custom assemblies are more difficult to deploy than code embedded in your report through the Code element. There are several reasons for this:

- Custom assemblies are not part of the report itself and must be deployed separately.

- Custom assemblies are not deployed to the same folder as the reports themselves.

- The built-in project deployment method in VS.NET will not automatically deploy your custom assemblies.

- Custom assemblies are only granted Execution permissions by default. Execution permission allows code to run, but not to use protected resources.

To use your custom assemblies with SRS, you will need to take the following steps to place them into a location where SRS can find them and to edit the files that control security policy. The location of the files depends on whether we want to use them in Report Designer within Visual Studio or on the report server itself.

1. You need to deploy your custom assemblies to the Report Designer or Reporting Services applications folder.

   - For Report Designer, the default is C:\Program Files\Microsoft SQL Server\80\Tools\Report Designer.

   - For Reporting Server, the default is C:\Program Files\Microsoft SQL Server\MSSQL\Reporting Services\ReportServer\bin.

2. Next, you need to edit the Reporting Services policy configuration files if your custom assembly requires permissions in addition to Execution permission.

   - For Report Designer, the default location is C:\Program Files\Microsoft SQL Server\80\Tools\Report Designer.

   - For Reporting Server, the default location is C:\Program Files\Microsoft SQL Server\MSSQL\Reporting Services\ReportServer.

For example, if you were writing a custom assembly to calculate an employee's cost per visit, you might need to read the pay rates from a file. To retrieve the rate information, you would need to add an additional security permission, FileIOPermission, to your permission set for the assembly. To grant this permission, we have to make the following two changes to the configuration file.

■Tip For more information about code access security and reporting services, see *Understanding Code Access Security in Reporting Services* in the SRS BOL.

To add permission to read a file called D:\Temp\EmployeeCost.xml, you first need to add a permission set in the policy configuration file that grants read permission to the file. You can then apply the permission to the custom assembly, as shown in Listing 5.4.

Listing 5-4. *Granting Read Permission on the EmployeeCost.xml File*

```
<PermissionSet class="NamedPermissionSet"
    version="1"
    Name="EmpCostFilePermissionSet"
    Description="Permission set that grants read access to my employee cost file.">
       <IPermission class="FileIOPermission"
           version="1"
           Read=" D:\Temp\EmployeeCost.xml "/>
       <IPermission class="SecurityPermission"
           version="1"
           Flags="Execution, Assertion"/>
</PermissionSet>
```

Next, as shown in Listing 5-5, we add a code group that grants our assembly the additional permissions:

Listing 5-5. *Granting File I/O Permission on the Employee Assembly*

```
<CodeGroup class="UnionCodeGroup"
    version="1"
    PermissionSetName=" EmpCostFilePermissionSet"
    Name="EmpCostCodeGroup"
    Description="Employee Cost Per Visit">
    <IMembershipCondition class="UrlMembershipCondition"
        version="1"
        Url="C:\Program Files\Microsoft SQL Server\MSSQL\Reporting
Services\ReportServer\bin\Employee.dll"/>
</CodeGroup>
```

■Note The name of the assembly that you add to the configuration file must match exactly the name that is added to the RDL under the CodeModules element.

In order to apply custom permissions, you must also assert the permission within your code. For example, if you want to add read-only access to an XML file C:\CurrencyRates.xml, you must add the code shown in Listing 5-6 to your method:

Listing 5-6. *Asserting Permission with Code*

```
// C#
FileIOPermission permission = new
    FileIOPermission(FileIOPermissionAccess.Read,
    @" D:\Temp\EmployeeCost.xml");
try
{
    permission.Assert();
    // Load the XML currency rates file
    XmlDocument doc = new XmlDocument();
    doc.Load(@"D:\Temp\EmployeeCost.xml");
...
```

You can also add the assertion as a method attribute, as shown in Listing 5-7.

Listing 5-7. *Asserting Permission with a Method Attribute*

```
[FileIOPermissionAttribute(SecurityAction.Assert,
    Read=@" D:\Temp\EmployeeCost.xml")]
```

For more information, see ".NET Framework Security" in the *.NET Framework Developer's Guide*, available on the Microsoft Developer Network (MSDN) website at http://msdn.microsoft.com. You will also want to read about using the Global Assembly Cache (GAC) to store your custom assembly.

Troubleshooting

If you modify a custom assembly and rebuild it, you must redeploy it because Report Designer only looks for it in the Report Designer application folder. If you followed our suggestion in the "Debugging Custom Assemblies" section to change the output path, it should be in the correct location each time you rebuild it while debugging. If not, you will need to follow the instructions in the "Deploying a Custom Assembly" section to move it into to the Report Designer application folder. Remember, Visual Studio will not deploy your custom assembly to your SRS Server; it must be copied manually.

You may find that you have to exit the VS.NET IDE in order to replace the files, as they may otherwise be in use.

Finally, you may wish to keep the version of any custom assembly the same at least while you are developing it. Every time you change the version of a custom assembly, the reference to it must change under Report Properties References, as discussed earlier in this chapter. Once your reports are in production where you want to keep track of version information, you can use the GAC, which can hold multiple versions; this means you only have to redeploy reports that use the new features of the new version. If you want all of the reports to use the new version, you can set the binding redirect so that all requests for the old assembly are sent to the new assembly. You would need to modify the report server's Web.config file and ReportService.exe.config file.

Summary

In this chapter, we have looked at using custom code within your application and we have discussed some of the other programmatic aspects of dealing with reporting services. Chapters 6, 7, and 8 will build on this as we write applications to render, deploy and manage both the reporting solutions we have developed and the SRS server itself.

In subsequent chapters, we will look at other aspects of programmatically working with SRS, such as how to render reports from within a custom .NET application and how to deploy them to and secure them on the report server.

CHAPTER 6

■■■

Rendering Reports from .NET Applications

Report rendering is the process of outputting the results of a report into a specific format. You pass the appropriate parameters to SRS telling it what report you want to run, and optionally what format you want the output in, any user credentials, and the actual report parameters, and SRS renders the report and returns the results.

The manner in which you pass these parameters and how the results are returned depends on the SRS method that you're using to render the report. Once SRS has the information it needs, based on the particular report you're running, it queries the appropriate data sources. SRS uses the passed credentials and parameters if appropriate, renders the report into an intermediate format, and then renders and filters this intermediate format into the final display format requested.

With SRS, you can render reports in two ways from a .NET application:

- You can build a URL that allows the client to access the report on the report server, and supply any appropriate parameters, including rendering format, login information, report criteria, and report filters.

- You can use the Web services APIs to render the report. This returns the rendered data as a stream that you then display. This is a more difficult method of rendering. That's because the information you get back from the server is essentially a binary stream of data, and you don't have the benefit of having the server/browser combination to do the actual work of displaying the data. However, you can use the Web services APIs for more than just rendering; you can use them to access the report server's complete functionality. We'll use the Web services APIs in our solution to provide us with information about the reports we're rendering, such as the report parameters that they use.

The most common—and simplest—rendering method is via URL access. In this case, SRS provides some defaults for most reporting options. For example, SRS provides a default user interface for entering parameter and filter information. It prompts you for login information if necessary, and it defaults to rendering in HTML format. You get all this simply by passing the URL of the report from the browser. This is most useful if you're rendering your reports using just your web browser, with no other controlling application.

You can optionally pass parameters along with the URL to change these default behaviors, provide login information, change the default rendering, hide the parameter toolbar, and so on. This is useful if you have a custom application and want to control these options yourself rather than providing the default user interface.

You can do many of the same things using the Web services API, but there are no real defaults and the actual display of the returned data to the user is left up to the application developer. By using the web browser in an ASP.NET application, or embedded into a Windows Form, you get the benefits of the URL rendering method, but you can exercise control over it. This provides users with a more integrated experience. The methods covered in this chapter apply largely to both Windows Forms and Web Forms applications. The project we'll build is a Windows Forms-based report viewer that allows us to use SRS as the reporting solution for our application.

In this chapter, we'll do the following:

- Show you how to build a URL through which a client application can access a report on the report server. We'll use the Employee Service Cost report in our example (available with the code download for this chapter in the Downloads section of the Apress web site at `http://www.apress.com`).

- Discuss the reporting parameters that, when specified in the URL, control how the report is rendered. You can specify the actual format (for example, HTML or PDF). You can specify that a specific page in a report be rendered, or you can search for a particular word and start rendering on that page.

- Build a simple .NET Windows Forms application that accesses and renders our report, via a Web Browser control that we'll embed into a form.

- Use Web services API calls to query for the report criteria and filter parameters and allow us to display them on our Windows Form. We'll then use the Web services API again to see if the parameters have a list of values for the user to select from. If so, we'll use those values to populate combo boxes for each parameter. We'll also give the user a combo box to select a rendering format. We'll then display all the selections to the users and use their selected values to create a URL that contains all the information necessary to run the report. Finally, we'll use this URL with our embedded web browser to render the report with user-entered report parameters and rendering commands.

URL Access

In this section, we'll show you how to build a URL that accesses the desired reports on the report server and passes the appropriate parameters to the report.

The syntax for the entire URL breaks down into two parts. The first part specifies the path to the report file and the second specifies the parameters. The full URL syntax is as follows:

```
http://server/virtualroot?[/pathinfo]&prefix:param=value
[&prefix:param=value]...n]
```

Table 6-1 describes each component part of the URL.

Table 6-1. *URL Access Parameters*

Parameter	Description	Supported Values
server	Name of the SRS Web server	None
virtualroot	Virtual root of the SRS Web service	None
?	Separates the application virtual root from the parameters	None
[/pathinfo]	The optional path to a folder containing the report	None
&	Separates individual parameters	None
Prefix	When used, indicates that the following parameter is a command to the server itself versus a report parameter	rc: Rendering control rs: Report server command dsu: User dsp: Password
Param	Command parameter name when used with a prefix; otherwise a report parameter name	None
Value	The value of the parameter	None

Let's walk through the steps of building a URL to access the Employee Service Cost report.

URL Report Access Path Format

As indicated in the previous section, the path to access the appropriate report starts with the name of the report server itself, in this case http://hwc04. Following that is the name of the SRS virtual root folder, such as /reportserver (this is the default folder during install). This folder points to the SRS Web service; we'll use this one for rendering our reports.

■**Note** The /reports virtual root folder is mapped to the Report Manager application that ships with SRS. If you navigate to this URL, you'll find that it lists the folders and reports within them that are on your report server through Report Manager.

We then add a "?" to the path, to let SRS know that everything that follows in the URL is a parameter. Next is the optional path information where you can specify any subfolder within the base folder that you use to organize your reports, such as /prors. Finally, we have the name of the actual report itself, such as "employees."

So, in our example, the full path to access the Employee Service Cost report would be as follows:

```
http://hwc04/reportserver?/prors/employees
```

Let's now move on to the section of the URL where we specify any necessary parameters.

URL Parameters and Prefixes

We now need to pass the appropriate parameters to the report. We're interested in several categories of parameters:

- **Report parameters (no prefix):** These parameters are supplied to the report's underlying queries, and are used as filters for the information as it's rendered. Thus, they control exactly what data the report displays.

- **HTML Viewer parameters (rc:):** These parameters control what features of the web-based report viewer are active, and at what page in the report the report viewer starts displaying. For example, you can use the FindString parameter to have the viewer start displaying a report on the first page on which the word is found.

- **Report server command parameters (rs:):** These parameters control the type of request being made, and the format of the returned report. For example, we'll use the rs:Command=Render&rs:Format=HTML4.0 parameter to render our report in HTML format in our report viewer.

- **Credential parameters:** You use these parameters to pass in data source credentials such as User (dsu:) and Password (dsp:). You use them to provide credentials when a data source connection is set to prompt.

Report Parameters

Report parameters are the actual parameters passed to the underlying report itself, versus instructions being sent to the report server. You use them to pass in criteria to your report such as start and end dates, employee IDs, and so on. You can pass these parameters to the report's query, and they're created when you specify parameters for the data source. You can also use parameters as variables in the report and as values for filters.

HTML Viewer Parameters

You use HTML Control parameters to tell SRS how to render the report. You can use the commands in Table 6-2 to control how the viewer appears to the user, as well as certain aspects of how the report appears in the viewer.

Table 6-2. *URL Viewer Control Parameters*

Parameter	Description	Default
Toolbar	Shows or hides the toolbar	true
Parameters	Shows or hides the parameters area of the toolbar	true
DocMap	Shows or hides the report document map. For information on what a document map is, see the section "Document Mapping" in Chapter 4.	true
DocMapID	The document map ID to which to scroll	Not applicable

Parameter	Description	Default
Zoom	Sets the zoom value. You can use a number representing a percentage or a string with standard values such as Page Width and Whole Page	100
Section	Page number of the report to display	1
FindString	Text to search for in the report	Not applicable
StartFind	Page number to start the search on, specified by FindString	Last page of the report
EndFind	Page number to end the search on, specified by FindString	Current page
FallbackPage	Page number to display if a FindString or DocMapID fails	Not applicable
GetImage	Gets a particular icon for the HTML Viewer interface	Not applicable
Icon	Gets the icon for a rendering extension	Not applicable

Report Server Command Parameters

Report server command parameters are prefixed with rs: and tell the report server the type of request being made (see Table 6-3). You use them to retrieve report and data source information in XML and HTML format, and to retrieve child elements such as the current folder's report names. You also use command parameters to tell the server you want to render a report and in what format, and if you want to render that report based on a preexisting snapshot.

Table 6-3. *URL Command Parameters*

Parameter	Description	Supported Values
Command	Type of request being made	GetDataSourceContents GetResourceContents ListChildren Render
Format	Format to render the report in	HTML3.2 HTML4.0 HTMLOWC MHTML IMAGE EXCEL CSV PDF XML NULL
Snapshot	Renders a report based on a snapshot	Valid ID of a snapshot

Credential Parameters

You can use the credential parameters in Table 6-4 to supply the user name and password that the report server uses to connect to the data source, to retrieve data for the report. SRS uses credential parameters only if the credential settings for the data source in the report are set to prompt; otherwise they're ignored. If the report has multiple data sources, you can use the credential parameters to supply credentials for each one.

Table 6-4. *URL Credential Parameters*

Parameter	Description	Example
dsu	User name to use to access the data source	dsu:employee=walter
dsp	Password to use to access the data source	dsp:employee=password

Example URLs

Now that we've examined every component part of the URL, it's useful to take a look at a few complete example URLs. The following URL renders the report in HTML 4.0 and hides the HTML Viewer toolbar, by setting the rc:Toolbar parameter value to false:

```
http://hwc04/reportserver?/prosrs/employees&rs:Command=
 Render&rs:Format=HTML4.0&rc:Toolbar=false
```

The next example passes a report parameter for the employee ID and hides the input display of user-supplied parameters:

```
http://hwc04/reportserver?/prosrs/employees&rs:Command=
 Render&rs:Format=HTML4.0&rc:Parameters=false&EmpID=201
```

The next one uses the rs:Format parameter to set the default output format to be PDF:

```
http://hwc04/reportserver?/prosrs/employees&rs:Command=
 Render&rs:Format=PDF
```

The final example automatically positions us at mapping ID 201 in the report:

```
http://hwc04/reportserver?/prosrs/employees&rs:Command=
 Render&rc:DocMapID=201
```

We've taken a brief look at the commands you need to render a report through a URL. In the remainder of this chapter, we'll create our own report viewer. It uses URL commands to integrate an SRS report into a .NET Windows Forms-based application.

Integrating SRS with .NET Applications

Now that you have some understanding of how URL access works, let's create a Windows Forms SRS Viewer application that uses URL access to render reports for our application.

Building the Windows Forms Report Viewer

We'll create a simple Windows Form that contains our embedded browser, which we'll use to view a report. We'll then extend the application so that it uses Web service API calls to query the report server for the parameters the report can accept, and what values are possible for each. We'll use these parameters to create pick lists for the users of our Windows Form.

Creating the Viewer Form

Open VS.NET and create a Windows Forms application. In our example, we'll use C# to create the SRS Viewer.

Resize the blank form to around 900×700; add the Microsoft Web Browser control to the form; and anchor the control to the form's top, bottom, left, and right. If the Microsoft Web Browser control doesn't appear in your Toolbox under Windows Forms, you can add it easily by opening the Toolbox, going to Windows Forms, right-clicking, and selecting Add/Remove Items, as shown in Figure 6-1.

Figure 6-1. *Add/Remove Items*

Select the COM Components tab and scroll down until you find Microsoft Web Browser. Select it by placing a check in the check box, as shown in Figure 6-2.

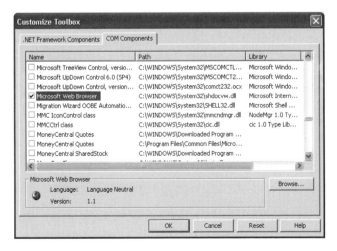

Figure 6-2. *Adding the Microsoft Web Browser control*

The Microsoft Web Browser control should now appear in your Toolbox, as shown in Figure 6-3.

Figure 6-3. *Microsoft Web Browser control in the Windows Forms Toolbox*

Now add a text box, a label, and a button, as shown in Figure 6-4.

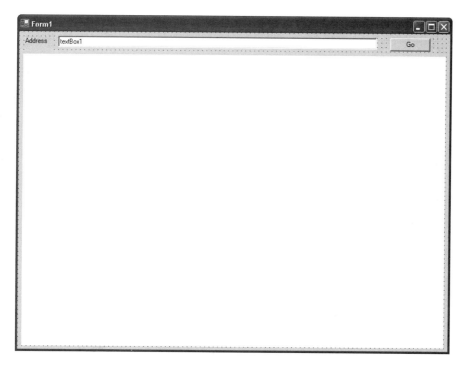

Figure 6-4. *Windows Form with all the controls*

Let's start adding the code necessary to use this custom "browser" to render our SRS reports.

Coding the Viewer Form

To start with, we need to add the following code to the form load event so that the browser control is properly initialized and points to about:blank when the form loads:

```
private void Form1_Load(object sender, System.EventArgs e)
{
    Object url = "about:blank";
    Object nul = null;
    axWebBrowser1.Navigate2(ref url, ref nul, ref nul, ref nul, ref nul);
}
```

Now we add some code to our button click event to make sure that we can browse to and view an existing report:

```
private void button1_Click(object sender, System.EventArgs e)
{
    object url = textBox1.Text;
    object nul = null;
    axWebBrowser1.Navigate2(ref url, ref nul, ref nul, ref nul, ref nul);
}
```

Now we run the project in debug mode. When the form displays, we enter the following URL into the text box:

```
http://hwc04/reportserver?/ProRS/EmployeeServiceCost
```

This renders the Employee Service Cost report. Of course, you need to use the name of your report server where we show hwc04 in the preceding URL. At this point, you should see something that looks like Figure 6-5.

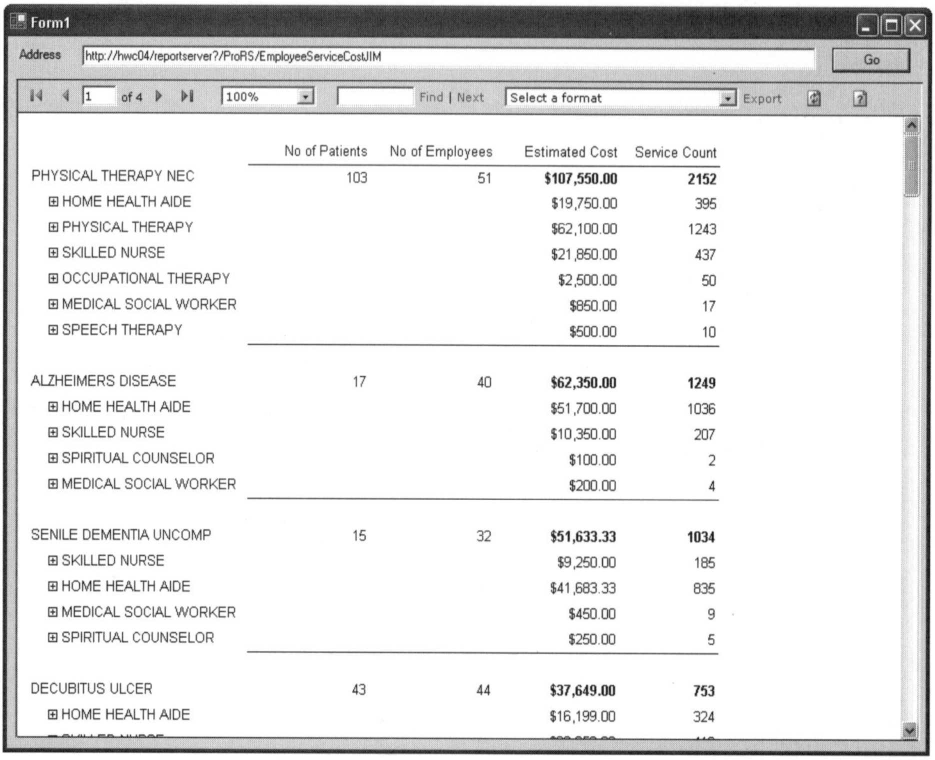

	No of Patients	No of Employees	Estimated Cost	Service Count
PHYSICAL THERAPY NEC	103	51	**$107,550.00**	**2152**
⊞ HOME HEALTH AIDE			$19,750.00	395
⊞ PHYSICAL THERAPY			$62,100.00	1243
⊞ SKILLED NURSE			$21,850.00	437
⊞ OCCUPATIONAL THERAPY			$2,500.00	50
⊞ MEDICAL SOCIAL WORKER			$850.00	17
⊞ SPEECH THERAPY			$500.00	10
ALZHEIMERS DISEASE	17	40	**$62,350.00**	**1249**
⊞ HOME HEALTH AIDE			$51,700.00	1036
⊞ SKILLED NURSE			$10,350.00	207
⊞ SPIRITUAL COUNSELOR			$100.00	2
⊞ MEDICAL SOCIAL WORKER			$200.00	4
SENILE DEMENTIA UNCOMP	15	32	**$51,633.33**	**1034**
⊞ SKILLED NURSE			$9,250.00	185
⊞ HOME HEALTH AIDE			$41,683.33	835
⊞ MEDICAL SOCIAL WORKER			$450.00	9
⊞ SPIRITUAL COUNSELOR			$250.00	5
DECUBITUS ULCER	43	44	**$37,649.00**	**753**
⊞ HOME HEALTH AIDE			$16,199.00	324

Figure 6-5. *SRS Viewer displaying report*

We'll use the same URL repeatedly in our examples to avoid having to type it in over and over again. Now, we'll create a new method called `Navigate`, which takes a string variable as its input that contains the URL to which we want the browser to navigate. It looks like this:

```
public void Navigate(string URL)
{
    object url = URL;
    object nul = null;
    axWebBrowser1.Navigate2(ref url, ref nul, ref nul, ref nul, ref nul);
}
```

Now we'll change the `Form_Load` event to use the new method:

```
private void Form1_Load(object sender, System.EventArgs e)
{
    Navigate("about:blank");
    textBox1.Text = "http://hwc04/reportserver?/ProRS/EmployeeServiceCost";
}
```

We've now created a report viewer in a Windows Form. We could stop at this point and just use the URL to tell the report to render and to display the report parameters, toolbar, and report. However, in this example, we want to use the SRS Web services API to get a list of parameters for the selected report and to display them to the user in a Windows Form. To get this list of parameters, we need to call a method on the SRS Web service called `GetReportParameters`.

Using the Web Services API

The SRS Web service is an XML-based Web service. It uses the Simple Object Access Protocol (SOAP) API to allow you to call a variety of methods on the report server and interact with them, using a rich set of objects provided by the service.

Web Services Method Categories

The Web service can control every aspect of the report server and consists of several categories of methods, as listed in Table 6-5.

Table 6-5. *Categories of Web Services Methods*

Category	Manages
Namespace management	Folders and items on the server and sets their properties
Authorization	Tasks, roles, and policies
Data source connections	Data source connections and credentials
Report parameters	Setting the retrieval parameters for reports
Rendering and execution	Report execution, rendering, and caching
Report history	Snapshot creation and history
Scheduling	Shared schedule creation and modification
Subscription and delivery	Subscription creation and modification
Linked reports	Linked report creation and management

The Web service uses many of these methods to control aspects of SRS that aren't directly related to the rendering of reports, so we won't cover them in this chapter. However, you should be aware of the level of control your custom application can have over SRS and the types of functions that can be performed, because you might wish to provide a user interface to them from your application. Keep in mind that the main SRS report server application itself is built using ASP.NET and these Web services.

For our SRS Viewer, we're using the URL method to render the report, but we want to provide a custom Windows Forms-based user interface to allow users to enter their report parameters and to select the format in which they want to render the report. The rest of this chapter concentrates on using methods from the report parameters category listed in the preceding table. We'll use these methods to obtain a list of the parameters that the report expects, and also to find out the possible values for those parameters. We'll use this information to create and populate combo boxes that allow the users to enter their choices from a Windows Form.

Creating the Parameters Form

We already have a form to render and display the report in our embedded browser. We'll now add a second form to our project that we'll use to display the report and rendering parameters and to allow the users to make their selections.

We add a Form2 to our project by selecting Project ➤ Add Windows Form. We name the form Form2.cs. Onto this form, we add a panel control and two button controls, and set the text for the buttons to OK and Cancel. When we're done the form should look like Figure 6-6.

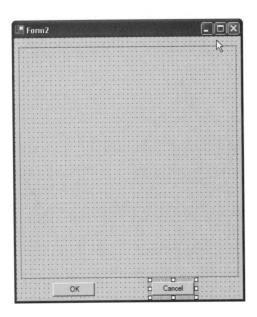

Figure 6-6. *Parameter dialog box form*

We now need to add a reference to the SRS Web service to our project. We do this by selecting Add Reference under the Project menu or right-clicking on the references in the Solution Explorer and selecting Add Web Reference. When the dialog box appears we enter the following URL:

```
http://hwc04/reportserver/reportservice.asmx
```

Substitute the name of your server for hwc04. Then click the Go button. You see a dialog box similar to the one in Figure 6-7.

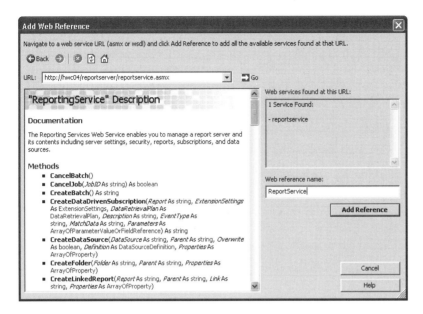

Figure 6-7. *Add Web Reference dialog box*

In the Web Reference Name text box, we enter **ReportService**, which is the name by which we'll refer to our Web service in our code.

Once this dialog is closed, we need to add the following `using` directives to our code. Note that if your project name is different than SRSViewer, you should change the reference to reflect the name of your project:

```
using SRSViewer.ReportService;
```

Now we can reference the Web service much more easily because we won't have to enter the fully qualified namespace. We also add this code:

```
using System.Web.Services.Protocols;
```

This allows us to access the Web services-specific functions more easily in our code.

Because we're going to use this form as a dialog to display the report parameters and their possible values, and allow the user to select them, we need a way to communicate between the two forms.

Coding the Report Parameters Form

When we instantiate the report parameters form (Form2), we do so by passing in the URL of the report the user has entered in the viewer form (Form1). We use this URL to determine the report server name and the specific report the user wishes to run. We need to know both of these for the calls to the report server Web service. Because we'll use this information throughout the rest of the code, in this class we store them in some class-level variables:

```
private string url;
private string server;
private string report;
```

In the Forms constructor, we break the report server and report name into two separate fields. We also use the url variable to pass the complete URL containing all parameters the user has selected back to our viewer on Form1. To break the URL into the server and report name, we use the string split method and create a constructor that looks like Listing 6-1.

Listing 6-1. *Report Parameters Form Constructor*

```
public Form2(string URL)
{
    //
    // Required for Windows Form Designer support
    //
    InitializeComponent();
    url = URL;
    string[] reportInfo = url.Split('?');
    server = reportInfo[0];
    report = reportInfo[1];
}
```

The Form2_Load Event

Now we get to the where the real work for this dialog is done: the Form_Load event. First we create a ReportingService object so that we can access SRS through the Web service that we added as a reference earlier. Next, we set our Windows credentials as the credentials to be used for calling the Web service:

```
ReportingService rs = new ReportingService();
rs.Credentials = System.Net.CredentialCache.DefaultCredentials;
```

■**Note** You can also use Basic Authentication using rs.Credentials = new System.Net.Network-Credential("username", "password", "domain");. The method that you use depends on the security settings for the report server virtual directory. By default, it's configured to use Windows Authentication.

Calling the Web Services GetReportParameters Method

The GetReportParameters method takes five parameters:

- **Report**: The full path name of the report.

- **ForRendering**: A Boolean value that indicates how the parameter values should be used. We must set it to true to get a list of the possible values for each parameter.

- **HistoryID**: The ID of the report history snapshot. We set it to NULL because we aren't running the report from a snapshot.

- **ParameterValues**: The parameter values (ParameterValue[] objects) that can be validated against the parameters of the report that are managed by the report server. We set this to NULL in our example.

- **Credentials**: The data source credentials (DataSourceCredential[] objects) that can be used to validate query parameters. We set this to NULL in our example.

The GetReportParameters method returns an array of ReportParameter[] objects that contain the parameters for the report. We use this information to render combo boxes that allow the user to select the parameter values they want to use when running the report.

The following code sets up the variables we need to use, and then calls the GetReportParameters method to retrieve a list of reports that the report expects:

```
bool forRendering = true;
string historyID = null;
ParameterValue[] values = null;
DataSourceCredentials[] credentials = null;
ReportParameter[] parameters = null;
    parameters = rs.GetReportParameters(report, historyID, forRendering,
            values, credentials);
```

Once we have our list of parameters back from SRS, we loop them using the values to create labels as we create our combo box for each parameter:

```
foreach (ReportParameter rp in parameters)
```

Each ReportParameter object has a read-only property called ValidValues. We can use the ValidValues property, which returns an array of ValidValue objects, to populate the items in each combo box:

```
if (rp.ValidValues != null)
{
    //Build list items
    ArrayList aList = new ArrayList();
    pvs = rp.ValidValues;
    foreach (ValidValue pv in pvs)
    {
        aList.Add(new ComboItem(pv.Label,pv.Value));
    }
    //Bind list items to combo box
    a.DataSource = aList;
    a.DisplayMember="Display";
    a.ValueMember="Value";
}
```

So, for each ReportParameter, we see if there are any ValidValues. If so, we loop through them, adding each item to the combo box. Because we want to retrieve the display name and the actual value for each item in the combo box, we have to create a combo box item class and bind the objects to the combo box. The combo box is shown in the complete code listing for the Form2_Load event in Listing 6-2.

Listing 6-2. *Get Report Parameters and Possible Values, and Display in Combo Boxes*

```
private void Form2_Load(object sender, System.EventArgs e)
{
    ReportingService rs = new ReportingService();
    rs.Credentials = System.Net.CredentialCache.DefaultCredentials;

    bool forRendering = true;
    string historyID = null;
    ParameterValue[] values = null;
    DataSourceCredentials[] credentials = null;
    ReportParameter[] parameters = null;
    ValidValue[] pvs = null;

    int x=5;
    int y=30;

    try
    {
        parameters = rs.GetReportParameters(report, historyID, forRendering,
                values, credentials);

        if (parameters != null)
        {
            foreach (ReportParameter rp in parameters)
            {
                this.SuspendLayout();
                this.panel1.SuspendLayout();
                this.panel1.SendToBack();
                // now create a label for the combo box below
                Label lbl = new Label();
                lbl.Anchor = (System.Windows.Forms.AnchorStyles.Top |
                    System.Windows.Forms.AnchorStyles.Left);
                lbl.Location= new System.Drawing.Point(x,y);
                lbl.Name = rp.Name;
                lbl.Text = rp.Name;
                lbl.Size = new System.Drawing.Size(150,20);
                this.panel1.Controls.Add(lbl);
                x=x+150;
                // now make a combo box and fill it
                ComboBox a = new ComboBox();
                a.Anchor = (System.Windows.Forms.AnchorStyles.Top |
```

```
                    System.Windows.Forms.AnchorStyles.Right);
                a.Location= new System.Drawing.Point(x,y);
                a.Name = rp.Name;
                a.Size = new System.Drawing.Size(200,20);
                x=5;
                y=y+30;
                this.panel1.Controls.Add(a);
                this.panel1.ResumeLayout(false);
                this.ResumeLayout(false);

                if (rp.ValidValues != null)
                {
                    //Build list items
                    ArrayList aList = new ArrayList();
                    pvs = rp.ValidValues;
                    foreach (ValidValue pv in pvs)
                    {
                        aList.Add(new ComboItem(pv.Label,pv.Value));
                    }
                    //Bind list items to combobox
                    a.DataSource = aList;
                    a.DisplayMember="Display";
                    a.ValueMember="Value";
                }
            }
        }
    }

    catch (SoapException ex)
    {
        MessageBox.Show(ex.Detail.InnerXml.ToString());
    }
}


    public class ComboItem
    {
        public ComboItem(string disp, string myvalue)
        {
            if (disp != null)
                display=disp;
            else
                display = "";
            if (myvalue != null)
                val=myvalue;
            else
                val = "";
        }
```

```csharp
        private string val;
        public string Value
        {
            get{return val;}
            set{val=value;}
        }

        private string display;
        public string Display
        {
            get{return display;}
            set{display=value;}
        }

        public override string ToString()
        {
            return display;
        }
    }
}
```

Upon loading, you'll see a form that displays a series of combo boxes, each containing the valid values for the report parameters. It looks something like Figure 6-8.

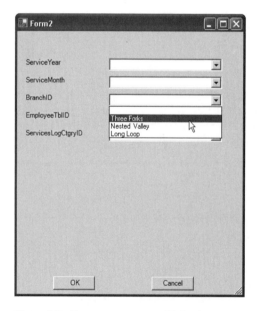

Figure 6-8. *Report parameter dialog box*

Rendering the Final Report

To finish up our SRS Windows Forms viewer application, we need to create the full URL necessary to render the report with the supplied parameters, the values of which the user has selected.

Our button1 click event handler, shown in Listing 6-3, starts out by adding the Render command and the HTML 4.0 format to the URL, as well as adding Parameters=false to prevent the parameter panel from being rendered in the browser. We then loop through the controls contained in our panel1 parent control and, for each combo box, read out the Name for the parameter name (remember, we set the name equal to our parameter name in the Form_Load event) and the SelectedValue property for its value. We append the SelectedValue property to the URL that we used to execute our report back in Form1.

Listing 6-3. *Click Event Handler for button1*

```
private void button1_Click(object sender, System.EventArgs e)
{
        string URL = url + "&rs:Command=Render&rs:Format=
            HTML4.0&rc:Parameters=false";

        string[,] myValues = new string[this.panel1.Controls.Count/2,2];
        int i = 0;
        foreach (Control ctrl in this.panel1.Controls)
        {
            if (ctrl.GetType() == typeof(ComboBox))
            {
                ComboBox a = (ComboBox) ctrl;
                myValues[i,0] = a.Name;
                if (a.SelectedValue != null &&
                    a.SelectedValue.ToString() != String.Empty)
                {
                    myValues[i,1] = a.SelectedValue.ToString();
                    URL += "&" + myValues[i,0].ToString() + "=" +
                            myValues[i,1].ToString();
                }
                else
                    myValues[i,1] = String.Empty;

                i++;
            }
        }

        url = URL;
        this.DialogResult = DialogResult.OK;
        Close();

    }
```

We also need to add some code to handle the button2 click event in case the user clicks the Cancel button:

```
private void button2_Click(object sender, System.EventArgs e)
{
    this.DialogResult = DialogResult.Cancel;
}
```

To finish up our parameter dialog box form, we need to add some code to allow us to pass the completed URL with all commands and parameters back to Form1:

```
public string URL
{
    get
    {
        return url;
    }
}
```

To bring it all together, we need to modify the button1 click event in Form1 to use the new Form2 dialog box, passing in the URL of the report we want to run. Then we read the complete URL with commands and parameters from the URL property of the Form2 dialog box and navigate to it:

```
private void button1_Click(object sender, System.EventArgs e)
{
    string URL = textBox1.Text;
    Form2 form2 = new Form2(URL);
    if (form2.ShowDialog() == DialogResult.OK)
    {
        URL = form2.URL;
        textBox1.Text = URL;
        Navigate(URL);
    }
}
```

All that's left to do now is to run our application and see how it works. When you run the application you should see something similar to the form in Figure 6-9.

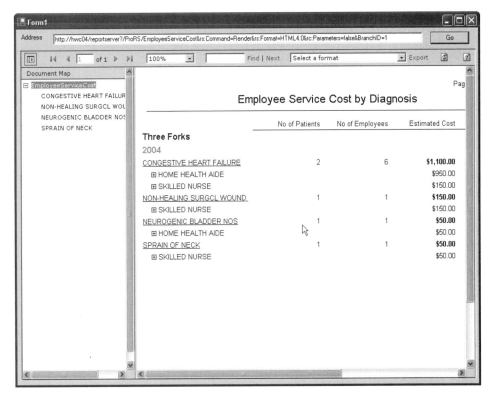

Figure 6-9. *Final report in custom Windows Forms viewer*

Now you have a foundation for a report viewer built for use with Windows Forms. This example has concentrated on using URL access for rendering the reports because it's straightforward to use and fairly simple to implement by embedding a browser control in our Windows Form. We've made our viewer a lot more user-friendly by using SRS's SOAP-based APIs to access the rich functionality of SRS features. This allows us to create a more familiar and responsive Windows-based user interface.

You can also render reports using the SOAP APIs directly. However, you lose the functionality of things such as the report toolbar with its built-in navigation and export functionality. This means you have to create these on your own if you use the SOAP APIs for rendering.

Summary

In this chapter, we used the URL-access capabilities of SRS to embed reports quickly into our applications. Beyond the Web Browser control, you can use other applications to render reports, such as the HTML Viewer web part in SharePoint Portal Server. By combining SharePoint and SRS, you can quickly build a portal that displays your reports without much code at all. Also, you learned how to make Web services API calls to create your own Windows Forms viewer application. This application allows you to type the URL of a report you wish to enter. It then uses the `GetReportParameters` method to retrieve a list of report parameters, and the `ValidValues` method to retrieve possible values. You then read the values selected by the user and construct the proper URL to run the report with the values selected, and use the URL rendering method to display the results on your embedded Web Browser control. In Chapter 8 we'll expand on this example by using the Web services API to allow the user to set the report to run on a schedule instead of immediately.

■■■

CHAPTER 7

Deploying Reports

Throughout the lifecycle of a report—from creation to maintenance—administrators, developers, and possibly users need to deploy reports continually to the SRS server. Deploying a report simply means placing the RDL file onto the SRS server so that your users can use it. (For more information on the specifics of the RDL format of these reports, see Chapter 3.) Fortunately, SRS provides several means for deploying reports:

- **Through your web browser using the Report Manager interface.** This method is simple to use and allows anyone with an RDL file to upload it to the SRS server. This can be especially useful if you're developing your report's RDL files in an application that does provide you with a method to upload them to the server. It's also useful if you want to make a quick edit of the RDL file—say to change a misspelled word—using an application such as Notepad, which doesn't offer a way to upload the report. We cover this scenario in Chapter 8, where we use Notepad to modify a report.

- **Using the Deploy option in VS.NET.** This method allows you to deploy your reports to the SRS server from directly within your development environment. If you're using VS.NET and have direct access to the report server to which you want to deploy your reports, this is by far the easiest option. However, using VS.NET is generally not a viable option if you have to distribute your reports outside the confines of your own network.

- **Using the rs command line utility.** The rs command line utility is a runtime environment used to execute VB.NET code in the form of specially formatted script files. This means that you use the same way of deploying the report with this method as we discuss in the next item. You can find out more about the rs command line utility in Reporting Services Books Online.

- **Programmatically, using the Web services API.** This method gives you complete control over the deployment process and gives you the added advantage of creating any type of user interface you want. Unlike the rs command line utility, you have your choice of languages and the full power of VS.NET to help you develop your custom interface. In Chapter 6 we used the Web services API to retrieve report parameter information about our reports from the SRS server, and then used that information to generate a Windows Forms user interface for parameter selection. In this chapter, we'll use the Web services API to publish reports to our SRS server. This type of interface is useful when you need to integrate the deployment of reports into your setup, installation, or runtime environment for your custom application.

Using Report Manager

To deploy reports using the Report Manager interface, simply open your browser and navigate to your SRS server using an address such as `http://hwc04/reports/`. You see a screen similar to the one in Figure 7-1.

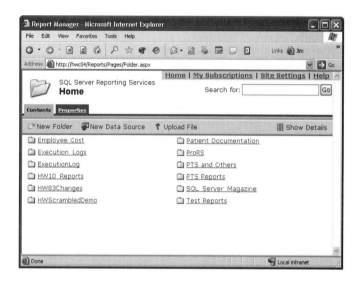

Figure 7-1. *Report Manager*

As you can see, an Upload File option is on the Report Manager toolbar. Selecting Upload File presents you with a standard browser-based upload-style dialog box such as the one shown in Figure 7-2.

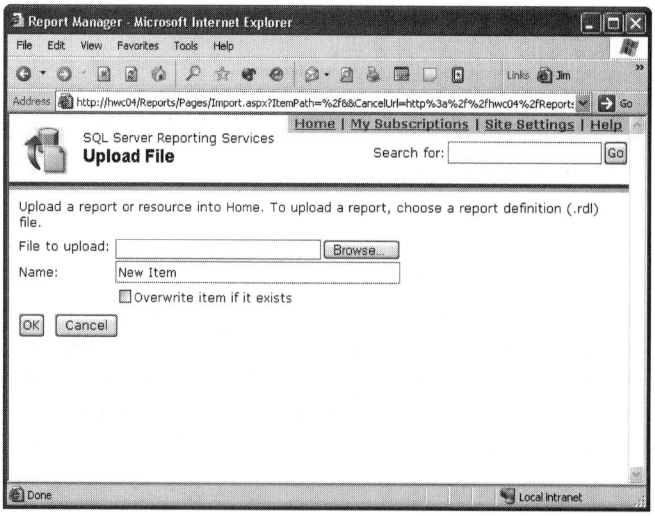

Figure 7-2. *Report Manager Upload File dialog box*

Using this dialog box, you can simply browse to the RDL file that you wish to upload and then upload it. Report Manager places it into the current folder (the one from which you initiated the upload process).

Once the report is uploaded, you can use the Report Properties page of Report Manager to modify the properties of the report, such as the name and description, as shown in Figure 7-3.

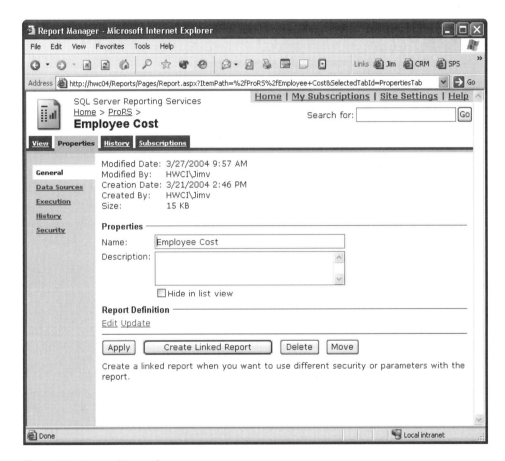

Figure 7-3. *Report Properties page*

This page also gives you the option to do the following:

- **Hide the report in the list view.** This can be useful if you don't want users with access to the SRS server to know that certain reports exist, or if you don't want them to see the detailed information about the report. Remember that this only hides the report in the summary view and not the detail view. You can combine the ability to hide reports with security when you need to prevent a user from running a report.

- **Edit the RDL and update it by uploading a new copy of the RDL file.** This can be useful when you want to make a minor modification to a report, such as changing the spelling of a word or modifying an expression. Keep in mind that this method only provides you access to the RDL file; you still have to use another program to edit the file and then you have to upload the modified file.

- **Delete the report and/or move it to another location on your report server.** This gives you the ability to remove reports that are no longer needed and to organize the reports into folders for organizational purposes as well as security purposes.

■**Note** You can perform many of these same operations in the detailed view by clicking the Show Details icon on the Report Manager toolbar.

Using VS.NET

You can also deploy reports using the Deploy option in VS.NET. This is convenient, because in many cases you'll probably be using VS.NET to develop your reports.

Configuring Report Deployment Options

VS.NET allows you to configure a different set of configuration properties for each project in your solution. You can also set these properties for each configuration available for your project, such as Debug, DebugLocal, and Release. For each configuration of a report project, you can uniquely define values for the following properties:

- **StartItem:** The name of the report to be displayed in the preview window, or in a browser window when the report project is run.

- **OverwriteDataSources:** A Boolean value indicating whether or not to overwrite an existing data source on the server. Set it to `true` to overwrite, which redeploys any data sources you have defined in your project each time you select Deploy. Set it to `false` if you don't want existing data sources overwritten.

- **TargetFolder:** The name of the folder in which to place your reports. By default, this is the name of the report project.

- **TargetServerURL:** The URL of the target report server, such as `http://hwc04/reportserver`.

What makes the different configurations convenient for the report developer is that you can set up different servers and/or folders for testing and deployment right in the same project. By default, when you create a report project, VS.NET creates three different configurations for you: Debug, DebugLocal, and Production. You can access the properties for these configurations through the project's Property Pages. To get to the configuration Property Pages, in Solution Explorer, right-click the project containing the reports and then click Properties. To see the property settings for each configuration option, select from the Configuration drop-down list at the top of the dialog box, as shown in Figure 7-4.

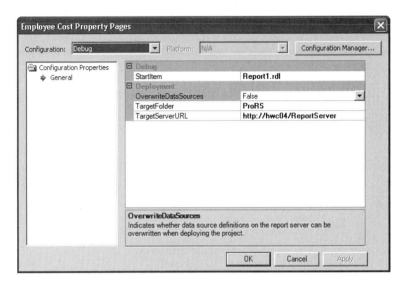

Figure 7-4. *Project Property pages*

Once you have the configuration information set up correctly in VS.NET, you can deploy reports to your server in two different ways. First, you can use the Build and Deploy options in the Configuration Manager, which decide if reports are built, deployed, or both when you start the project in VS.NET.

To open Configuration Manager, in Solution Explorer, right-click the project containing the reports and then click Properties. From there, click Configuration Manager. You see a dialog box that looks similar to the one in Figure 7-5.

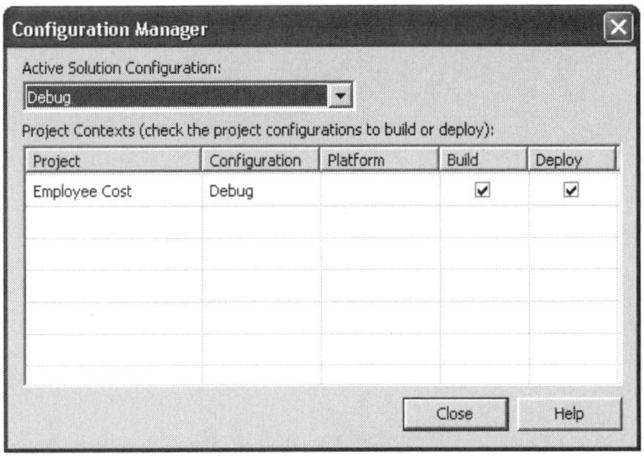

Figure 7-5. *VS.NET Configuration Manager*

By default you see the setup for the currently active configuration. You can select other configurations by selecting from the Active Solution Configuration drop-down list. As you can see, for each project in your solution, check boxes are in the Build and the Deploy columns.

Each time you start the project you want to build it, so you run the latest version of your report. If the Deploy check box is also checked, then whenever you start the project in that configuration, VS.NET deploys the reports to the specified server. However, for certain configurations, such as when you're debugging locally, you won't necessarily want to deploy your report to the server.

Deploying Reports Through Solution Explorer

You can also deploy reports from Solution Explorer. A list of options follows for deploying from Solution Explorer. You deploy your reports by right-clicking each of the following items and selecting Deploy:

- **The solution:** Deploys the reports in all the projects in your solution to the server that has been set up in each project's properties.

- **The project:** Deploys the reports in the specific project in your solution to the server that has been set up in the specified project's properties.

- **The report:** Deploys an individual report from a project in your solution to the server that has been set up in the project properties containing the report you're deploying.

Figure 7-6 shows an example of deploying all the reports in a project.

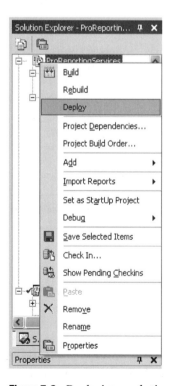

Figure 7-6. *Deploying a solution through Solution Explorer*

Using the Web Services API

The primary method provided by SRS for deploying reports programmatically is through the use of the Web services API (introduced in Chapter 6 when we wrote our report viewer). In this section, we'll take a look at deploying reports to SRS through the use of a Windows Forms application that simulates what customers would need to do once they have an RDL file ready for deployment:

- Select a report server to which to publish their report.

- Select from a displayed list of folders on that server to determine which folder on the server we'll publish the report to.

- Browse to the RDL file that is to be uploaded to their report server.

We'll use the Web services API to get a list of folders on the server and then upload the report to the server. In our example, we'll upload some of the reports we've created for the healthcare provider. In our healthcare setting, we want to maintain strict control over the report folders and their permissions on the server, so we won't allow the users to create a new folder, only to upload to the existing folders for which they have permission to do so.

The CreateReport method of the Web services API allows us to deploy our report to the report server by creating a copy of the report on the server from an RDL file that we provide to it, using the following parameters:

- **Report:** The name of the new report. SRS uses this name, and it appears in the SRS Report Manager.

- **Parent:** The full path name of the parent folder to which to add the report.

- **Overwrite:** A Boolean expression that indicates whether an existing report with the same name in the location specified should be overwritten.

- **Definition:** Byte array containing the report definition to publish to the report server. This is an in-memory representation of our report that's created by reading the RDL file from disk.

- **Properties:** An array of Property[ ] objects that contains the property names and values to set for the report. Property[ ] objects are simply name/value pairs that hold the report's properties. You can use them to set the description of your report; for example, by using the Description property.

■**Note** The CreateReport method might pass sensitive data, including user credentials, over the network. You should use SSL encryption whenever possible when making Web service calls with this method.

First we'll create a new C# Windows Forms solution with VS.NET. We'll call this solution Report Publisher.

Accessing the Web Service

We need to add a reference to our SRS Web service, which is the same as we did in Chapter 6 for our report viewer. We do this by selecting Add Reference under the Project menu or right-clicking the references in the Solution Explorer and selecting Add Web Reference. When the dialog box appears you enter in the following URL:

```
http://hwc04/reportserver/reportservice.asmx
```

Substitute the name of your server for hwc04 in the preceding URL. Then click the Go button. You see a dialog box similar to the one in Figure 7-7.

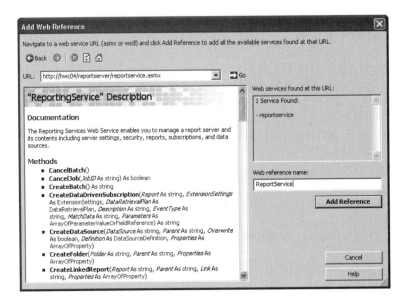

Figure 7-7. *Add Web Reference dialog box*

In the Web Reference Name text box, we enter **ReportService**, which is how we'll refer to our Web service in our code.

Once this dialog is closed, we add the following using directives to our code:

```
using ReportPublisher.ReportService;
```

Now we can reference the Web service much more easily because we don't have to enter the fully qualified namespace. We'll also add two other using directives that allow us to access the Web services and I/O-specific functions more easily in our code:

```
using System.IO;
using System.Web.Services.Protocols;
```

Laying out the Form

Next we add a Label and a TextBox control. We set the text property of the Label control to Report Server Name. We use this text box to allow the user to enter the report server name that they wish to deploy the report to. We add Go, Open, and Cancel buttons to the form that accept the users' input or allow them to exit without performing any operations.

Next we add a TreeView control to the form, so that when we enter in a server name and click Go we get a list of available folders on the server where we can upload our report. Then we add an openFileDialog control to the form so that we can give the users a way to search for the file that they wish to upload to the report server. Once we've added all these controls, the form should look something like Figure 7-8.

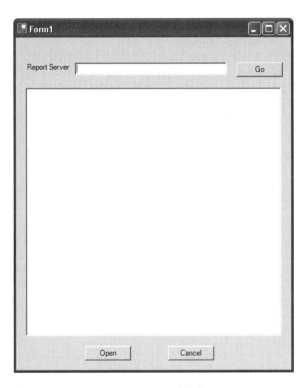

Figure 7-8. *Form1, our report publisher*

Coding the Form

Now that we have our form laid out, we'll add code to handle the functions necessary to allow our users to do the following:

1. Enter in a server name.

2. Get a list of the folders available on that server.

3. Select the folder to which to upload.

4. Select a report RDL file to upload.

Identifying the SRS Server

When a user types in a server name on our form, our code needs to build the URL that fully identifies the SRS server to which to deploy the RDL file.

First we create a class-level variable to hold our reference to the report server, much as we did in the SRS Viewer in Chapter 6. We do this by adding this definition to the class variables:

```
private ReportingService rs;
```

To build the URL that identifies the server, based on the user input, we first instantiate our Web service and then set the URL property to reflect the name of the server that the user entered into textBox1. We then create a short function to check the name and append the rest of the path name to make up the complete URL necessary to reference our Web service on the desired server. By constructing the URL based on the user's input, we can use our report deployment application to deploy our reports on any SRS server where we have permission to do so:

```
private string GetRSURL()
{
    if (textBox1.Text.StartsWith("http://"))
        return textBox1.Text + "/reportserver/ReportService.asmx";
    else
        return "http://" + textBox1.Text
            + "/reportserver/ReportService.asmx";
}
```

Populating the TreeView Control

We'll now use the SRS Web services API to retrieve a list of objects from the server and use them to populate our TreeView control.

We use the URL that we just constructed in the GetFolders click event, as shown in Listing 7-1, to retrieve a list of objects from the server, and place a call to the Web service's ListChildren method. The ListChildren method takes two parameters:

- **Item:** The full path name of the parent folder.

- **Recursive:** A Boolean expression that indicates whether to return the entire tree of child items below the specified item. The default value is false.

■**Note** The ListChildren method returns all objects on the report server, including data sources and reports, not just folders. In our example, we'll filter out everything but the folders because we're only interested in the folders. We do this by using the ItemTypeEnum enumeration object and test it against the Type property of the CatalogItem.

Listing 7-1. *Code to Populate TreeView Control*

```
private void GetFolders_Click(object sender, System.EventArgs e)
{
    rs = new ReportingService();
    rs.Credentials = System.Net.CredentialCache.DefaultCredentials;
    CatalogItem[] items = null;
    rs.Url = GetRSURL();;

    TreeNode root = new TreeNode();
    root.Text = "Root";
    treeView1.Nodes.Add(root);
    treeView1.SelectedNode = treeView1.TopNode;

    // Retrieve a list of items from the server
    try
    {
        items = rs.ListChildren("/", true);
    }

    catch (SoapException ex)
    {
        MessageBox.Show(ex.Detail.InnerXml.ToString());
    }

    int j = 1;

    // Iterate through the list of items and find all of the folders
    // and display them to the user
    foreach (CatalogItem ci in items)
    {
        if (ci.Type == ItemTypeEnum.Folder)
        {
            Regex rx = new Regex("/");
            int matchCnt = rx.Matches(ci.Path).Count;
            if (matchCnt > j)
            {
                treeView1.SelectedNode =
                    treeView1.SelectedNode.LastNode;
                j = matchCnt;
            }
            else if (matchCnt < j)
            {
                treeView1.SelectedNode = treeView1.SelectedNode.Parent;
                j = matchCnt;
            }
            AddNode(ci.Name);
```

```
            }
        }
        // Make sure the user can see that the root folder is selected by default
        treeView1.HideSelection = false;
}
private void AddNode(string name)
{
        TreeNode newNode = new TreeNode(name);
        treeView1.SelectedNode.Nodes.Add(newNode);
}
```

We'll also use a regular expression to help us determine how deep each folder is in the hierarchy, so we need to add the following using directive to our project:

```
using System.Text.RegularExpressions;
```

We tell the ListChildren method to start at the root folder by passing in a "/" as the starting point, and also set the recursive option to true, which causes the ListChildren method to iterate through all the folders and subfolders on our SRS server. We use this information to create nodes in our TreeView control to display each folder in a hierarchy that represents the hierarchy of the folders on the server. We use a regular expression to look for the number of "/" characters in the path of each CatalogItem to determine how deep we are in the hierarchy (one level, two levels, and so on).

Opening the Report RDL File and Uploading It to the Server

Now we need to add some code to use with the Browse dialog box. We want to limit the user to searching for files ending in "RDL" by default, because this is the native extension for SRS report definition files. We also want to read the selected node in our treeview so that we know what folder to deploy our report to on the SRS server.

We start out by reading the path of the selected node from the TreeView control and turning it into a path name we can use with SRS's CreateReport method:

```
string pathName = treeView1.SelectedNode.FullPath;

if (pathName == "Root")
    pathName = "/";
else
{
    pathName = pathName.Substring(4,pathName.Length-4);
    pathName = pathName.Replace(@"\", "/");
}
```

This section of code gets the full path from the TreeView control, strips the word Root off the front of the path, and then replaces all occurrences of a backslash in the string with the forward slash we need for SRS.

Next we open a Browse dialog box when the user clicks the Open button on our form. We read in the file using a file stream and convert it into the byte array form that SRS's CreateReport method requires:

```
byte[] definition = null;

openFileDialog1.Filter =
    "RDL files (*.rdl)|*.rdl|All files (*.*)|*.*" ;
openFileDialog1.FilterIndex = 1;
if(openFileDialog1.ShowDialog() == DialogResult.OK)
{
    try
    {
        // Read the file and put it into a byte array to pass to SRS
        FileStream stream = File.OpenRead(openFileDialog1.FileName);
        definition = new byte[stream.Length];
        stream.Read(definition, 0, (int)(stream.Length));
        stream.Close();
    }
    catch (Exception ex)
    {
        MessageBox.Show (ex.Message);
    }
}
```

We set the options for our openFileDialog control so that it browses by default for files with the RDL extension and then displays the dialog to the user. If the user makes a selection, we then open the file using a FileStream object and read from the stream into a byte array. That's because the SRS CreateReport method expects the contents of the RDL file to be passed in as a byte array.

Next we read the filename that the user selected and use it as the title for the report in SRS. Once we have a title, we have everything we need to upload the report, which we do by calling the CreateReport method with the values we've created. You can see at the end of Listing 7-2 where we have added the necessary code into the complete listing.

Listing 7-2. *Code for Browse Dialog Box*

```
private void OpenFile_Click(object sender, System.EventArgs e)
{

    // Get the full pathname from the treeview control
    string pathName = treeView1.SelectedNode.FullPath;

    if (pathName == "Root")
        pathName = "/";
```

```csharp
else
{
    // Strip off the Root name from the path
    // and correct the path separators for use with SRS
    pathName = pathName.Substring(4,pathName.Length-4);
    pathName = pathName.Replace(@"\", "/");
}

byte[] definition = null;
Warning[] warnings = null;
string warningMsg = String.Empty;

openFileDialog1.Filter =
    "RDL files (*.rdl)|*.rdl|All files (*.*)|*.*" ;
openFileDialog1.FilterIndex = 1;
if(openFileDialog1.ShowDialog() == DialogResult.OK)
{
    try
    {
        // Read the file and
        // put it into a byte array to pass to SRS
        FileStream stream =
            File.OpenRead(openFileDialog1.FileName);
        definition = new byte[stream.Length];
        stream.Read(definition, 0, (int)(stream.Length));
        stream.Close();
    }
    catch (Exception ex)
    {
        MessageBox.Show (ex.Message);
    }

    // We are going to use the name of the RDL file
    // as the name of our report
    string reportName =
        Path.GetFileNameWithoutExtension(
            openFileDialog1.FileName);
```

```
// Now let's use this information to publish the report
try
{
    warnings = rs.CreateReport(reportName, pathName,
        true, definition, null);
    if (warnings != null)
    {
        foreach (Warning warning in warnings)
        {
            warningMsg += warning.Message + "\n";
        }
        MessageBox.Show("Report creation failed with the warning:\n"
            + warningMsg);
    }
    else
        MessageBox.Show(String.Format(
            "Report: {0} created successfully
            with no warnings", reportName));
}
catch (SoapException ex)
{
    MessageBox.Show(ex.Detail.InnerXml.ToString());
}
}
}
```

To complete our report publisher, we need to add some code to our Cancel button to exit the application if Cancel is selected:

```
private void button3_Click(object sender, System.EventArgs e)
{
    Application.Exit();
}
```

Running the Application

Now let's run our example. Start the project and when the form displays, enter the name of your report server in the Server text box and press Go. Your form now looks similar to Figure 7-9, with the folders on your SRS server displayed and the Root folder highlighted.

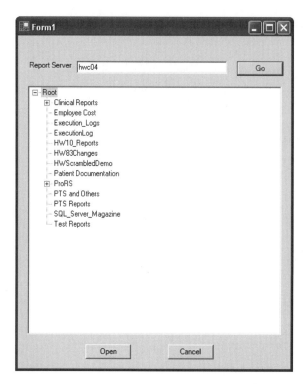

Figure 7-9. *Complete report publisher showing folders on SRS server*

By default, the Root folder on your server has been selected. If you want to place your report in a different folder on your server, highlight the node in the treeview with the name of the folder you want to place your report into. Once you've selected the folder to use, click Open and select an RDL file (you can pick one from a previous example or create your own). When you click Open, our report publishing application uses the Web services API's `CreateReport` method and publishes the report to the selected server.

In this case, we've selected the ProRS folder on the hwc04 server, and we're uploading a report called Daily Schedule.rdl. If you navigate to that folder with your web browser, you'll see something similar to the screen shown in Figure 7-10 (note that Report Manager marks it as "!NEW" to indicate that it has just been deployed).

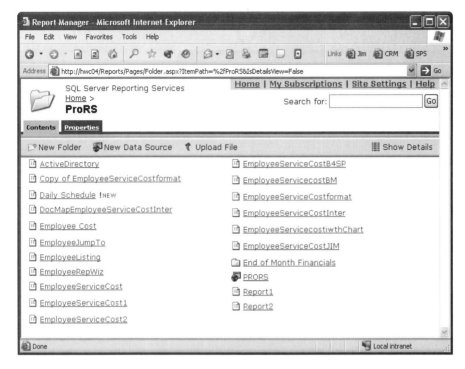

Figure 7-10. *Report Manager showing uploaded report*

You now have a Windows Forms application that allows files to be uploaded to your report server. This can be a handy way to add the ability to upload or update reports from within an application without needing the user to interact with the SRS Report Manager directly.

This can be especially useful if you want users to interact with all aspects of SRS from within your application. In Chapter 6, we developed an application that allows users to display reports from within the application. By combining that application with this report publisher, you can handle a number of non-administrative tasks directly from your application. You could also expand on this example by providing the user with some additional options:

- You could allow the user to create shared data sources.

- You could allow the user to enter in the name of the report to publish instead of taking the name from the RDL file itself. For example, you could add another text box to the form and read it for the report title. So, instead of the following code:

```
// We are going to use the name of the RDL file
// as the name of our report
string reportName =
    Path.GetFileNameWithoutExtension(openFileDialog1.FileName);
```

You could do the following:

```
// We are going to read the contents of textbox2
// as the name of our report
string reportName = textbox2.text
```

- You could allow the user to set other properties of the report, such as it being hidden in the list view on the report server. For example, you could add a Description property:

```
Property[] itemProps = new Property[1];
Property itemProp = new Property();
itemProp.Name = "Description";
itemProp.Value = "Employee Service Cost by Patient";
itemProps[0] = itemProp;
```

You could then change your call to CreateReport from the following code:

```
warnings = rs.CreateReport(reportName, pathName,
    true, definition, null);
```

You could change it to the following code instead:

```
warnings = rs.CreateReport(reportName, pathName,
    true, definition, itemProps);
```

As you can see, with SRS Web services APIs there isn't much you can't do.

Summary

In this chapter, we used the SRS Web services APIs to list the folders on the selected server, and then allowed the user to select an RDL file and update it to the user-specified folder on the selected report server. We also examined some of the additional features you could provide the application by using a few of the many methods and properties exposed by SRS.

CHAPTER 8

■■■

Report Management

In many reporting solutions prior to SRS, management of reports required little more than delivery of the completed report file to the end user, via a file share or embedded in a third-party application. SRS is a full reporting environment with features such as scheduled report execution, report subscription services, snapshots, content caching, and on-demand web access.

With these added benefits comes an additional level of management responsibility. Depending on the size of the organization, some management tasks can be delegated to other users, such as departmental managers, who might maintain report folders for their departments, as well as to system administrators and DBAs. Fortunately, SRS provides several means of managing the report server at all levels. In this chapter, we will continue to work with built-in tools such as Report Manager and command-line utilities, as well as with custom .NET management tools that take advantage of the SRS programming models to administer an SRS deployment.

We can subdivide the management roles for a SRS deployment into four basic categories:

- Content management

- Performance

- Report execution

- Error logging

In our experience, it is always best practice to perform a test deployment of any application—in our case, an Internet-hosted application—before placing it in a production environment. Because our company provides services through the Internet to a wide range of users, special management considerations, such as how to provide report subscriptions to the same report for different companies, were imperative and various scenarios needed to be tested to ensure proper functionality in each case. Let's begin by looking at the three management categories and how we implemented and tested them to make sure that when deployed to production, there would be few (if any) unexpected consequences. These tasks were all done using the built-in administration tools with SRS and Visual Studio .NET. Later in the chapter, we will show how to build a management application interface with .NET that provides much of the same functionality.

Content Management

To effectively manage content on the SRS report server, you need to be familiar with the management tasks available. There are several aspects of report management that are available only after the report has been deployed. We will cover each aspect in detail as we deploy our healthcare reports for selected users:

- Shared schedules

- Report parameters and data sources

- Report snapshots and history

- Subscriptions

For each content management task, we will give specific real-world scenarios, continuing with our healthcare agencies as an example. Up to this point, we have deployed several reports, data sources, and other report items, such as graphic images and code, that we have developed throughout the book. Now it is time to put on our administrator's cap and take advantage of all of the features that make SRS a unique and powerful report-delivery system in addition to providing a rich report-authoring environment.

Shared Schedules

Generally speaking, a *shared schedule* is very much like a shared data source in that it is available systemwide to users who have permission to access it. A shared schedule can be created specifically for a certain job type. It is possible to configure a shared schedule to execute by the hour, day, month, and week, or to run only once. In our case, we have financial reports that will execute at the end of each month. It is important that a history be maintained for these reports so that the values can be frozen at any point in time, or for auditing capabilities, such as understanding which user viewed a report and what he or she saw in the report.

Report snapshots are reports that are executed at a specific time, either when initiated by a user or as part of a schedule, and that collectively make up the report history. We will cover snapshots in more detail later. For now, let's create a shared schedule that will be used to run the financial reports on the last day of each month to provide the following benefits:

- We can schedule the reports to execute at a predetermined time.

- We can store a snapshot of each report, to maintain an historical perspective of the data.

One financial report that customers might run at the end of the month is the AR Reconciliation report. This report lists financial transactions that occurred during the current accounting period, such as 2004–05. This report is one of several reports that will need to execute on the same schedule. Other financial reports might include an Aged Trial Balance report and an AR Aging report. We will use the AR Reconciliation report to demonstrate the management tasks in the following sections.

To create the shared schedule in Report Manager, click Site Settings, and then select Manage Shared Schedules at the bottom of the page. Click New Schedule and name the schedule End of Month Financials. In the Schedule details section, you will see that you are presented with the standard scheduling options: Hour, Day, Week, Month, or Once. For our report, we will choose Month.

The first challenge when configuring a shared schedule to run on the last day of each month is to overcome the built-in data validation on the Shared Schedule form. Though it is possible to tell SRS to execute the report on the last Sunday of every month, it is not possible to select the last day of each month), because the last day is variable (i.e., it could be 28, 29, 30, or 31, depending on the month). Well, it should be possible to create a single schedule to encompass all four dates, right? Not exactly. Choosing 31 causes an error when all the days of the month are selected, as shown in Figure 8-1, because not all months have 31 days.

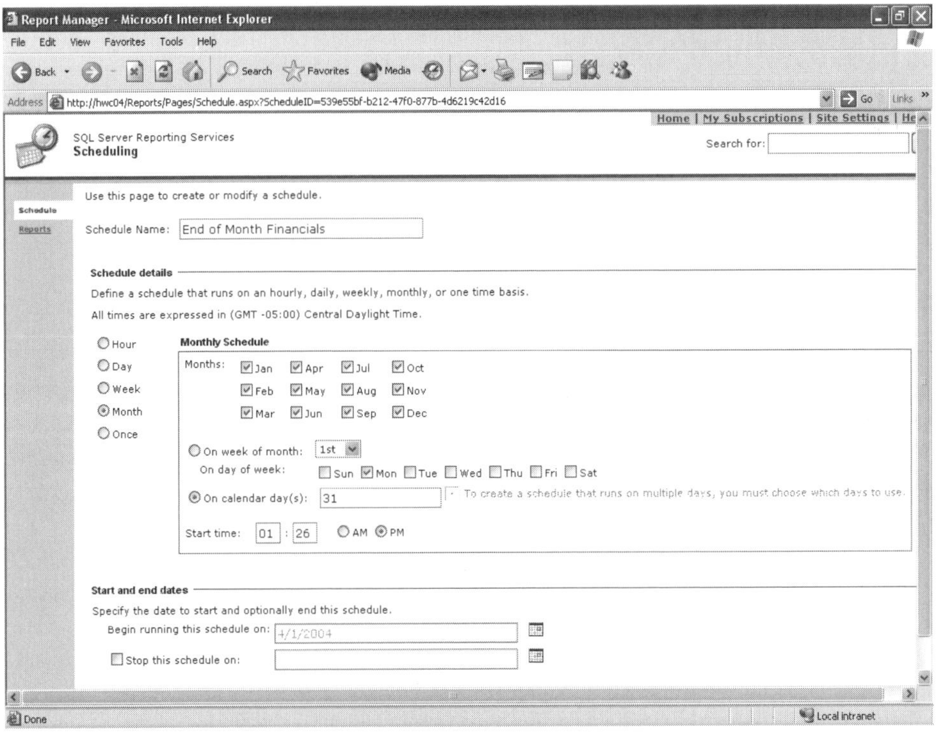

Figure 8-1. *Choosing the last day of the month*

The solution in our case, since we know that no activity will occur after 12:00 AM on the last day of the month, is to set the schedule to run on the first day of the month at 12:01 AM. This essentially gives us the last day for every month.

Next, we select an appropriate start date and end date for the schedule (in this case, we don't specify an end date), and then click the Apply button. Now we can move on and prepare the report itself to use the new schedule.

> **Note** It is important to note that when a job is scheduled to run within SRS, such as a subscription or an execution snapshot, a SQL Server job is created using SQL Server Agent. Jobs can be monitored through Enterprise Manager or Report Manager.

Configuring a Report to Use a Shared Schedule

The AR Reconciliation report contains report parameters, so we will need to supply appropriate values for these parameters at the time the report is executed. If we do not properly configure default values (such that we do not require user input), the report will not execute successfully from the shared schedule. There are six report parameters for the AR Reconciliation report, as shown in Figure 8-2.

Figure 8-2. *AR Reconciliation report parameters*

For every parameter except AcctPeriodYear and AcctPeriodMonth, we left the default values of None in the Report Parameters property page when designing the report. However, as we did in Chapter 4, we are returning a NULL value in the data set that populates the parameter input fields with user-selectable values. By returning a NULL value for each parameter, SRS will render the report automatically and not require the user to first select a parameter in the browser. This will allow SRS to use the shared schedule to run the report unattended.

For the parameters AcctPeriodYear and AcctPeriodMonth, we want to add default non-NULL parameter values such that we return a data set that includes only records for the current accounting period. To do this, we use two functions:

- DATEPART: Returns an integer representing one of the component parts of a date, such as year, quarter, month, or day

- TODAY: Returns the current date

Used together in an expression, these functions will allow us to set the desired default values for our two parameters. For `AcctPeriodYear`, we simply set the default value to the current year, as follows:

```
=DATEPART("yyyy",TODAY())
```

For `AcctPeriodMonth` we essentially do the same thing, but we need to subtract 1 from the expression value to return the data for the correct month. For example, the expression `=DATEPART("m",TODAY())`, when run at 12:01 AM on June 1, would return a value of 6, when the current accounting period is 5 (May). So the correct expression is

```
=DATEPART("m",TODAY()) -1
```

Updating and Uploading the RDL File Using Report Manager

We could very easily add the `AcctPeriodYear` and `AcctPeriodMonth` expressions using Report Designer in VS.NET, and then redeploy the report. As we have not as yet discussed the use of Report Manager to upload RDL files to the SRS server, now would be a good time to do so.

For this section, we will assume that the AR Reconciliation report is already deployed to the SRS server in a folder called End of Month Financials, as shown in Figure 8-3. The names have been intentionally scrambled.

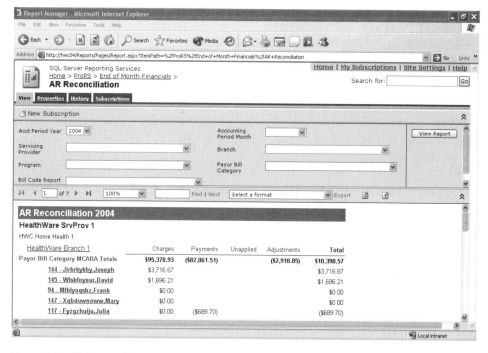

Figure 8-3. *AR Reconciliation report in Report Manager*

On the Properties page for the AR Reconciliation report are two buttons, Edit and Update, that administrators can use to modify the RDL directly without having to redeploy reports through other means (such as through use of custom code, the authoring environment, or the rs command-line utility). Click the Edit button to open the RDL file in the default text-editor (typically Notepad). Figure 8-4 shows the RDL file for the AR Reconciliation report. Notice the AcctPeriodYear and AcctPeriodMonth parameters in the RDL.

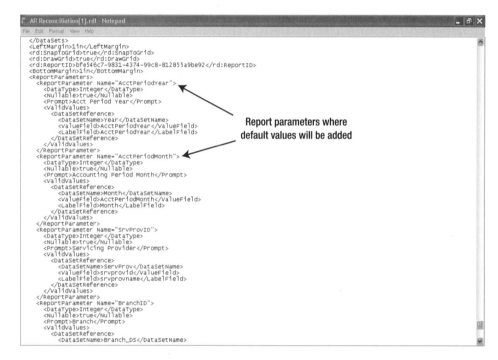

Figure 8-4. *RDL file edited in Notepad*

To update the report to include the default parameter values that we created in the previous section, we can place RDL code directly in the file and save it. The section of the RDL that generates the default values for each parameter is only five lines long, as you can see in Listing 8-1, which shows the default value section for the AcctPeriodYear parameter.

Listing 8-1. *RDL Default Value Section*

```
<DefaultValue>
    <Values>
        <Value>=datepart("yyyy",TODAY())</Value>
    </Values>
</DefaultValue>
```

Figure 8-5 shows the RDL file after the default value code was inserted for both parameters.

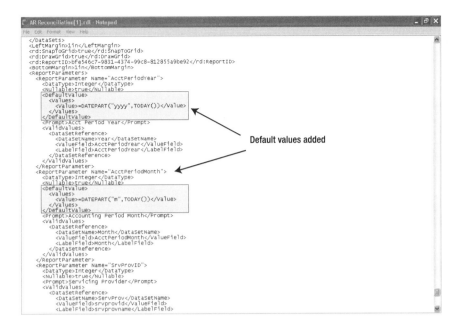

Figure 8-5. *RDL file with default parameters*

Now we have to save a copy of the RDL file to disk, as we are not able to save directly back to the SRS server from Notepad. Any accessible location is fine, such as a network share. Once the file is saved, we can click the Update link, locate our updated RDL file on disk, and select OK to update the existing report. When we execute the report now, we should see that the report will have the correct defaulted values, as shown in Figure 8-6.

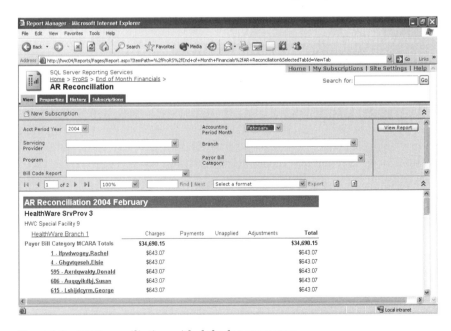

Figure 8-6. *AR Reconciliation with default parameters*

Updating the report through Report Manager doesn't overwrite other properties of the report such as history, schedules, and execution methods.

■**Caution** When you use default values based on variables, such as we are using for dates, it is important to note that the returned value will have to coincide with available values. In our case, if we were to return a value of 5 for May, but there were no value for May that could be selected, the report will force the user to make a selection, as opposed to executing and returning no data. We chose to limit the data to values actually stored in the database.

Setting Up a Data Source for the Report

We will be setting up this report to generate a history that will allow users to view the report as it was at the point in time at which it was executed. Also, because SRS will run the report at a prescheduled time, SRS will need to know what credentials to use to access the data for the report. We need to create a new data source to accommodate this.

We first navigate to the folder that contains the report and select New Data Source. Because this is a SQL Server–based connection, we supply the appropriate connection string, which includes the server name and database or catalog for the connection. Next, we need to choose to store the credentials securely on the server, and supply a name and password—in this case, SQL Authentication credentials. Finally, we choose to hide the data source in list view so that we can prevent users from accidentally selecting it when browsing. Figure 8-7 shows the selections for the new data source in Report Manager. After we click the Apply button to create the data source, all that we need to do is associate the report to the new shared data source, which we will do in the following sections.

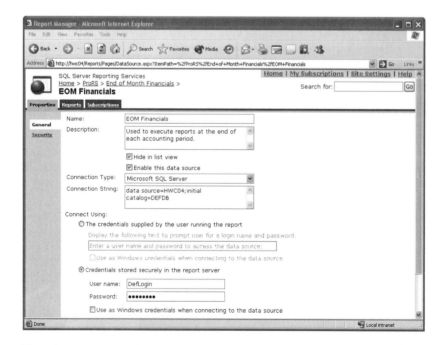

Figure 8-7. *Data source selections*

Note Microsoft recommends using Windows Authentication when connecting to SQL Server. We chose SQL Authentication in this example simply because our healthcare application was originally developed with SQL Authentication.

Creating Snapshots for the Report History

Our goal for the AR Reconciliation report was to allow it to execute at a specified time of month, during off-peak hours for performance benefits, and to maintain a historical picture of each month's processing. To this point we have created the shared schedule, End of Month Financials, and now it is time to make use of a very beneficial feature of SRS, which is the ability to process a report as a *snapshot*.

A snapshot is a static "point-in-time" copy of a report. There are two types of snapshots in SRS: those generated as execution snapshots and those generated to be stored in History. In this section, we are concerned with configuring the AR Reconciliation report to generate snapshots for report history, so that we can generate a series of historical financial reports.

We will use Report Manager to configure the History properties for the AR Reconciliation report so that a snapshot of the report is generated each time the report is processed, according to the End of Month Financials schedule.

Let's begin by looking at the available settings for report history. As you can see in Figure 8-8, there are several settings that effect not only the creation of snapshots, but also how the snapshots will be stored in the report history. You can navigate to the History property page for any report by selecting the Properties of the report and then selecting History in the left frame.

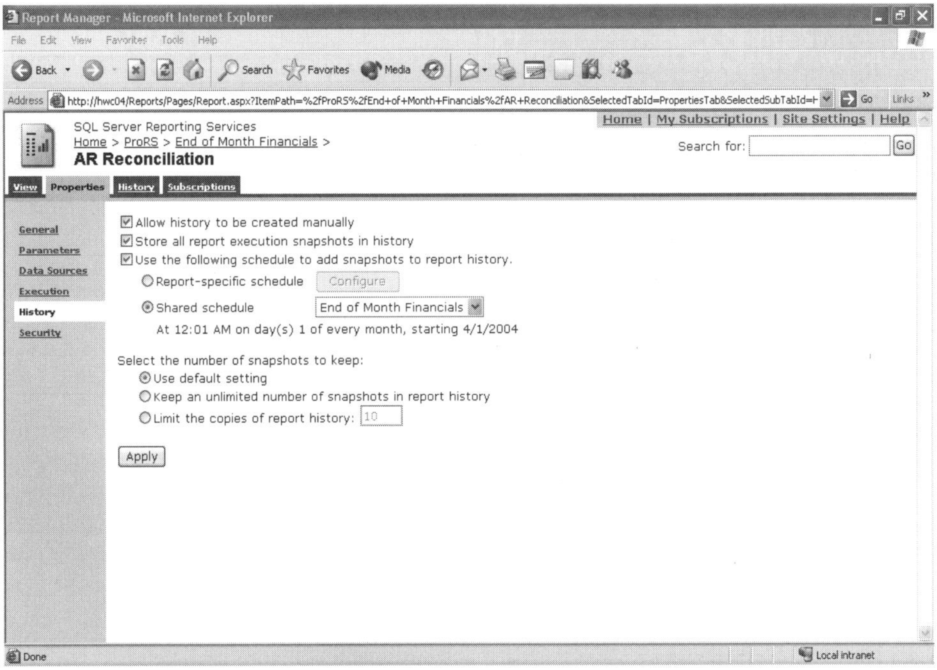

Figure 8-8. *Report History Properties settings*

For the AR Reconciliation report, we want to set the History properties such that:

- Users will not be able to create snapshots for the report history.

- Report execution snapshots will not be stored in the report history. This option is related to report Execution properties, which we cover in the next section.

- We use the End of Month Financials shared schedule.

- We use the Default setting for the number of snapshots to keep in the report history. The Default setting keeps an unlimited number of reports, but this can be changed via Site Settings in Report Manager. If a specific number of snapshots is selected to be kept, such as 10, then older snapshots will be removed first to make room.

Having made the selections, as shown in Figure 8-9, we click OK.

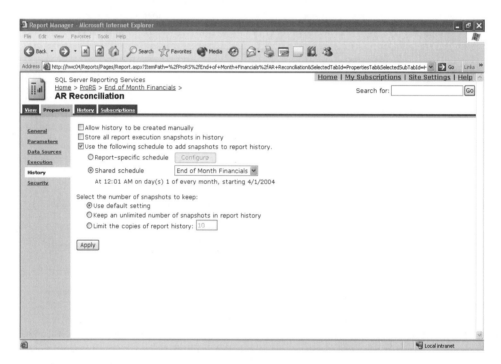

Figure 8-9. *Report History settings for the AR Reconciliation report*

Over time, the snapshots will be created in the report history. Users who have access to the report history can access the snapshots through Report Manager by navigating to the History tab for the report. The History tab for the AR Reconciliation report, as shown in Figure 8-10, indicates that over a two-month period, we have generated two snapshots, as expected.

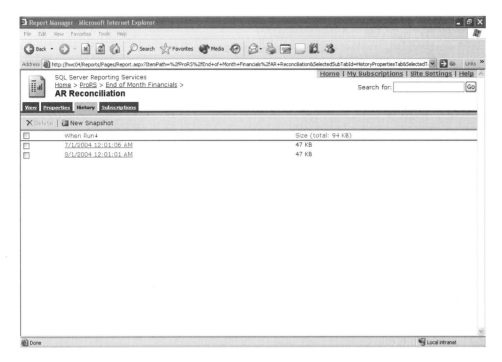

Figure 8-10. *AR Reconciliation report snapshots created on schedule*

It is beneficial for performance to render a report from the history, first because the report has been preprocessed, and secondly because there is no need to query the data source for the report, as both the data and layout information are stored in the snapshot. When generating large reports, such as financial reports with hundreds of pages, we highly recommend using snapshots, as well as other performance-enhancing features of SRS such as report caching, which we cover next.

Report Execution and Caching

Our report AR Reconciliation is now set up to be delivered from a schedule, and to be rendered from a snapshot, and saved in report history. This report will also be used by employees to be run *on-demand*, meaning that users can view the report with the most recent data. Because this is a potentially a resource-intensive financial report, we want to ensure that performance isn't affected when the report is rendered for multiple users simultaneously. We'll use Report Manager to configure the settings that control how the report will be executed.

The first step is to navigate to the Properties tab for the AR Reconciliation report, and then select Execution in the left frame. Figure 8-11 shows the available settings for report execution.

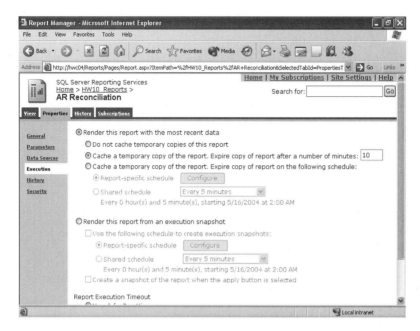

Figure 8-11. *Execution Properties settings*

The first execution selection, "Render this report from the most recent data," has several options that control report caching.

Caching is an SRS feature that allows temporary copies of a report to be stored and rendered to a user. The main advantage related to creating a cached copy of a report is increased performance. Users who access a report that is set to be cached will generate the first cached instance. Every subsequent user will receive the cached copy if certain conditions are met. The conditions for a user to receive the cached copy are as follows:

- The subsequent user must access the report within the time internal before the cached report is set to expire. When the cached report expires, a new copy must be created by the next user.

- If the report that's set to be cached has parameters that change during subsequent executions, and each user receives a new report based on that parameter, each report that's generated becomes a cached copy specific to the parameter value.

- The report's data source isn't set to Windows Authentication or to prompt the user for login credentials. Reports can't be cached with these authentication methods.

For our report, we instruct SRS to cache a temporary copy of the report, and expire the cached copy after ten minutes. Ten minutes is generally a good length of time to maintain cached reports, although it really depends on the time-sensitivity of your data. The data in a cached report will, of course, reflect the time at which the report was rendered rather than the current time and, short of printing the execution time on the report, there is no way for users to know if they're viewing a cached or live report.

The second selection, "Render this report from an execution snapshot," shouldn't be confused with a snapshot that creates a report history. An execution snapshot, unlike a history snapshot, is viewed from a report folder in Report Manager just like on-demand reports would be viewed. History snapshots, on the other hand, are viewed from the History tab of the report and can accumulate many copies.

Execution snapshots don't expire like cached reports; rather, they're refreshed at a specified interval. If you choose to generate an execution snapshot for a report, then that report can't be cached. In our case, we won't select this option.

The final report execution option sets the timeout interval for the report, either at a default setting, which is typically 1800 seconds (30 minutes), or at a specified value. This is an important setting because long-running reports use valuable system resources. We will use the Default value for the AR Reconciliation report.

We mentioned the trade-off involved in using caching for reports with time-sensitive data. There is another important consideration when choosing to use either snapshots or cached reports: disk space. Over time, history and cached reports set with lengthy expiration times can accumulate. We feel, however, the cost of disk storage compared to the performance and subsequent productivity increase is negligible and shouldn't stop anyone from taking advantage of these beneficial features of SRS.

Managing Subscriptions

Subscription services for SRS provides a means for delivering pre-executed reports to specified locations, either to a user via e-mail or to a network file share. There are several key benefits to using subscriptions. Internally in an organization, employees need key information at a certain times, such as daily or at the end of a month. Externally, customers may wish to receive newsletters or financial statements on a predetermined schedule. Subscriptions can accommodate both of these needs easily.

Setting up subscriptions has the added benefit of allowing you to schedule the processing of resource-intensive reports at off-peak hours, thus ensuring that there will be little or no degradation to performance during periods of heavy usage. There are two types of subscriptions that we will be working with in this section:

- **Standard subscriptions**, statically set up for one or more users

- **Data-driven subscriptions**, whereby subscriber lists can be derived from multiple data source locations and be generated from a custom query

---

▪**Note** Data-driven subscriptions are by far the most powerful form of subscriptions. They're available only in the Enterprise Edition of Reporting Services.

Standard Subscriptions

We will begin by setting up a standard e-mail subscription for employees in a healthcare organization that provides home-care services to patients. The report, called Patient Recertification Listing, was designed for employees who are responsible for tracking patient documentation.

It is a requirement that the patient's documentation, in this case an HCFA 485, be completed and signed by the attending physician. The report is essentially a daily work list for these employees, where any documentation that is unsigned becomes a work item.

Because this report needed to be generic enough for on-demand viewing in addition to being used for subscriptions, a report parameter was added that works with a report filter to show patients with both signed and unsigned documentation. There are other parameters for this report as well, as shown in Figure 8-12. As you will see, the parameters will be used when we generate the subscription.

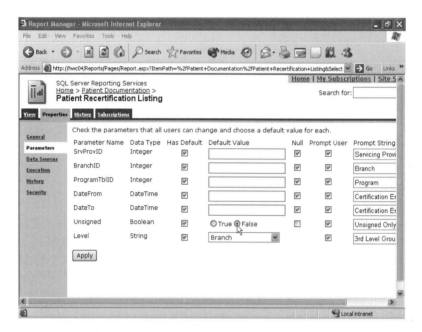

Figure 8-12. *Patient Recertification Listing report with parameters*

Creating a Standard Subscription

The first step in manually creating a subscription is to run Report Manager and navigate to the report for which you wish to create the subscription.

In our case, we navigate to the Patient Certification Listing report, which is in the Patient Documentation folder on the report server HWC04. Each report has a number of configurable values under four different pages: View, Properties, History, and Subscriptions.

We select the Subscriptions page and create a new subscription for the report. A subscription that is delivered via e-mail provides standard delivery options for Cc, Bcc, Reply-To, Subject, Priority, and Comment, which will be the body of the e-mail message. It is also possible to send the entire report in the e-mail, a link to the report, or both. Since we know that the user who will be receiving this subscription will have network access to the report server, we opt to send just a link to the report. Sending the report itself via e-mail does have benefits, especially when working with users who will need the report offline, such as traveling staff. We will demonstrate this in the next section when we set up a data-driven subscription.

■**Note** During installation of SRS, an SMTP server and default e-mail address are configured, which SRS will use to send e-mail based subscriptions.

Configuring the Subscription

Subscriptions are configured to execute at a scheduled time. The schedule can be customized for individual reports or based on a shared schedule. This report needs to be delivered to staff members in the morning, and it can be run anytime after 5:00 PM so that it's delivered by the next business day. For our needs, a schedule of 9:30 PM every day except Saturday is sufficient, as shown in Figure 8-13.

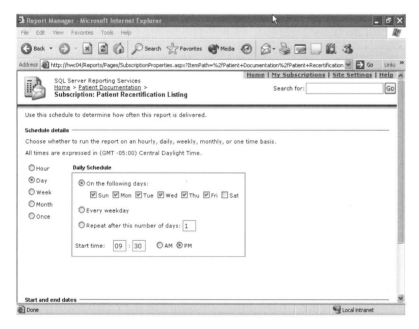

Figure 8-13. *Daily schedule for Patient Certification Listing*

Next, we configure the parameters for the report. As mentioned earlier, this particular report has a parameter called Unsigned, which is a Boolean data type (either True or False), which shows both signed and unsigned documentation. When this report is rendered, by default it is rendered to include all patients, whether signed or unsigned documentation exists. The subscribers of this report, however, will be interested in seeing only unsigned documentation, so we will set the parameter for Unsigned to be True. Because this report has been designed to provide populated drop-downs for the parameter values that are based on individual data sets, these values are available to us here, as shown in Figure 8-14. For now, we leave all of the other parameters with their default NULL values.

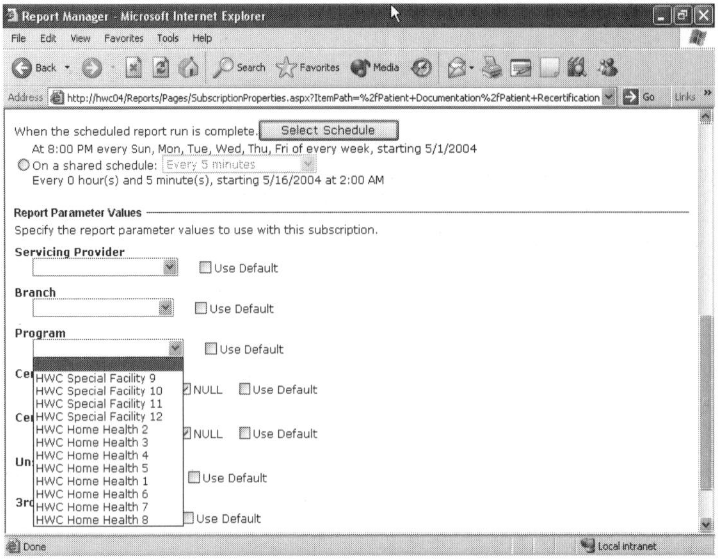

Figure 8-14. *Subscription parameter drop-downs*

To verify that the subscription is indeed working the way we anticipate, we made rodneyl@healthware.com the sole recipient of the mail for testing. In Figure 8-15, you can see standard e-mail options for To, Cc, Bcc, and Reply-To. In the To field you add the recipient's e-mail address, and then click OK to add the subscription. Once you verify the subscription's success, you modify the attributes of the subscription to add in the real subscribers by navigating back to the report in Report Manager, selecting Subscriptions, and then selecting Edit.

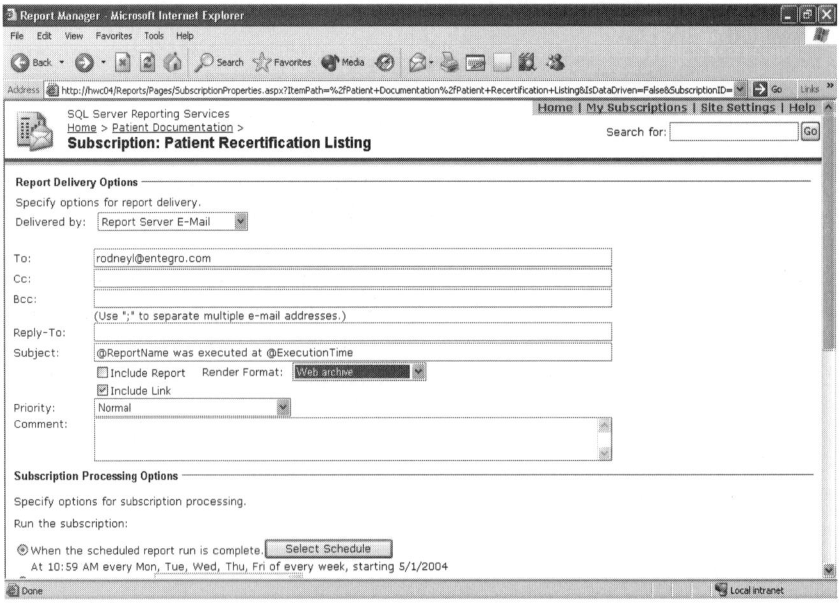

Figure 8-15. *Assigning recipients to subscriptions*

At the scheduled time, the recipient received the e-mail with the link to the report as expected, as you can see in Figure 8-16. We can now go back and assign multiple recipients, separated by a semicolon (;), or we can have the mail sent to any legitimate e-mail address—a public folder in Exchange Server, for example—or a distribution list address.

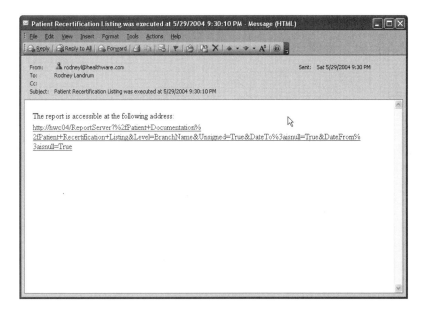

Figure 8-16. *E-mail subscription with a link*

Using Office Web Components with Subscriptions

We wanted to create a subscription that would e-mail a performance report to the administrator once per week to present an overview of report activity and investigate possible performance issues. The one issue with the subscription is that standard subscriptions support all rendering formats except HTMLOWC, which is the rendering format for Office Web Components (OWC) that would provide PivotTable functionality.

The administrator would have to execute the report in HTML, the default rendering format, and then export the report to OWC to gain the PivotTable functionality. To overcome this, we used a small "trick" that embeds the HTML reference to the report in the Comment field of the subscription. We unchecked the options Include Report and Include Link so that all the administrators would receive is an e-mail that contained a subject of the report name and execution time, and a link to the OWC-rendered report where the Comment field would have been included. Figure 8-17 shows a section of the HTML reference that we pasted directly into the Comment field.

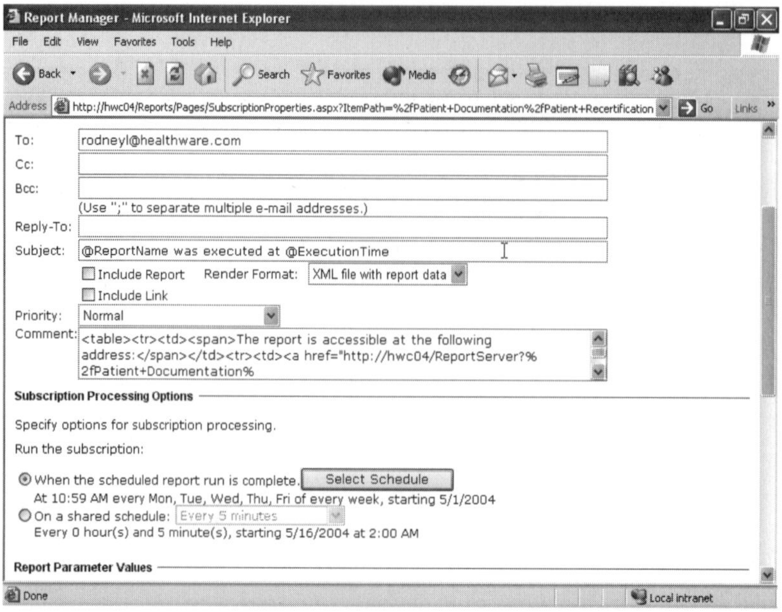

Figure 8-17. *Section of HTML code for a custom subscription*

■**Note** You can derive the source for the HTML code by clicking View Source in the e-mail message that sends the basic link to the report.

Data-Driven Subscriptions

Standard subscriptions will address the needs of many companies that want to set up custom subscriptions for both their employees and their customers. However, there is another, much more flexible method for delivering reports: the data-driven subscription. Data-driven subscriptions allow administrators or content managers to query a data source—a SQL Server table, for example—to return a list of subscribers that meet a specific set of criteria. This is the ideal way to deliver reports to a wide-ranging list of subscribers. Plus, you have to manage only one subscription for all subscribers, and those subscribers could have different parameters that are used to generate personalized reports.

We knew that we would want to let our customers and their employees take advantage of data-driven subscriptions and, fortunately, we had long ago structured our application database to include employee information that would be useful for just this purpose. By storing the employees' e-mail addresses as well as other data, such as geographical locations and certifications, we had all we needed to provide a flexible delivery system, via e-mail, to traveling staff. The employees that we initially targeted were clinicians who had a daily schedule of patients to see. Most of the clinicians operated laptops or PDAs as part of their daily routine.

Designing the Subscription Query

The first step was to redesign a report in SRS so that it would provide clinical employees with their daily schedules, and parameterize it in such a way that it would be employee-specific each time it was executed. As part of the data-driven subscription, the report would be processed and delivered to employees as both an embedded, printable format, and as a link to connect to the SRS report server if they were online. Figure 8-18 shows the report we created, Daily Activity.

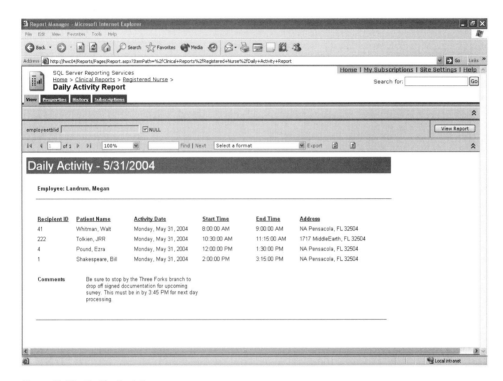

Figure 8-18. *Daily Activity report*

Because data-driven subscriptions are based on just that, data, a query to drive the subscription is essential. It is important to design the query to have very selective criteria, because SRS will deliver a copy of the report for every record that is returned from the data source.

For our recipient list, we use the query in Listing 8-2. Essentially, the query will return all employees who have an e-mail address and who also have scheduled activities for the day following the date of report execution. The report will be processed and delivered after hours. It is unusual in our environment that an employee's schedule will change after 9:00 PM, so we set up the report to execute at that time.

Listing 8-2. *T-SQL Query to Return the Subscriber List*

```
SELECT
    DISTINCT EmployeeTblID,Email,HWUserLogin,ActivityDate
FROM
    Employee INNER JOIN
    Activity ON Employee.EmployeeTblID = Activity.ProviderID
WHERE
    Email IS NOT NULL AND
    ActivityDate BETWEEN GETDATE() AND GETDATE () + 1
```

The output of the query yields six rows of data, as you can see in Table 8-1, indicating that six clinicians have activities for the next day. There are many ways to format and compare datetime values. However, in this case, using the GETDATE function to compare the current date with the ActivityDate field value was the best choice. It was necessary to use BETWEEN with GETDATE because the ActivityDate value defaults to 00:00:00 for the time value, whereas GETDATE returns the current time. The comparison values wouldn't match in a one-to-one comparison.

Table 8-1. *Output of a Data-Driven Query*

EmployeeTblID	Email	UserLogin	ActivityDate
15	NurseC@healthware.com	hwci\Nursec	2004-05-09
34	Lottah@healthware.com	hwciLottah	2004-05-09
44	MaryElizah@healthware.com	hwci\MaryElizah	2004-05-09
147	Fayel@healthware.com	hwci\Fayel	2004-05-09
155	Brendanl@healthware.com	hwci\brendanl	2004-05-09
159	Ethanl@healthware.com	hwci\Ethanl	2004-05-09

Creating the Data-Driven Subscription

Now we can step through the procedure for creating the data-driven subscription in Report Manager. Open the browser and navigate to the Daily Activity Report, and from there select Subscriptions. On the toolbar, select New Data-driven Subscription. There are seven steps to walk through to complete the data-driven subscription:

1. Choose a name, delivery method, and data source type.

2. Choose the data source location or define a new data source.

3. Choose the command or query to return a list of recipients.

4. Choose the settings for the Report Server Delivery Email delivery extension.

5. Choose the report parameters.

6. Choose when the subscription will be processed.

7. Set up a schedule for the report.

The most important of these steps is step 4, in which you specify the settings for the delivery extension. This is where you will use the data from the driving query to instruct SRS how to send the subscription. Every selection in step 4 has the option to retrieve the value derived from the query in used in step 3, which is much more versatile than a standard subscription.

We paste our query into the query box in step 3, as you can see in Figure 8-19, and verify it by clicking the Validate button. From this point, the fields we selected in the query, namely EmployeeTblid, Email, HWUserLogin, and ActivityDate, can all be used as criteria in the remaining steps.

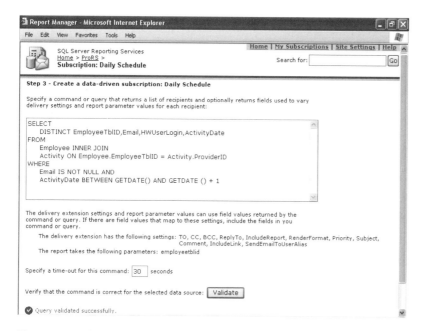

Figure 8-19. *The verified query that drives the subscription*

In step 4, there are several settings that control how the report will be sent to subscribers: To, Cc, Bcc, ReplyTo, IncludeReport, RenderFormat, Priority, Subject, Comment, and IncludeLink. For each setting, it is possible to choose a static value, a database value, or no value, as you can see in Figure 8-20. We assign the To field to the Email field from the subscription query. We leave the values for all of the other fields at their default settings. By leaving the defaults, the subscription will automatically include the report itself and the link to the report in the e-mail to the subscribers.

■**Tip** All of the report-rendering formats are available for subscriptions, except for HTML Office Web Components. With data-driven subscriptions, unlike with standard subscriptions, the rendering format can be controlled per subscriber because it too is a data-driven setting. If you need to control the rendering format per user, you can add a field to store this value in the Employee table and select this value in the query.

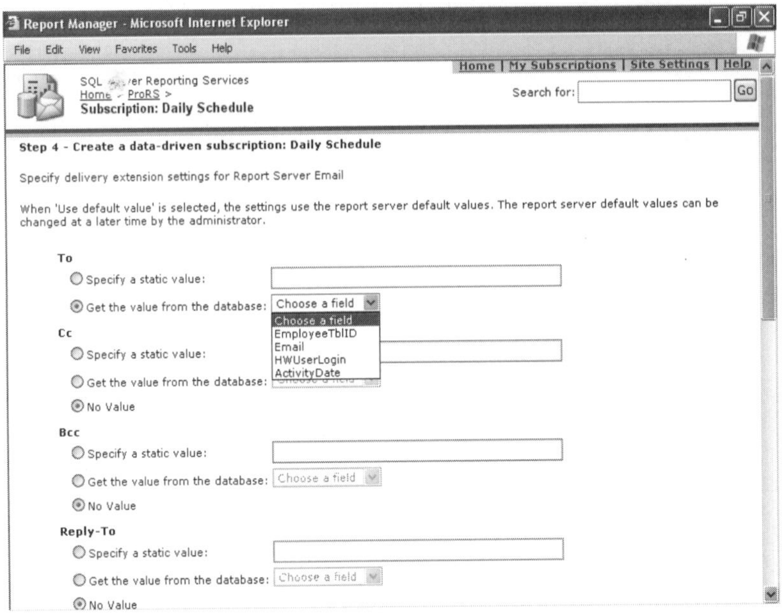

Figure 8-20. *Subscription settings*

The EmployeeTblid field is used for the one parameter in the report. Because we've selected this field in our query and passed this as a parameter input, each report will be automatically generated with data specific to the employee who subscribed to the report. The other field, HWUserLogin, is put in the driving query, which we will ultimately compare to the Windows login name of the user executing the report. This will be accomplished, as you will see in Chapter 9, by using the User global collection.

For the final step, we create a schedule that processes the report each weeknight at 9:30 PM, as described earlier. We can create another shared schedule to process the subscription and test it to verify that the e-mail is being delivered successfully. Once that is complete, we're finished with the subscription configuration.

■**Note** The default rendering format for subscriptions is Web Archive, but for many types of reports, this isn't the ideal choice. Other printable reports are better suited for Adobe Acrobat PDF files or static image files such as TIFF.

Execution Auditing and Performance Analysis

As you deploy SRS in both test and production environments, gauging performance will involve a variety of benchmarking and analysis tools. Based on the performance analysis, administrators will be armed with the knowledge of what stress levels their servers can endure, and they'll be able to configure the environment accordingly. We'll put the components of our SRS deployment to the test, and using standard tools we'll analyze the output.

Many agencies like ours need to monitor and archive the details of user activity. This is especially important if we suspect there's undesired access to data. SRS provides a built-in logging feature that captures several key pieces of information. This information is useful in two ways:

- We can capture performance information about the reports, such as the processing duration and record count.

- We can capture security information, such as who executed the report and whether or not they were successful.

Our first goal in this section is to set up and extend the built-in logging functionality of SRS using tools provided in the SRS installation. We'll need to log all activity so that we may pinpoint the reports and users that are most impacting the server. We have created a custom SRS report, Report Execution Log, that will deliver the logging statistics to administrators and contain dynamic column groupings based on a report parameter and be rendered in HTMLOWC for PivotTable analysis. We'll show how you can use this report for your SRS deployment.

Our second goal in this section is to perform benchmarking tests on the SRS servers in our test web farm to ensure there won't be any unexpected performance problems when SRS is deployed to a production environment. We'll work with a web application stress-test utility called Application Center Test (ACT) to gauge performance.

Configuring SRS Logging

Getting to the execution log information in SRS is a fairly straightforward procedure. It consists of a main table in the SRS database called, appropriately enough, ExecutionLog. When SRS is installed by default, execution logging is enabled. However, the data in the table, though useful by itself, isn't ideally formatted for direct querying. Since one of our aims is to build a custom SRS report to deliver report execution information to administrators, we'll need to be able to query the log data. Fortunately, SRS provides a means of transforming the data in the ExecutionLog table into several tables that can be queried more easily to produce valuable output.

Transforming the ExecutionLog Table

Setting up SRS to transform the logging data is a simple step-by-step procedure. We will quickly step through the process in our environment here. All the files that you'll need to create and transform the SRS logging data can be found in the path *<drive letter>*:\Program Files\Microsoft SQL Server\80\Tools\Reporting Services\ExecutionLog. The first step is to create the database where the execution log data will be stored. The database may reside on the same SQL Server as SRS, but you can create it on another database server if desired. The script to create the database is called CreateTables.sql. You can load the script and execute it in Query Analyzer. By default, the database that is created is named RSExecutionLog.

After creating the database that will store the log data, you load and execute the DTS package called RSExecutionLog_Update.dts, which populates the tables in the newly created database, as shown in Figure 8-21.

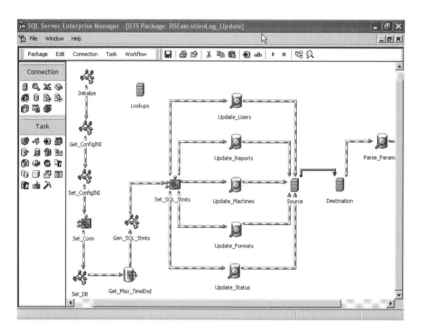

Figure 8-21. *RSExecutionLog_Update DTS package*

This package uses an initialization file that specifies the source and destination databases and their locations—typically ReportServer and RSExecutionLog, respectively—on the local server. These values can be modified if the default names and locations were not used to create the execution log database.

■**Tip** It is important to note that the package needs to be executed regularly to keep the transformed log data current. In our situation, we created a scheduled job for this purpose that runs the DTS package every evening.

Microsoft provides a set of sample reports that can be used with the ExecutionLog database. These reports are on the SRS CD at the following location: \extras\Execution Log Sample Reports. The sample reports are useful for giving administrators information, such as report execution by user and report size, among other things. There are seven SRS execution log sample reports in all, one of which, ReportsByMonth, is shown in Figure 8-22.

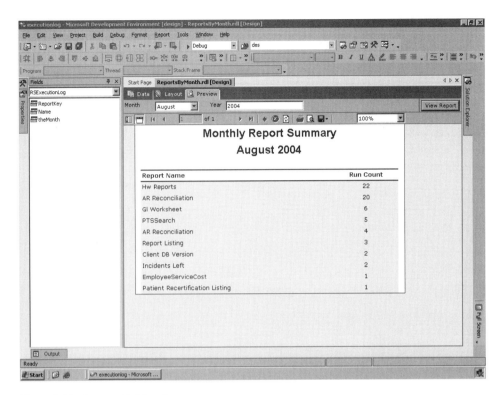

Figure 8-22. *ReportsByMonth*

Designing the Log Report

We knew that we were going to need a single report that contained all of the execution log information, and it should be one that administrators could easily analyze. Thus, we created a matrix-style report using data from a single query. We needed to use the OWC rendering format to take advantage of the user interactivity and drag-and-drop capabilities of the PivotTable control.

For measuring performance from information contained in the execution log, we're interested in several statistics:

- **Total time to retrieve the data:** How long did it take to retrieve data?

- **Total time to process:** How long did the report take to process?

- **Total time to render:** How long did the report take to render?

- **Byte count:** How many bytes are in the report?

- **Row count:** How many rows of data are in the report?

In addition, it will also be useful to know when the report was executed. For the row groupings in the matrix, we want to see what report was executed, who ran the report, and from which client machine the report was run. For the column group, we will want to have two possible selections: either rendering format, such as HTML 4.0, OWC, or PDF, or source types, meaning how SRS generated the report (Live, Cache, or Snapshot, for example). Source_Type is an important field to monitor, because how SRS generates reports directly impacts performance. Generating reports from a cached copy or a snapshot, which are both preprocessed copies of reports, is a performance benefit. If SRS is always generating live or on-demand reports for users, performance may suffer.

To accomplish the dynamic column groupings in the matrix, we will use a parameter called Column_Group that takes the values of the field names in the query, Format or Source_Type. We will use a default value of Format so that the report will automatically be rendered when previewed. Both the column grouping and heading values will use the following expression to make the column dynamic based on the parameter:

```
=Fields(Paramter!Column_Group).Value
```

When the report is rendered, as you can see in Figure 8-23, it will default to the Format field, but you can change it dynamically by changing the parameter drop-down to Source Type.

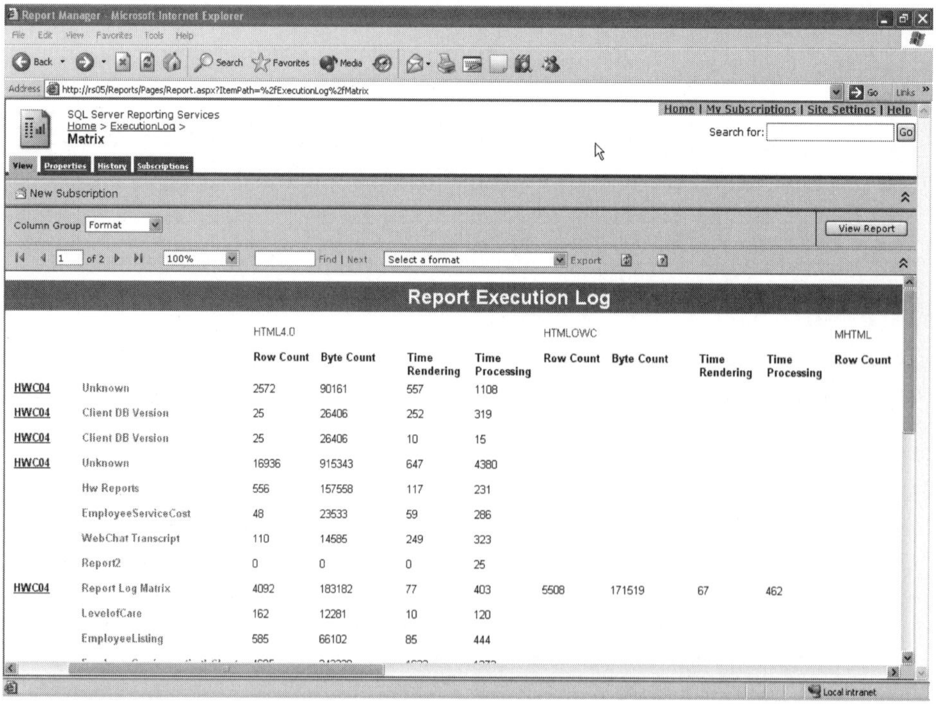

Figure 8-23. *Report Execution Log report*

One problem remains: automatically rendering the report in OWC instead of the default HTML 4.0. To accomplish this goal, we can simply append the Format command to the base URL that calls the report so that the URL will look like the following: http://hwc04/ReportServer?%2fExecutionLog%2fMatrix&Column_group=Format&rs%3aCommand=Render&rs%3AFormat=HTMLOWC.

When administrators execute the report from this URL, they will have the ability to dynamically work with the report to gain a clear picture of the longest running reports overall, as well as the report that contained the most data. Having the ability to group by user and machine will further narrow down potential bottlenecks. We could gather additional performance measures to report on if we chose to, such as the parameter value that the user selected. This would be useful when a pattern is discovered, such as that a particular user runs a certain report and always chooses the same parameters that return over 10,000 records. Thousands of possible combinations of data views exist for the administrator within the PivotTable. Further, if the administrator would like to save a custom view of the report, he or she can export the PivotTable from OWC directly to Microsoft Excel.

Figure 8-24 shows the Report Execution Log report rendered in OWC. We have included this report for download on the Apress website, so that you can use it directly with your SRS deployment.

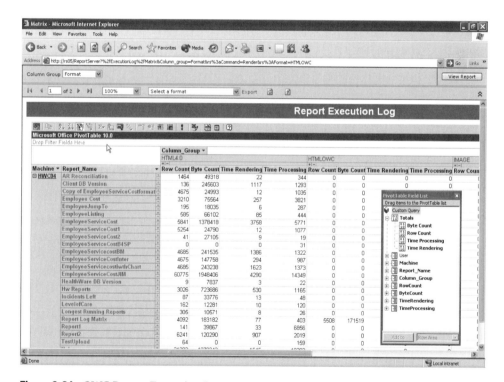

Figure 8-24. *OWC Report Execution Log*

Performance Testing

Of course, no one wants to experience the frustration of building a solid reporting solution in a development environment only to find out that when deployed to the masses it can't hold up under the strain. Generally, it is a best practice to put a simulated load on your servers to gain a better understanding of how the systems will function. Also, when you roll out a full solution, it is a common practice to roll out several pieces at a time to a limited number of users. That is what we have done in our online models.

The strategy for rolling out should also include a plan for which reports will be available on demand versus which ones will be provided by way of report snapshots or subscriptions, as we've done up to this point in the chapter. Since we have a working testbed, complete with a wide enough variety of reports for a valid simulation, we can step through the process of testing how our solution will work when users begin to use it.

By stress testing the components of our SRS solution, we will be able to see how the machines themselves will respond, in addition to the individual reports. In this section, we use a web application stress-testing tool called Microsoft ACT to verify that our SRS deployment will stand up to the rigors of many simultaneous users. We also use `rsconfig` and `rsactivate` to join an SRS server to a web farm to see how offloading resources to another system will enhance performance.

Setting Up Microsoft Application Center Test

As previously mentioned, for our test we use the ACT tool that is a part of Visual Studio .NET. This stress-test application records calls to a website made from a browser and then plays back the recorded session on a single client machine or multiple client machines, emulating the load of many simultaneous users.

Before we create our test, there is one issue that we must overcome with ACT and how it works with sites that incorporate Integrated Windows Authentication. ACT creates requests based on HTTP 1.0, which does not support "keep-alive" connections, which are required for Integrated Windows Authentication. Unless we change the default directory security for the ReportServer virtual directory in IIS to Basic, we will receive an authorization error when navigating to the reports within the browser when we attempt to record the test. The workaround is to change the security to Basic Authentication, record the test, change back to Integrated Windows Authentication, and make a few global changes to the resultant test script:

1. Run Internet Information Services Manager on the SRS web server, navigate to the ReportServer virtual folder, and select Properties. On the Directory Security tab, click the Edit button in the "Authentication and access control" section, check Basic authentication, and uncheck Integrated Windows.

2. Open Application Center Test and select New Test. Step through the wizard until you get to the Browser Record form, where you can start recording. When you click Start Recording, the browser will launch and you can navigate to and execute the reports that you want for your tests. When you're finished you can close the browser and click the Stop Recording button. Name the test RS05_Test_Load.

3. You now have a VBScript file that will initiate requests to your SRS server that are identical to what you've just done manually in the browser. You can make your global changes to the VBScript file. First, comment out all instances of the line `oHeaders.Add "Authorization",...` by placing a single quote before each line. You'll also need to change all instances of `HTTP/1.0` to `HTTP/1.1`, as you can see in Figure 8-25.

4. Change the directory security for the ReportServer virtual directory back to Integrated Windows Authentication in IIS. Now you're ready to run the test, RS05_Test_Load.

Figure 8-25. *RS05_Test_Load in ACT*

Running the Performance Test on a Single Machine

Before you start the test created in the previous steps, RS05_Test_Load, you need to assign users to the test project. You do this in the properties of the test itself. In our case, we'll add the user for the test domain. A password is also required, which we'll add for each user that we set up. By adding the same user three times, we'll be able to run the script for three simulated users. We'll click Start Test and monitor the connections that are created on the SRS server that we're connecting to, RS05.

On the target SRS server, we can quickly assess the performance impact by monitoring the server with Task Manager. Unfortunately, we see that our test has pushed the server to 100% CPU utilization. Analyzing the individual processes that are taxing the processor, we ascertain that they are SQL Server and the Web service W3WP.exe. Figure 8-26 shows the CPU usage jumping to 100% as the test is running.

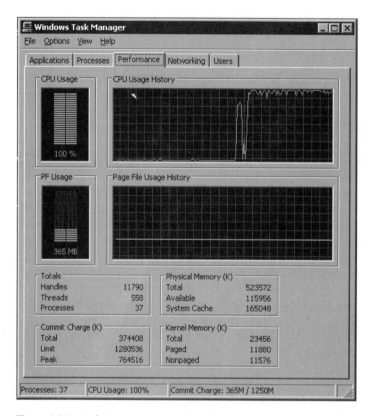

Figure 8-26. *Task Manager at 100%*

We know that our SRS server is a single processor system with over 500MB of RAM. In this case, it is the CPU that is the bottleneck. Because our deployment of SRS won't mirror the setup of this server (in other words, the production server will be a high-end multiprocessor system with at least 2GB of RAM), we can take that into consideration.

However, there is one other factor that will have a substantial impact on the difference in performance between the production and test environments. In the test environment, the SRS Web service and SQL Server are on the same system, RS05. What if we were to configure the SRS Web service to use a remote SQL Server instance for its database? Any performance degradation caused by accessing the ReportServer database over the network instead of a local database would be negligible if the CPU utilization percentage were to drop down to a more manageable number.

If you have two SRS servers, then moving an SRS server from one instance to another is quite simple. We have two SRS servers in the test environment, RS05 and HWC04, so the move should be easy enough. To instruct the Web service on RS05 to use the SRS databases on HWC04, we will use the command-line utility rsconfig. Rsconfig and rsactivate are both required when first joining one SRS Web service to a web farm that uses the same ReportServer database. The syntax for the rsconfig command is as follows:

```
rsconfig -c -s HWC04 -d ReportServer -a SQL -u username -p password
```

We run the `rsconfig` command on RS05, where we would like to reset the connection to use HWC04. We then run `rsactivate` on HWC04 to connect to the remote Windows ReportServer service to activate the Web service. The syntax for `rsactivate` is as follows:

```
rsactivate -m RS05 -u username -p password
```

Rsactivate is required to set the encryption keys that are stored in both the RSReport-Server.config file and in the ReportServer database. We will cover managing encryption keys for SRS in more depth in Chapter 9.

Now that RS05 is using the remote SQL Server database, we can initiate another test to see if the CPU utilization has improved. As you can see in Figure 8-27, CPU utilization has improved substantially and is now under the 60% average.

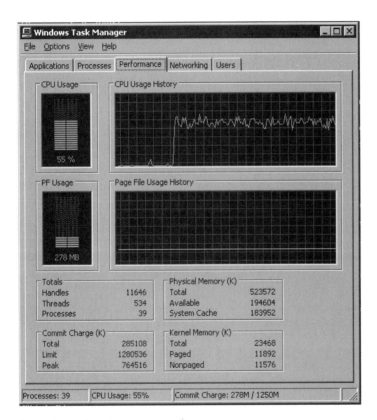

Figure 8-27. *Task Manager with improvements*

We can now view the results of the test in ACT. We can see that we have an average of 48 requests per second from the client browser on HWC04, as shown in Figure 8-28. In the real world, we know that it's not likely that we'll see that many requests per second over an extended period of time, but it's a good benchmark to see how the server would react under that stress load. We now know that our production deployment must have SRS Web service offloaded to its own server and not shared with the SRS database server. In many cases having both services running on the same system may be a viable option for many smaller companies.

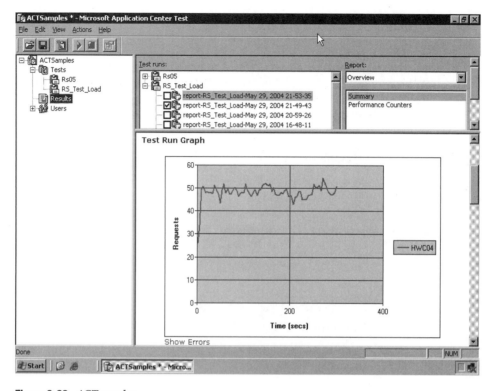

Figure 8-28. *ACT results*

■**Note** Specific licensing guidelines are available for the SRS deployment and the location of the databases and data sources. For more information, visit http://www.microsoft.com/sql/reporting/howtobuy/howtolicensers.asp.

Controlling Reporting Services Programmatically

SRS offers two main methods of controlling SRS through code:

- Web services

- Windows Management Interface (WMI)

In this section, we're going to take an introductory look at using both of these technologies to deal with report management from code. We'll use the Web services API to add subscription functionality to the SRS viewer we created in Chapter 6, and we'll extend it to allow our users to add subscriptions for the reports we've developed and deployed so far. This has two main benefits. First, it allows us to offload some of the processing activity from our SQL Server and our SRS server during the day, when they are used most heavily. Second, it will save the executives who want to receive the reports from spending time navigating to our report server, entering in the parameters, and waiting for the results.

Controlling Reporting Services with SOAP

SRS Web services offers a feature-rich way of interacting with and controlling your reporting server. Based on SOAP and operating over HTTP, Web services are a simple and yet powerful way to access the features of the server. In fact, the Reporting Services reports interface is built using ASP.NET and SRS Web services.

Using the Web services API, you can create custom applications that control all aspects of the server and cover the entire reporting life cycle:

- Folder and resource management

- Task, role, and policy management

- Data sources and connections

- Report parameters

- Report rendering

- Report history

- Report scheduling

- Report subscriptions

- Linked reports

Adding Subscription Functionality to SRS Viewer

We've already used the Web services API to provide us with a list of report parameters and their possible values, and to deploy reports in Chapters 6 and 7. In this chapter, we'll take a look at using the Web services API to schedule reports to run automatically each morning before the office opens.

As you saw in the earlier part of this chapter, you can set up subscription services through the UI of the report server itself. You may, however, want to provide this functionality within your customized Windows Form (or web) application. In our example, we will expand on our previous Windows Form application to allow the user to provide the parameters that they want to run the report with, as well as schedule the time to run the report and indicate the delivery mechanism to use.

In our example, we're going to allow the users to pick only a shared schedule that has already been defined by the systems administrator. Because we want centralized control over when scheduled reports will be run, we won't give users the ability to define their own schedules. We're also going to allow them to select to trigger a subscription based on a snapshot. This allows them to receive their subscribed report whenever a snapshot is created for it. See the "Creating Snapshots for the Report History" section earlier in this chapter for details.

Accessing an Existing Shared Schedule

Let's get started. First, open the SRS viewer project from the previous chapter. To this, you'll add a second panel to Form2 from the previous chapter, and then to that add a label and a combo box. Also widen the form a bit, because the schedule descriptions can get long. Set the label text to Schedule and make sure that the combo box is named comboBox1. When you're done, you should have a form that looks like Figure 8-29.

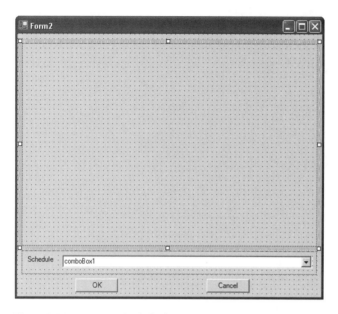

Figure 8-29. *Create Schedule dialog box*

Now you'll modify the Form2 Load event to query the SRS server for the shared schedules that are available.

■**Note** You'll need to set up these shared schedules in advance using Report Manager on your SRS server. You can add and edit shared schedules by navigating to your SRS server with your web browser, selecting Site Settings, and then under Other selecting Managed shared schedules. See the "Shared Schedules" section earlier in this chapter for details.

To get a list of available shared schedules from your SRS server, you'll use the ListSchedules method of the Web services API. The ListSchedules method returns an array of Schedule objects, so once you call the method you'll need to loop through the array to populate your combo box. Since you're expanding the existing viewer, you still want the user to be able to run the report immediately. You also want your users to be able to trigger the subscription whenever a snapshot of the report is created. To do this, add a "Do not schedule" choice and a "Schedule with snapshot" choice to your combo box.

■**Note** Snapshots will also be set up through Report Manager web interface of your SRS server.

Use the `ComboItem` class that you created in Chapter 6 to add the items to combo boxes. Go just below the last line of the current Form2_Load function, and add the code in Listing 8-3.

Listing 8-3. *Adding the ComboItem Class*

```
Schedule[] schedules = null;

try
{
    schedules = rs.ListSchedules();
    if (schedules != null)
    {
        //Build list items
        ArrayList aList = new ArrayList();
        // Now add the Do not schedule item
        aList.Add(new ComboItem("Do not schedule", "NS"));
        // And the Snapshot schedule
        aList.Add(new ComboItem("Schedule with Snapshot", "SS"));
        foreach (Schedule s in schedules)
        {
            aList.Add(new ComboItem(s.Description, s.ScheduleID));
            Debug.WriteLine(String.Format("Desc: {0} - ID: {1}", s.Description,
                    s.ScheduleID));
        }
        //Bind list items to combo box
        comboBox1.DataSource = aList;
        comboBox1.DisplayMember="Display";
        comboBox1.ValueMember="Value";
    }
}
catch (SoapException ex)
{
    MessageBox.Show(ex.Detail.InnerXml.ToString());
}
```

Scheduling the Report

Now that you have the list of available scheduling options, you need to add some code to handle the case in which the user has selected to schedule the report to be delivered based on one of the shared schedules or on the creation of a snapshot. To do this, you'll use another method of the SRS Web service API, `CreateSubscription`. The `CreateSubscription` method of the API takes six different parameters:

- **Report**: The full path name of the report for which to create a subscription.

- **ExtensionSettings**: An ExtensionSettings object that contains a list of settings specific to the delivery extension.

- **Description**: A meaningful description displayed to users.

- **EventType**: The type of event that triggers the subscription. The valid values are TimedSubscription and SnapshotUpdated.

- **MatchData**: The data that is associated with the specified EventType parameter. This parameter is used by an event to match the subscription with an event that has fired.

- **Parameters**: An array of ParameterValue[] objects that contains a list of parameters for the report.

In your report scheduler, you'll create a new method, ScheduleReport, which is called whenever the user selects to have a report scheduled. This method will set these parameters to the appropriate values and then call the CreateSubscription method of the SRS Web service. Most of the values are just strings and are very straightforward to set.

First, check to see if the user selected a subscription and, if so, whether it is based on a shared schedule or a snapshot. You'll use this to set the EventType accordingly. If the user selected Shared Schedule, then set the variable matchData to the ScheduledID. If not, set the variable to NULL to tell SRS to trigger it based on a snapshot.

```
if (comboBox1.SelectedValue.ToString() == "SS")
{
    eventType = "SnapshotUpdated";
    matchData = null;
}
else
{
    eventType = "TimedSubscription";
    matchData = comboBox1.SelectedValue.ToString();
}
```

To set up a subscription, you have to provide SRS with some information about how to deliver the subscription. To do this, you set the delivery extensions through an ExtensionSettings object, which itself contains ParameterValue objects. ParameterValue objects are essentially name/value pairs, making the ExtensionSettings object essentially an array of name/value pairs.

To use the ExtensionSettings object, create ParameterValue objects (your name/value pairs) with your delivery settings, and then add them to the ExtensionSettings object. You'll then call the CreateSubscription method and pass in the ExtensionSettings object to give SRS the subscription specifics. See Listing 8-4 for details.

If the user decides upon a subscription based on a shared schedule, and the report accepts parameters, then you'll need to collect them from your report viewer interface so that you can set them in the subscription. These will be the values that the report will run with whenever it's run by the subscription. You'll get the report parameters by calling a method that you'll move from inline code to a separate method from the code in Chapter 6. This refactored code is shown in Listing 8-4. The only other item you need is the report itself, which you already have as a class-level variable that was set in the Forms constructor. The final method should look like Listing 8-4 and should be added to Form2.

Listing 8-4. *Report Scheduler*

```
private void ScheduleReport()
{

    // See if the user wants to schedule this vs. run it now
    if (comboBox1.SelectedValue.ToString() != "NS")
    {
        string desc = "Send report via email";
        string eventType = String.Empty;
        string matchData = String.Empty;
        // If the user selected SnapShot then set up the parameters for a snapshot
        if (comboBox1.SelectedValue.ToString() == "SS")
        {
            eventType = "SnapshotUpdated";
            matchData = null;
        }
        // otherwise the user is using a subscription
        else
        {
            eventType = "TimedSubscription";
            matchData = comboBox1.SelectedValue.ToString();
        }

        ParameterValue[] extensionParams = new ParameterValue[8];

        extensionParams[0] = new ParameterValue();
        extensionParams[0].Name = "TO";
        extensionParams[0].Value = "someone@company.com";

        extensionParams[1] = new ParameterValue();
        extensionParams[1].Name = "ReplyTo";
        extensionParams[1].Value = "reporting@company.com";

        extensionParams[2] = new ParameterValue();
        extensionParams[2].Name = "IncludeReport";
        extensionParams[2].Value = "True";

        extensionParams[3] = new ParameterValue();
        extensionParams[3].Name = "RenderFormat";
        extensionParams[3].Value = "MHTML";
```

```
extensionParams[4] = new ParameterValue();
extensionParams[4].Name = "Subject";
extensionParams[4].Value = "@ReportName was executed at
    @ExecutionTime";

extensionParams[5] = new ParameterValue();
extensionParams[5].Name = "Comment";
extensionParams[5].Value = "Here is your @ReportName report.";

extensionParams[6] = new ParameterValue();
extensionParams[6].Name = "IncludeLink";
extensionParams[6].Value = "True";

extensionParams[7] = new ParameterValue();
extensionParams[7].Name = "Priority";
extensionParams[7].Value = "NORMAL";

ParameterValue[] pvs = ReportParameters();

ExtensionSettings extSettings = new ExtensionSettings();
extSettings.ParameterValues = extensionParams;
extSettings.Extension = "Report Server Email";

try
{
    rs.CreateSubscription(report, extSettings, desc, eventType, matchData,
        pvs);
}

catch (SoapException e)
{
    Console.WriteLine(e.Detail.InnerXml.ToString());
}
    }
}
```

Now let's take a look at the revised button1 click event of the SRS viewer and the new ReportParameters method created when you refactor the code. First, you need to modify the button1 click event to check if the user wants to run the report now or schedule the report to run later using a subscription. You're also going to refactor the code a bit to move some common code into methods you can call separately. This will prevent you from duplicating the code inline for the ScheduleReport method and in the button1 click event. It will also make your code much cleaner and easier to maintain in the future. To do this, you modify the button1 click event, as shown in Listing 8-5.

Listing 8-5. *Modifying the button1 Click Event*

```
private void button1_Click(object sender, System.EventArgs e)
{
    //See if the user wants to run now (Not Scheduled)
    if (comboBox1.SelectedValue.ToString() == "NS")
    {
        string URL = ReportParametersURL();
        url = URL;
        this.DialogResult = DialogResult.OK;
        Close();
    }
    else
    {
        ScheduleReport();
        this.DialogResult = DialogResult.Cancel;
        Close();
    }
}
```

Next, you'll take part of the code that you pulled out of the button1 click event used to get all of the report parameter values entered by the user and put it into its own method. This now gives you a single common way to get the report parameter values entered by the user. You've already used this new method in the ScheduleReport method shown in Listing 8-6, and you'll use this new method to create the ReportParametersURL method shown in Listing 8-6. Because SRS uses these values in the form of an array of ParameterValue objects, most of the time you'll make the return value of your method an array of ParameterValue objects.

Listing 8-6. *ReportParametersURL Method*

```
private ParameterValue[] ReportParameters()
{
    int numCtrls = (this.panel1.Controls.Count/2);
    ParameterValue[] pvs = new ParameterValue[numCtrls];
    int i = 0;

    foreach (Control ctrl in this.panel1.Controls)
    {
        if (ctrl.GetType() == typeof(ComboBox))
        {
            ComboBox a = (ComboBox) ctrl;
            pvs[i] = new ParameterValue();
            pvs[i].Name = a.Name;
            if (a.SelectedValue != null && a.SelectedValue.ToString() !=
                String.Empty)
```

```
        {
            pvs[i].Value = a.SelectedValue.ToString();
        }
        i++;
    }
}


return pvs;


}
```

You'll also create another method that uses the array of `ParameterValue` objects returned by the `ReportParameters` method to construct your report URL, as shown in Listing 8-7. As you saw in Listing 8-6, the button1 click event can now use the new `ReportParametersURL` method to do the work of getting the report parameters and generating the URL necessary to display your report should the user still want to run the report interactively versus on a schedule.

Listing 8-7. *Using an Array of ParameterValue Objects*

```
private string ReportParametersURL()
{
    ParameterValue[] pvs = ReportParameters();
    string URL = url +
        "&rs:Command=Render&rs:Format=HTML4.0&rc:Parameters=false";
    foreach (ParameterValue pv in pvs)
    {
        if (pv.Value != null && pv.Value != String.Empty)
            URL += "&" + pv.Name + "=" + pv.Value;
    }
    return URL;
}
```

Report Delivery

In our example, we've used the HTML format to deliver the report to our subscription user. We've also hard-coded the e-mail address, which isn't practical in the real world. One other issue we're concerned with, especially in our healthcare setting, is HIPAA compliance and protecting patient information.

We could give the user a text box with which to enter the e-mail address that the user wants the report delivered to. However, it is possible that the user could type in an incorrect e-mail address and possibly deliver the report to the wrong person. It would be great if we could fill in the user's e-mail address automatically, knowing it would be the correct address. We could do this by pulling the address from a field in a table in our database similar to the example given earlier in the report where we pulled the e-mail address from the employee table. However, in this case, the user pulling the report may not be in our database table, and we want to report delivered automatically to the user scheduling it. Fortunately, the .NET Framework and Active Directory offer us an easy way to do this. For many organizations using Microsoft Exchange Server 2000 or 2003, e-mail addresses are integrated with Active Directory. If you aren't using

Exchange Server, e-mail addresses aren't integrated with Active Directory, but you can still enter them into Active Directory manually.

Let's create a method that will determine the e-mail of the currently logged-in user. Then we can use it to provide the To e-mail address for our subscription. We need to start out by adding a new reference to our project for System.DirectoryServices. Next, we add using statements to simplify our typing, as follows:

```
using System.DirectoryServices;
using System.Security.Principal;
```

To find the current user's e-mail address, we use the DirectorySearcher, which allows us to perform queries against Active Directory, as in Listing 8-8. We'll start at the root level of the directory and look for the user by name. When we find the user's name, we return the first e-mail address that we find for the user.

Listing 8-8. *Code to Query Active Directory*

```
private string GetEmailFromAD()
{

    DirectoryEntry rootEntry;
    DirectoryEntry contextEntry;
    DirectorySearcher searcher;
    SearchResult result;

    string currentUserName;
    string contextPath;

    WindowsPrincipal wp =
        new WindowsPrincipal(WindowsIdentity.GetCurrent());
    currentUserName = wp.Identity.Name.Split('\\')[1];

    rootEntry = new DirectoryEntry("LDAP://RootDSE");
    contextPath =
        rootEntry.Properties["defaultNamingContext"].Value.ToString();

    rootEntry.Dispose();
    contextEntry = new DirectoryEntry("LDAP://" + contextPath);

    searcher = new DirectorySearcher();
    searcher.SearchRoot = contextEntry;
    searcher.Filter =
        String.Format("(&(objectCategory=person)(samAccountName={0}))",
        currentUserName);
    searcher.PropertiesToLoad.Add("mail");
    searcher.PropertiesToLoad.Add("cn");
    searcher.SearchScope = SearchScope.Subtree;
```

```
    result = searcher.FindOne();

    return result.Properties["mail"][0].ToString();
}
```

To use this, all we have to do is modify the TO parameter for the delivery extension in the
ScheduleReport method we wrote earlier to use the new method we just wrote. So our previous
code for the TO parameter becomes this:

```
extensionParams[0] = new ParameterValue();
extensionParams[0].Name = "TO";
extensionParams[0].Value = GetEmailFromAD();
```

Now when we run the SRS viewer, select 2004 for the Service Year parameter, and choose
a schedule from the shared schedules, it will create a subscription that will be e-mailed to
us on the schedule we selected. If we navigate to the server now using our browser and select
the EmployeeServiceCost report, and then select the Subscriptions tab, we should see our
subscription. If we click Edit, we see that it has provided all of the parameters that we selected,
and it inserted our e-mail address in the To field. It should look something like Figure 8-30.

We haven't looked at all of the possible options that we can use when scheduling reports
such as our Employee Cost report, but we've given you a good start to schedule and deliver
reports and add other functionality. Some possibilities include the following:

- Allow the user to decide the format the report will be delivered in.

- Allow the user to attach the report or just provide a link.

- Allow the user to create schedules on the fly.

You can use the SRS Web services API to control many more aspects of the report server
and of the reports under its control. We have just scratched the surface here of what you can do,
but be aware that the basic aspects of dealing with the report server through the Web services
API are the same for nearly all of the functions.

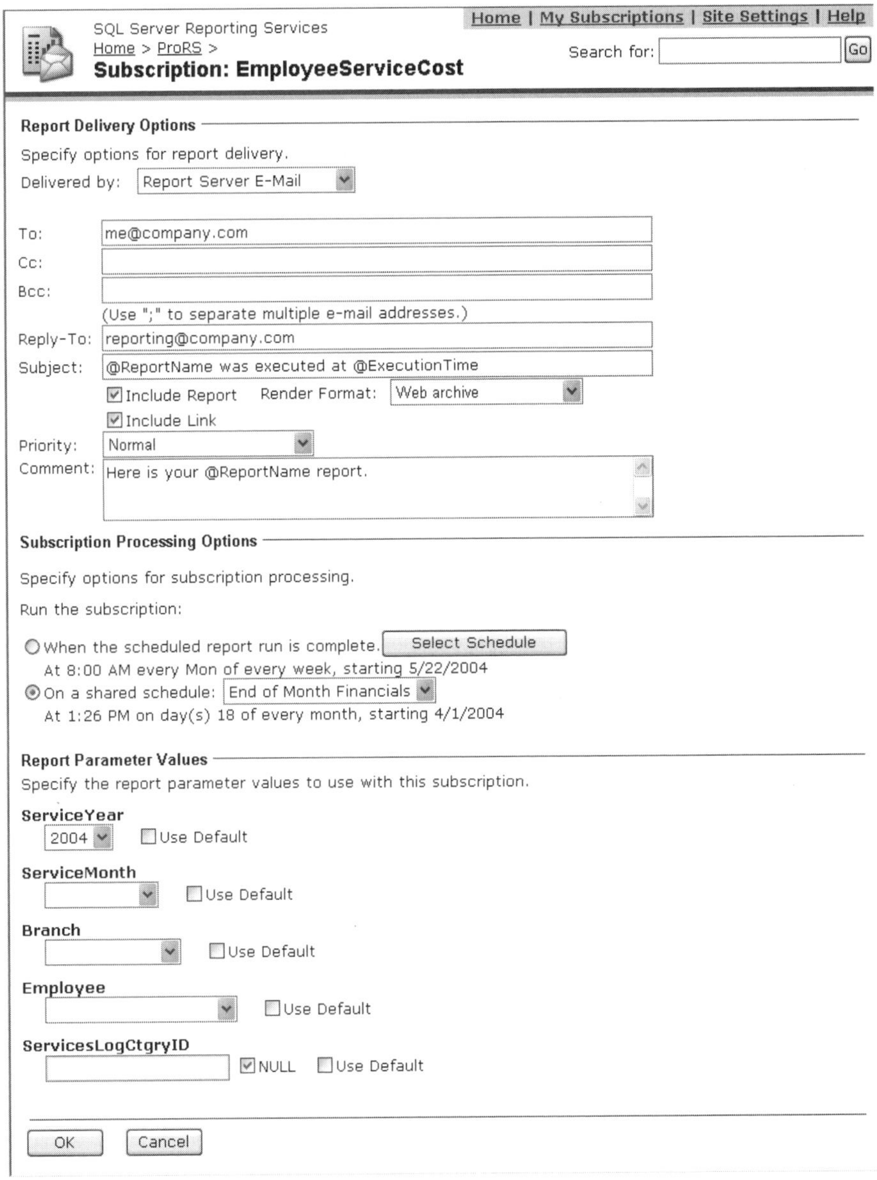

SQL Server Reporting Services

Home > ProRS >

Subscription: EmployeeServiceCost

Search for: [   ] [Go]

Report Delivery Options

Specify options for report delivery.

Delivered by: [Report Server E-Mail ▾]

To: [me@company.com   ]
Cc: [   ]
Bcc: [   ]
           (Use ";" to separate multiple e-mail addresses.)
Reply-To: [reporting@company.com   ]
Subject: [@ReportName was executed at @ExecutionTime]
           ☑ Include Report   Render Format: [Web archive   ▾]
           ☑ Include Link
Priority: [Normal   ▾]
Comment: [Here is your @ReportName report.   ]

Subscription Processing Options

Specify options for subscription processing.

Run the subscription:

○ When the scheduled report run is complete. [Select Schedule]
   At 8:00 AM every Mon of every week, starting 5/22/2004
◉ On a shared schedule: [End of Month Financials ▾]
   At 1:26 PM on day(s) 18 of every month, starting 4/1/2004

Report Parameter Values

Specify the report parameter values to use with this subscription.

ServiceYear
[2004 ▾] ☐ Use Default

ServiceMonth
[▾] ☐ Use Default

Branch
[▾] ☐ Use Default

Employee
[▾] ☐ Use Default

ServicesLogCtgryID
[   ] ☑ NULL ☐ Use Default

[OK]   [Cancel]

Figure 8-30. *Subscription as it appears in SRS*

Controlling Reporting Services with WMI

Before we finish this chapter, we should also briefly discuss how you can manage Reporting Services using two WMI classes. These classes are used more for administrative tasks and allow you to programmatically access server settings. WMI is not used for manipulating reports or report settings.

WMI offers a standardized way to monitor and control systems and services running anywhere on your network. Using the WMI provider, you can write code that allows you to query the current settings of a SRS server and also to change those settings through properties and methods of the classes providing these services.

Essentially, these providers allow you to change the settings of the configuration files on the server programmatically. So, as you might guess, the properties of these classes correspond almost directly to the elements within the XML files that hold SRS configuration information.

The two classes provided by SRS for use with WMI are shown in Table 8-2.

Table 8-2. *SRS Classes for Use with WMI*

Class	Controls	Configuration File
MSReportServer_ ConfigurationSetting	Report Server	RSReportServer.config
MSReportServerReportManager_ ConfigurationSetting	Report Manager	RSWebApplication.config

You can use the MSReportServer_ConfigurationSetting class to determine and/or configure most of the database settings used by SRS itself—that is, for the database that Reporting Services uses to store the reports, snapshots, and so on. This class doesn't control the data source connection information used in your reports, although you can set the login information that the server uses to run a report in unattended mode. You can also work with things such as the database server name, database name, and login credential information in this class. This class can also be used to configure the SRS service instance name, pathname, and virtual directory it maps to in IIS.

You can use the MSReportServerReportManager_ConfigurationSetting class to determine the instance name, pathname, and virtual root of the SRS Report Manager, as well as to read or set the URL of a particular instance.

To access this information through the SRS WMI providers, you will use the System.Management namespace, which provides access to WMI.

■**Note** If there is more than one instance of a report server installed, you'll need to locate the correct instance before reading and setting properties. The `PathName` property is the key property, and it uniquely identifies a particular instance.

Summary

SRS provides many tools for management tasks, and we covered several of them in this chapter. Because SRS is a full reporting solution, administrators may find it difficult to manage the entire site single-handedly without some level of automation or divided tasks. Fortunately, administrators and, to some extent, SRS users. In the next chapter, we will explore configuring security roles for SRS.

CHAPTER 9

■■■

Securing Reports

If there is currently a topic that is more on the minds of OS makers, application developers, and system administrators than security, I would be hard pressed to name it. We all know that security threats come in many flavors and levels of severity, from the innocuous pop-up web pages to the invasive worms and viruses that wreak havoc on systems and take their toll on productivity by wasting time and resources.

These threats are often anonymous scripts or executables—automatons—whose human creator has released them into the wild. But what of the security violations from real individuals? These are not just elusive system crackers bent on destruction, but can be the overlooked disgruntled employee who left the company with a notebook full of passwords and the determination to make a point about the insecurity of the company's vital data.

Securing systems takes time and effort—and sometimes, unfortunately, takes a backseat to other important daily tasks. However, if your company, like ours and thousands of others, is affected by the regulations imposed by the Healthcare Insurance Portability and Accountability Act (HIPAA), meeting stringent security standards is a requirement, not just a recommended practice. Most companies have policies and procedures in place that will meet HIPAA compliance, which is set to take effect in April 2005, but many are still in the implementation phase.

As a roles-based application, SRS will take advantage of the underlying authentication and network already at work in your organization, especially if you are running a Windows 2000 or 2003 domain. There are three important components to the SRS security model:

- Data encryption

- Authentication and user access

- Report auditing

Our goal in this chapter is to meet the challenge of effectively setting up and testing each of these security components in our SRS deployment.

When we first decided to incorporate SRS in our business, we knew that we would have to deploy it in two different environments: the first is an internal deployment to a secure intranet site for our employees and the second is as an Application Service Provider (ASP) to our Internet customers who use our healthcare application via a hosted Terminal Services connection. Though each model requires unique security considerations, which we will discuss in the deployment section, fundamentally our three security checkpoints—authentication, encryption, and report auditing—apply to both.

When we made the decision to deploy SRS to our clients, it was not without much consideration and testing. We had already determined, through the beta test cycles with Microsoft, that the report design aspects of SRS met our needs. But until we could actually deploy and monitor the access and execution of the reports that we would be rewriting for our healthcare application, we could not be certain that we would be able to deploy for each of our required models. Each model presented its own challenges.

Universal Security Challenges

When working with confidential data of any kind, the chief concern is that the only people who can see that data are those who need to see it and who have been specifically granted permission to see it. This is especially true of "PI," or patient identifiable, data, as defined by HIPAA, with which we as a software development company had to be concerned. Let's start with the first of the three main challenges that we defined as crucial to a successful secure deployment of SRS: data encryption.

Data Encryption

In today's mixed-technology networked environment, data encryption comes in many varieties. However, regardless of the technology, the encryption algorithms must meet a high standard for complexity and reliability. Fortunately, many applications provide built-in levels of encryption. Following is a brief list of technologies that companies may have in place.

- **Wireless:** Uses WEP, or Wireless Encryption Protocol, with shared key to encrypt data transmitted through Wireless Access Points.

- **Internet Information Services:** Uses a server certificate, generally from a trusted authority such as VeriSign, to provide encryption over Secure Sockets Layer (SSL). SSL is used when transmitting data with HTTPS instead of HTTP.

- **Terminal Services:** Uses Remote Desktop Protocol (RDP) for remote connection from a client workstation to a terminal server. Provides both low and high levels of data encryption.

- **Virtual Private Networks:** Allows accessibility to internal networks from VPN client systems. Encapsulates and encrypts PPTP and L2TP tunneling protocols.

- **IPSec:** Standard security protocol for TCP/IP traffic. Adds several layers of security, including data encryption.

In our two deployment scenarios for SRS we utilize several of the encryption technologies listed here. In the Internet-hosted deployment model, for example, we make use of both SSL and Terminal Services encryption. For the internal deployment, on an intranet server, we set up a VPN solution, configured a Wireless Access Point to encrypt data packets transmitted to and from wireless devices, and also provided SSL pass-through from a Microsoft Integrated Security and Accelerator (ISA) server.

Securing Network Traffic Using SSL

In this section we will set up the SRS server to use SSL. By having an SSL server certificate installed on the server, all data transferred between the client application (which can be a browser or custom application) and the report server will be encrypted. This is essential when transmitting confidential data such as patient identifiable information over the Internet. Having a certificate from a trusted authority such as VeriSign or Thawt also ensures that the registered domain name used to access the web server has been validated and can be trusted to be from the legitimate company that it claims to be from.

Before we actually install the certificate on the SRS server, it would be a good idea to look at what data is being transmitted at the packet level to our SRS server through HTTP requests. In this way, when we do actually install the certificate, we will be able to compare the data packets before installation and after to verify that the certificate is working as it is supposed to. To begin, we will use a tool that is included with most versions of Windows, called Network Monitor.

Analyzing HTTP Traffic

Network Monitor is a packet analysis utility that will allow us to capture all of the data packets transferred to and from the target server and client. The version of Network Monitor that is installed with Windows is unlike other network capture tools, such as the version of the same tool included in Systems Management Server, in that it can only listen to traffic that is destined for the machine on which it is executed.

On the SRS server, we will launch Network Monitor from Administrative Tools. If more than one NIC card is installed on the machine, as it is in our case, make sure you select the card on which you will be testing. Figure 9-1 shows the main screen of Network Monitor and the traffic that it is capturing on the network, including broadcasts and local packets. Network Monitor can be daunting to the uninitiated, as it was designed to be used by network administrators who have more than a cursory understanding of network protocols.

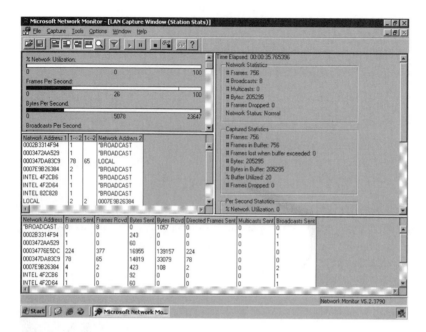

Figure 9-1. *Network Monitor*

We can filter out any unwanted traffic, which we will do because we will be capturing data through a Remote Desktop session that sends a steady stream of Remote Desktop Protocol (RDP) frames on ports 3389 and 3381; we only want to see HTTP traffic on port 80. I could actually go to the server's console to run Network Monitor, which would preclude capturing unwanted RDP frames, but that would require leaving my office chair and thus interrupt my sedentary lifestyle that has been exacerbated—or should I say enhanced—by the creation of Remote Administration features of Windows. So I will lazily apply a filter.

We could, for example, define a capture filter that uses a pattern match in the data packet to limit the results of the capture. Alternately, we could capture everything and then configure a display filter to limit the results. In this case, it is worth the effort of setting up a capture filter to exclude RDP protocol traffic. To do this, you must know two important values, the pattern and the offset. The pattern is a hexadecimal value that represents the port numbers, 3389 or 3381. The offset is the location pointer of the pattern in the frame. Both of these values can be gleaned by running a capture with no filters applied. In Figure 9-2 you can see a frame that has a source port of 3389 (OD3D in hex) and the offset location. We will use these values, as well as the values for port 3381, to now exclude all RDP traffic and then open Report Manager from our client machine and navigate to our reports to capture SRS-specific traffic.

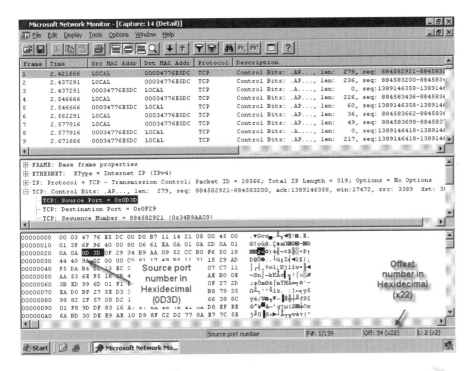

Figure 9-2. *Offset and pattern location*

On the Network Monitor toolbar, click the Edit Capture Filter button. In the capture filter window, click Pattern and type in our pattern for port 3389 as a hexadecimal value, 0D3D. For the Offset, we will use a value of 22 and leave From Start Of Frame checked. Next, because we want to exclude these frames, select each of the patterns and click NOT to add the exclusion in the tree, as shown in Figure 9-3.

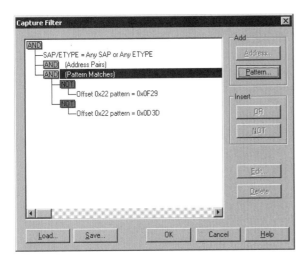

Figure 9-3. *Capture Filter properties*

Now, click the Start Capture button and let the capture run as we view a report with Report Manager. We will want to make sure that we access a report that could have identifiable information in it. The Employee Service Cost report that we have been working with does, so we will use it for this purpose. We are concerned not only with capturing user login information potentially passed on a URL but also with any information that may provide the identity of a patient. If this is the case, and we allow access to the report over the Internet, we know that we would have a serious problem and be out of compliance with HIPAA regulations.

After executing the report, analysis of the captured frames reveals the disturbing news. We can see the name of one of our patients (whose true identity has been altered to be Bill Shakespeare) returned directly in an HTTP frame, as clearly shown in Figure 9-4. In this case, we have not analyzed other types of traffic, such as SQL requests on port 1433, to see if other protocols are potentially sending plain text information, but we can use the same tool to do that.

■**Tip** Though we will not be performing the steps to configure SQL Server itself to encrypt network traffic, as we will be doing with Internet Information Services, it is important to mention that SQL Server uses SSL as well and that by having a certificate installed, SQL Server can very easily be configured to transmit encrypted data. There is a minimal performance hit associated with encryption.

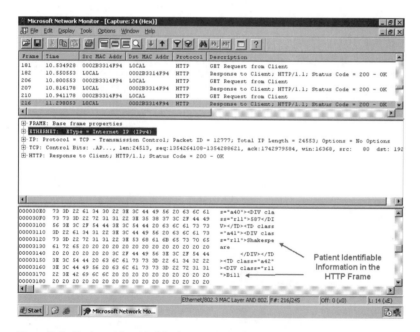

Figure 9-4. *Patient identifiable data captured*

Applying the SSL Certificate

Now it is time to apply a certificate to our SRS server and rescan the traffic to make sure that the viewable data in clear text will be encrypted.

There are several companies that provide server certificates that can be installed on a web server and verified directly over the Internet from the trusted site that issued the certificate. By using the certificates issued from these trusted sources, such as VeriSign, the client will automatically trust the site. Other certificates, such as those generated through Certificate Services in Windows, may require that the certificate be installed on the client machine, because the client will not automatically trust the certificate if it cannot reach the certificate authority. Generally, for Internet use, it is more practical to pay the fee to use the commercial certificate. Our online deployment uses a server certificate issued from a commercial certificate authority. However, for our temporary test environment, we can use SelfSSL, a handy little utility that comes as part of the IIS 6.0 Support Tools.

SelfSSL will generate and automatically apply a temporary certificate to a website. You run SelfSSL from the command line on the server on which you want to add the certificate. Typical syntax will be of the following format:

```
Selfssl.exe /N:CN=RS05 /V:10 /T
```

The /N:CN=RS05 option indicates that the common name on the certificate will be the name of the server (RS05). The /V:10 indicates that the certificate is valid for 10 days. The /T option instructs SelfSSL to add the certificate to the Trusted Certificates list so that the local browser will automatically use the certificate when connecting to the site. We can manually install a local copy of the certificate on other client machines that will access this server. Because SelfSSL installs the certificate that it generates, there is no need to go through the process of generating a certificate request, which would normally be sent to a commercial certificate authority. We can view the installed certificate in Internet Information Services Manager. To do this, right-click the default website, select Properties, and then click on the Directory Security tab. Next, select View Certificate. As you can see in Figure 9-5, the certificate is good for 10 days and is issued to our server, RS05.

Figure 9-5. *SelfSSL-assigned certificate*

Capturing HTTPS Traffic

Now that we have the certificate installed, let's return to Network Monitor and capture running the reports, but this time using HTTPS, which instructs the browser to connect to the site with SSL on port 443, instead of HTTP on port 80.

The first thing we notice when we navigate directly to the report is a warning that the certificate has not passed all of the criteria to be trusted because it does not come from a known certificate authority (see Figure 9-6).

Figure 9-6. *Warning for nontrusted security certificate*

We can select Yes to continue because we do indeed trust the site. We could also install the certificate on the local machine by clicking on the lock at the bottom of the browser and selecting Install Certificate so that we will not be prompted with this message again. Installing the certificate in the local client's certificate store causes the browser to automatically trust the site. These steps are not required for known certificate authorities such as VeriSign, but are required for our self-assigned certificate.

The next security warning message we receive informs us that the page contains both secure and nonsecure items, as Figure 9-7 shows. We have the option to proceed or to choose not to view the page. If we choose to view the page, the data will not be encrypted as we expect. The reason for this is that although we have installed the certificate and can use it within SRS for basic secure access, we still need to instruct the Web service itself to utilize the certificate.

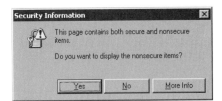

Figure 9-7. *Warning for nonsecure items*

We can control the level of security that SRS will use via the service config file, RSReportServer.config, located in the installed folder, typically DriveLetter:\Program Files\ Microsoft SQL Server\MSSQL\Reporting Services\ReportServer. Open the file in Notepad and look for the following entry:

```
<Add Key="SecureConnectionLevel" Value="0"/>
```

There are four values that control the level of security, 0 through 3. The default for a deployment that does not configure SRS for SSL during installation is 0, which is the least secure. A value of 3, the most secure, requires every web method to use SSL. When we set the value to 3 in the RSReportServer.config file and refresh our report in the browser, we are no longer prompted to accept the nonsecure items. All calls to the server will now automatically use port 443 and encrypt the data, including the URL string itself. When we capture the frames in Network Monitor we see that all of the previous HTTP frames on port 80 are now using SSL on port 443, as shown in Figure 9-8.

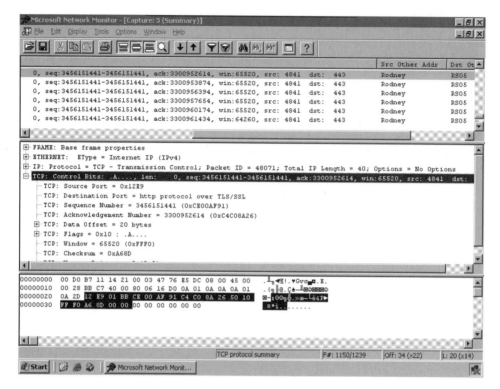

Figure 9-8. *Network Monitor with encrypted packets*

SRS and Secure Data Storage

While it is important to ensure that network traffic is encrypted, that is only one aspect of maintaining a secure environment. SRS requires that sensitive data, such as account information that is used for data access, be stored securely. Since this data is stored in different locations, such as database tables and configuration files, SRS uses a symmetrical key encryption process to securely store and access this information. What this means is that the authentication information in the database and configuration files is stored in an encrypted format and SRS uses the encryption keys that it generates to decrypt the information when needed.

Let's take a look at these two locations and use another SRS utility, RSKeyMgmt, to back up the keys so that if something were to occur that caused the server to be rebuilt we could reapply the keys to the installation. The encryption keys are generated when SRS is installed or with the command-line utility RSActivate. Figure 9-9 shows the RSReportServer.config file, which contains sensitive authentication credentials required to connect to SRS server components.

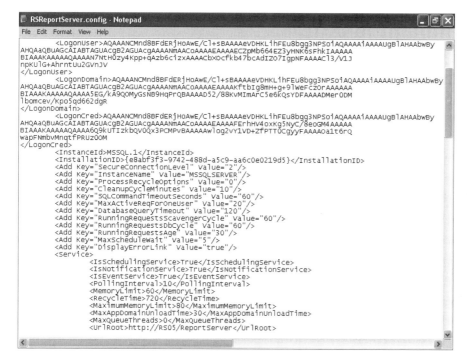

Figure 9-9. *RSReportServer.config encrypted values*

When a server is activated using the RSActivate command, as we did in the previous chapter, the keys used to access the encrypted data are stored in the Keys table in the Reports database. There should be two entries for each SRS web server—a row for the authentication credentials of the ReportServer Windows service, and a row for the SRS Web service. In our case, we now have two servers, HWC04 and RS05, using a single Reports database, thus we have four rows in the Keys table that are specific to the two servers, as seen in Figure 9-10. There is a default record as well, as you can see, which is the first record in the list.

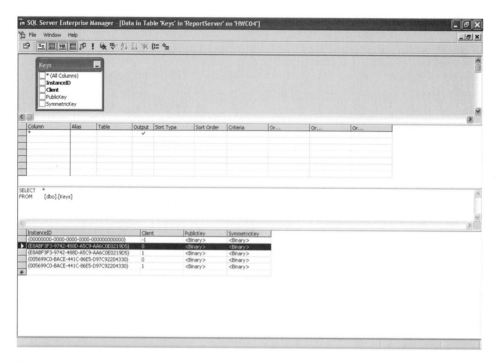

Figure 9-10. *Encryption keys stored in the ReportServer database*

We will use the RSKeyMgmt utility to extract the key for the HWC04 SRS installation. The command is

```
RSKeyMgmt -e -f D:\Temp\HWC04_SRS_Key -P Password
```

The "-e" option tells RSKeyMgmt to extract the key to the file HWC04_SRS_Key in the D:\Temp folder. The password option is required. If we needed to, we could reapply the key to the server using the same command. After execution of the command, you are timidly instructed to SECURE THE FILE IN A SAFE LOCATION!

Authentication and User Access to Data

Access to confidential electronic data, no matter where it resides, begins and ends with user authentication. Having security users or roles properly configured is critical to a secure deployment of SRS. In a Windows 2000 or 2003 domain environment, SRS can then take advantage of the authentication provided by Active Directory's security groups and users. The SRS administrator is responsible for configuring SRS-specific security roles that link to AD security accounts. In this section, we are going to set up a test Windows account for an employee who will have limited access to the SRS report server. We will discuss the following:

- **SRS roles:** These dictate what permissions the users will have when they access the SRS server. An AD security account, either a group or user, is assigned to either one of four predefined SRS roles or to a new role that the SRS administrator may create.

- **SRS role assignment:** These are the actual SRS tasks that a user who is assigned to an SRS role may perform.

- **Configuring and testing permissions for SRS objects:** Each report folder and its objects maintain individual permissions that can be set at the folder level and propagated to all children objects, or set specifically per object. We will set up two folders for our test user account and add report objects that are to be secured.

- **Report filtering:** It is possible to limit what data is displayed within a report based on the AD login account that is accessing the report server. This is accomplished by associating the value returned from an SRS global collection, User!UserID, with a field value in the data set of the report. User!UserID returns the current login account.

- **Data source authentication:** In addition to the Windows login account and SRS role assignments, data sources maintain their own authentication properties, which we will discuss.

- **Setting permissions on the data source database objects:** You may recall from Chapter 2 that we created a stored procedure, `Emp_Svc_Cost`, to use with the Employee Service Cost report but we did not assign user-specific permissions. We will assign the permissions settings in this section.

SRS Roles

By default, the SRS Web service installed in IIS uses Windows Integrated Authentication to access reports and report content. Windows user or group security accounts stored in AD must be associated with an SRS role before they will have access to the SRS server. Administrators can assign the Windows accounts to SRS roles with Report Manager. In our test scenario, we will set up a test Windows account in AD, called junderling, whom we will assume is a registered nurse in our healthcare organization who makes home visits to patients.

All of the clinical staff, including nurses such as junderling, are associated with security groups within AD for the domain. We will make junderling a member of the RN security group. In addition to the security group RN, all registered nurses, including junderling, will be contained with an Organizational Unit (OU) inside of AD, as you can see in Active Directory Users And Computers in Figure 9-11. Though we will not use OUs when assigning a user or group to a role in SRS, it is important to note that OUs can be used to configure Group Policy settings that apply to security as well, such as locking down the user's Desktop or Internet Explorer.

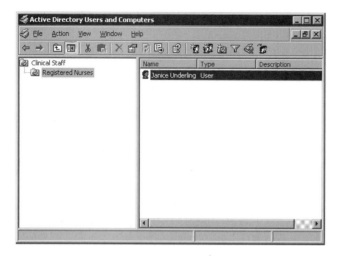

Figure 9-11. *Test Windows account in AD*

Before we assign our test Windows user to an SRS role and test the permissions settings, let's take a look the four predefined roles:

- **Browser:** Users assigned to the Browser role may only view reports, folders, and resources. They may also manage their own subscriptions.

- **Content Manager:** Administrators are assigned to the Content Manager role by default. Users assigned to this role can perform every task available for SRS objects such as folders, reports, and data sources that they manage.

- **My Reports:** The default role that is automatically assigned to a user when the My Reports feature is enabled on the SRS server, discussed later in this section.

- **Publisher:** Users assigned to this role have by default enough privileges to publish reports and data sources to the report server. Typically this role is used for report authors who work with Report Designer to create and deploy reports.

SRS roles are defined by the tasks that users assigned to each role may perform. SRS tasks, shown in the following list, provide content management permissions and define which SRS objects are viewable by the user:

- Create linked reports

- Manage all subscriptions

- Manage data sources

- Manage folders

- Manage individual subscriptions

- Manage report history

- Manage reports

- Manage resources

- Set security for individual items

- View data sources

- View folders

- View reports

- View resources

Each predefined role is configured by default, with a specific combination of allowable tasks. Users assigned to the Publisher role, for example, may manage folders, reports, resources, and data sources as well as create linked reports. To view the allowable tasks for each role, you can open Report Manager and navigate to the Site Settings page from the Home folder. On the Site Settings page, click Configure Item-Level Role Definitions. From here you may select any of the four predefined roles and see the tasks available to each. Figure 9-12 shows the default tasks available for the My Report role.

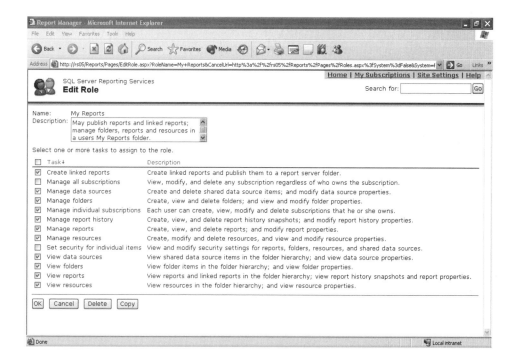

Figure 9-12. *My Reports role assignments*

My Reports is a feature in SRS that creates individual report folders specific to the Windows user. My Reports is useful for companies that need to provide a workspace for employees to create and manage their own reports. The feature is disabled by default and can be enabled in the Site Settings area of Report Manager. When it is enabled and a logged-in user clicks the My

Reports link, SRS creates a folder structure based on the user's login name and automatically navigates the user to that folder. A Users Folders folder is also created that can be used by the administrator to manage the My Reports folders for each user, as you can see in Figure 9-13.

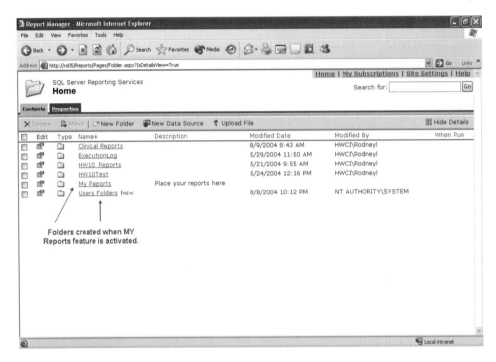

Figure 9-13. *My Reports folder*

Testing SRS Role Assignments

In this section, we are going to go through the process of adding folders and report objects that would be in line with what our nurse, junderling, would use. We will want to ensure that she will not have the ability to navigate to other folders and run other reports that may contain confidential information.

The first step in testing junderling's access to the reports that have been defined for her security group, RN, is to publish the reports to a folder on the SRS server that will contain reports for registered nurses. As the administrator for the test, we will open Report Manager and create two new folders, one in the root folder called Clinical Reports and then one inside of the Clinical Reports folder called Registered Nurse. To do this, we will simply click New Folder in Report Manager. Because both of these folders, by default, are inheriting permissions from the parent folder, which currently is configured for administrator access only, we will alter the permissions manually so that the new folder, and the reports and data source we will add to it, will maintain their own security settings.

To publish reports to the new folder, we could use any method that we have already covered, but for this test we will simply upload a report that we have already worked with, Daily Schedule (available with the code download for this chapter), and create a data source called RN_DS for the purposes of testing security.

Figure 9-14 shows the folder structure and report objects setup for the initial test that we will perform. At this point we have not added either the Windows account, junderling, or the security group, RN, of which she is a member.

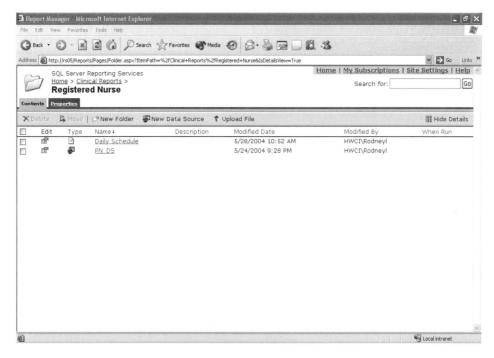

Figure 9-14. *Report objects for registered nurses test*

■**Note** Though shared data sources, with a file extension of RDS, are legitimate SRS objects, they cannot be uploaded successfully through Report Manager, unlike reports. Additionally, objects cannot be "copied" to other locations within the Report Manager UI; they can only be moved or deleted.

To begin the test, we will log in as junderling and run Report Manager and paste in the link to the Registered Nurses folder that we created previously. As you can see in Figure 9-15, we receive an error message indicating that our user does not have permissions to view the resources in the folder.

Figure 9-15. *Error message for insufficient permissions*

Running Report Manager as an administrator again, we are now going to set the permissions for our test user. Security settings are controlled on the Property tab for each folder as well as on individual report items. In our case, we will set permissions at the folder level for the Registered Nurses folder. We will navigate to this folder and click the Properties tab and then select Security. As you can see in Figure 9-16, the default security group is BUILTIN\administrators which is assigned to the Content Manager role.

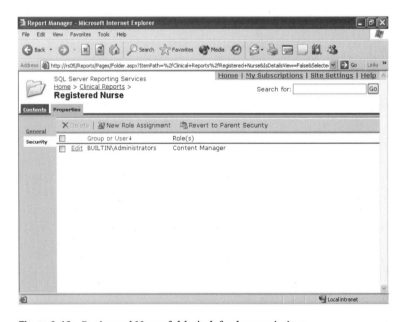

Figure 9-16. *Registered Nurse folder's default permissions*

To set permissions for the RN group, click on New Role Assignment and add the HWCI\RN security group as the group name on the New Role Assignment form. For the role assignment, we will choose Browser, which will allow the users assigned to the RN group to view the Registered Nurse folder and all of its child nodes, view reports and resources, and configure their own subscriptions. Now when we access the Registered Nurse folder logged in as junderling, all that we see are the reports that have been deployed to that folder, not the data source. In addition, all of the properties for the objects that we can view have limited accessibility and content. If we click on the properties of the Daily Schedule report, for example, we will only see the General properties information, such as the Created and Modified dates of the Daily Schedule report. By contrast, an administrator viewing the same Properties page would be able to see and modify other report property settings such as Parameters, Data Sources, Execution, and Security, as you can see in Figure 9-17.

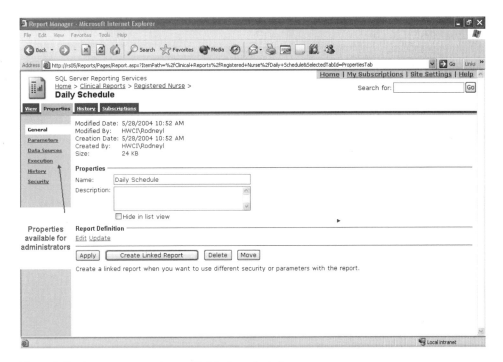

Figure 9-17. *Report properties available for administrator*

To complete the test, we will simply execute the Daily Schedule report as junderling. The report executes successfully. However, there is one issue. Though she would be able to enter an EmployeeID parameter value that would limit the data on the report to only her data, she would still be able to see other employees' schedules by entering their IDs, assuming she knew what they were. Though this might be an acceptable practice for many companies, in the next section we will go a step further to ensure that she will be able to view her schedule only.

■**Tip** When building a testing environment, there are a number of available resources that will simplify the process. In my testing I made extensive use of Remote Desktop Client and the Remote Administration features of Windows 2003 server. Since this would be the environment that I would ultimately deploy in—i.e., Terminal Services—it was beneficial also to see how SRS would work in this scenario. Microsoft's Virtual Server is another beneficial tool for testing, as it allows you to run multiple operating systems simultaneously on a single machine.

Filtering Report Content with User!UserID

For the Daily Schedule report, we have decided that we want the users to only be able to view their own schedule. SRS allows us to accomplish this by creating a report filter that uses the value of the login account for the user executing the report. The login name value is returned from a global collection in SRS. We have been using global collections all along—for example, when we use an expression like =Fields!FieldName.Value we are actually returning a value from the Fields global collection. The global collection that we will use for the report filter is User and the value we are interested in is UserID. The expression will therefore be =User!UserID.

To make use of the User!UserID in the filter, we will need a field in the data set that will equal the UserID value. In the data set for the Daily Schedule report, you may recall that we have a field called HWUserLogin that we can use for this purpose. When compared by the filter, the two values will be identical, one value delivered with the data set and the other at execution time of the report. After the filter is applied, the report will only display records where the username of the employee executing the report matches the value of the HWUserLogin field returned with each record of the data set.

Unlike parameters, filters cannot be set through Report Manager. To set up a filter, you will need to modify the report itself, either in the RDL file directly or through Report Designer. Notice that we used the RTRIM function in Listing 9-1 to strip off the trailing spaces; otherwise, the comparison may fail.

Listing 9-1. *RDL Filters Section*

```
<Filters>
    <Filter>
        <FilterExpression>=rtrim(Fields!HWUserLogin.Value)</FilterExpression>
        <Operator>Equal</Operator>
        <FilterValues>
            <FilterValue>=User!UserID</FilterValue>
        </FilterValues>
    </Filter>
</Filters>
```

Because this report may return several hundred records even though it will filter automatically for each user, it is a good idea to cache the report for 10 minutes. Caching, which is discussed in Chapter 8, will help alleviate the performance hit of requerying the data source every time a new user accesses the report.

Setting Data Source Security

Once the data source has been deployed to the report server, you can specify its connection properties. This is an important consideration because the property settings determine how both the user and SRS will connect to the data source. When executing unattended reports—for example, for a user subscription—SRS will control passing authentication credentials to the data source and must have access to valid authentication credentials.

There are four connection options for the data source available in Report Manager:

- **The credentials supplied by the user running the report:** With this option, users are always prompted to log in to the data source when executing the report.

- **Credentials stored securely in the report server:** SRS uses authentication credentials stored in the ReportServer database. The sensitive login information is encrypted.

- **Windows NT Integrated:** This option passes the login information for the current user to the data source. This option should not be chosen if the data source will be used for unattended installs or if Kerberos is not configured for the Windows domain.

- **Credentials are not required:** This is the least secure option and is used when the data source does not require authentication.

Setting SQL Server Permissions

In Chapter 2, when we created the stored procedure called `Emp_Svc_Cost`, we set the permissions to allow public execution while designing the report. The environment we were working in was otherwise secure, as it was isolated from other networks and there was no fear of it being compromised.

Now that we are deploying the stored procedure in a production environment, we will need to lock down the stored procedure as well. This can be done through SQL Enterprise Manager by right-clicking the stored procedure and selecting Properties. Next, click the Permissions button. Uncheck the EXEC checkbox for the public role and check the EXEC checkbox for valid security groups in our domain, including the RN security group. We do not need to explicitly grant EXEC rights to our test user junderling, as she is a member of the RN security group.

Report Auditing

Having the ability to know the details of report execution, specifically for undesired access, is an essential piece of the security puzzle. In Chapter 8, on Report Management, we set up the extended execution monitoring feature, provided with SRS. Having an audit trail of report execution is essential for gaining insight into user behavior and possible security breaches.

SRS Auditing

In this section, we'll look at how to audit the following in SRS:

- **Report execution activity:** Which user executed which report and when, and whether a user was denied access to a report because of permissions

- **Parameter inputs for reports:** Which parameters were keyed in by a user

The latter is important because even though SRS contains validation for certain types of parameters, such as integer and datetime, when a report parameter uses a string, it is susceptible to a SQL injection attack. SQL injection attacks are made possible when a web page or service takes input from a user or program that could contain injected code that could execute on the SQL Server. These types of attacks can be malicious in nature or cause the report or page to deliver back more data than was intended.

We will use a modified version Report Execution Log Report that we created in Chapter 8 for performance measuring. In the modified version, we are interested primarily in report execution for a security audit. We need to know which user executed which report and when. We have a generic report that shows the user and report name, as well as the times the report was executed. This report is driven from the same data source, RSExecutionLog, that we have already used.

We have simply made the report a table instead of a matrix, which was more in line with our PivotTable analysis for performance. In this modified report, called Report Execution Audit, which you can download from the Apress website, we will also include the parameters that the user has selected.

In Figure 9-18, you can see the times that the selected reports were executed as well as the parameter name and value that were used. Our user hwci\junderling has naughtily attempted to key in questionable parameter values. In addition to showing how the user interacted with the report via the parameters field, the Report Execution Audit also shows from what machine the report was accessed. Having this level of auditing is a valuable ally in the struggle to maintain security for confidential information. With HIPAA, it is also necessary to maintain an audit trail of user access to data. If there is suspicion that someone is accessing information that they are not authorized to view, this report can serve as the audit trail, along with other normal auditing procedures such as the Windows Event Log.

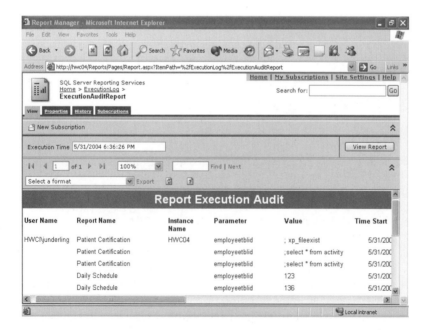

Figure 9-18. *Report Execution Audit Report*

Windows Auditing

In addition to report auditing, SRS supports two other types of logging: standard Windows Event logging and trace file logging. Both of these resources can be used to search for errors and warnings as well as other important information, such as security information.

All of the trace files are stored in the default installation location Drive:\Program Files\ Microsoft SQL Server\MSSQL\Reporting Services\LogFiles. There are three different types of log files: ReportServerService, ReportServerWebApp, and ReportServer. Each file is named with a timestamp, such as ReportServerService_05_31_2004_17_00_30.log, and contains information specific to its individual service. There are five different levels of trace log information that can be gathered—0 through 4—which are controlled in the ReportingServicesService.config file. Selecting 0 will disable tracing, while a 4 will enable verbose mode. Whenever there is any issue with SRS, the administrator can generally isolate the problem by looking in either the Event Log or one of the trace files.

Deployment Models

We will examine two deployment scenarios, one an application hosted on the Internet combining Terminal Services and SRS and the other an internal deployment of SRS that serves the reporting needs of employees on the intranet and through VPN. As you will see in both deployment strategies, much of the security benefits are gained by the logical layout of the systems themselves.

You may note as we go through each model that we will not be deploying SRS so that it is directly exposed to the Internet. The primary reason for this is that the version of SRS released for SQL Server 2000 does not directly support authentication other than Integrated or Basic, meaning a valid Windows login is required to access reports and objects. Although other authentication methods can be created by building a custom security extension, SRS does not, for example, provide forms-based authentication natively, which would be ideal for full Internet deployment. It is certainly feasible to create a limited Internet deployment for a select group of users. Using a preexisting infrastructure with Terminal Services hosted on the Internet was the ideal solution for integrating SRS within our application.

Implementing SRS with Terminal Services

When our company decided several years ago to host our SQL Server–based application on the Internet, the one solution that was most evident at the time was Windows Terminal Services. The reason that this technology was the best choice for us was that our application was not yet web-enabled. We needed a thin-client solution for our then fat-client application. Servers were added over the years to support more users, and technology advancements in Windows Server and .NET made available many benefits that were natively supported. Technologies such as Active Directory, Network Load Balancing, and Internet Printing allowed us to provide a secure and reliable service to our customers.

When SRS was released, we were already poised to integrate it within our Internet-hosted application. Let's take a look at a design for Internet access using Terminal Services. As you can see in Figure 9-19, the terminal servers are positioned to reside on the Internet zone as well as a DMZ (Demilitarized Zone), which is inaccessible to the outside world. In the DMZ are placed several key components that all work together to provide services to the terminal servers, namely SQL Server, SRS, and Active Directory. Users log in to the terminal servers directly, authenticating to one of two domain controllers. Once authenticated, they are allowed to utilize the services of the domain.

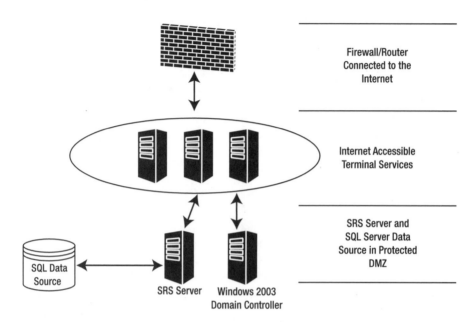

Figure 9-19. *SRS with Internet-hosted Terminal Services*

Several additional security measures are in place besides Windows authentication. Each Windows 2003 terminal server has its built-in firewall capabilities enabled on the Internet-facing network card to only allow network traffic on a specific port, 3389 for terminal services. All other network packets, including PING requests, will be dropped. This setup lessons the likelihood of this server being "discovered" using port scan tools. The networking components that provide Windows networking services, such as Client for Microsoft Networks and File and Printer Sharing for Microsoft Networks have been disabled on the Internet.

On the DMZ-facing network cards, we can be more liberal with our service abilities. In the DMZ, we still need to encrypt data, so we have applied a server certificate to our SRS server, as demonstrated earlier in the chapter, the only difference being that we are using a commercial certificate from a trusted authority.

Terminal Services in Windows Server 2003 provides two levels of security at the network packet level. The first level comes from the fact that, by its very nature, Terminal Services sends data that constitutes only screen shots, keystrokes, and mouse clicks. In order to glean confidential information from the RDP stream, which Terminal Services uses, you would need to capture and replay the packets. It is certainly possible but unlikely. Secondly, Terminal Services provides four levels of encryption, the lowest being 56-bit and the highest being FIPS Compliant, as shown in Figure 9-20. By turning on High encryption, clients that do not support the maximum encryption level of the server will be unable to connect.

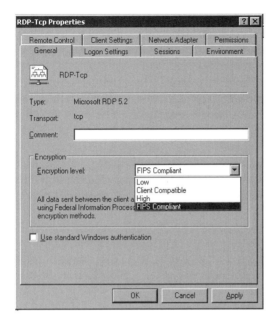

Figure 9-20. *Terminal Services encryption levels*

Finally, we have implemented several other security techniques in the Internet-hosted model by taking advantage of Terminal Services configurations through the use of Group Policy. Two important settings for controlling client behavior with Terminal Services are

- Forcing each user to only connect to one Terminal Services session at a time.

- Automatically executing an application when the user logs in. In our case, every time the user logs into a session, they will only see our healthcare application and not a desktop.

By configuring Terminal Services in this way, we can be assured users cannot share their logins to gain access simultaneously to the server. Equally important, our users will not be allowed to interact with a desktop. All of the tasks that they will need to perform will be available within the UI of the healthcare application. Further, because we have built our own .NET report viewer that is executed from within our application, users will not need to access Internet Explorer or another browser because they will view the reports from a web control within a Windows form.

In the future, as SRS matures into an application that will have other authentication methods supported, we will look to provide reports directly on the Internet. For now, the Terminal Services model is the best solution for us and fits in ideally with a preexisting infrastructure.

Implementing for Internal Access

In this scenario, each business maintains, through an internal IT staff, their security policies, servers, and applications. We knew that, as a third-party solution provider, we had the responsibility to offer recommendations for secure deployments of SRS within their businesses that would take advantage of their existing security infrastructure. To that end, we decided to embed our reports inside a custom report viewer that could be accessed through our application. This would serve to provide a browser control that we could lock down through code and pass the authentication that they had used initially to access our main application. This method of deployment was also identical to how we had previously deployed Crystal reports. Clients could now have the control over which reports the users could actually see from their menu choices. This did not address the concern about being able to access the SRS Web service from a browser and launching the report. However, because we would deploy all of our reports to a single known folder, the client maintained the ability to secure this folder at the user and role level, as demonstrated earlier.

An internal deployment of SRS requires the same roles-based security as in the Internet-hosted model. A Windows domain controller with Active Directory will contain the security grouping to associate with the SRS roles. The main difference between the two models is that, instead of using Terminal Services entirely, users will have the ability to access the reports through a browser. In addition, each company may employ traveling or offsite personnel who need access to the reports. This will be accomplished in one of two ways, either through VPN access or via secure redirected HTTPS traffic through a firewall, such as Microsoft Integrated Security and Accelerator Server. With VPN access, clients will connect to the internal network through a VPN client and will then use the native encryption on that connection, such as PPTP or L2TP, to access the SRS server to view reports. Microsoft Integrated Security and Accelerator (ISA) server supports SSL bridging, which allows incoming SSL requests to be redirected to any internal website, providing, in our SRS deployment, a means of encrypting the data from users directly on the Internet. The client's Windows credentials for which they will be prompted can be passed through the ISA server. Further, the ISA server can limit the connections to a list of users or known IP address sets.

Another technology consideration when deploying an SRS server internally is wireless access. Wireless has its own level of encryption through the use of Wireless Encryption Protocol (WEP), but not all default installations have this setting enabled by default. It is always best practice to have a server certificate installed on the SRS server with a SecureConnectionLevel set to 2 or higher when working with any confidential data.

As you can see in Figure 9-21, the internal deployment allows for secure connection within many points of the company. Administrators can control access to the server via standard Windows domain authentication policies while maintaining limited and secure external access from known sources.

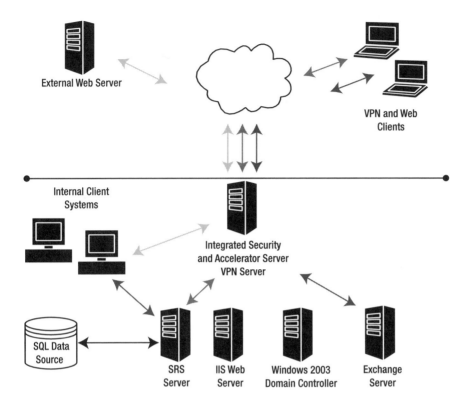

Figure 9-21. *Internal SRS deployment*

Summary

In this chapter, we have examined three of the security components essential to secure SRS deployment: encryption, authentication, and auditing. We looked at how we chose to implement SRS, both internally and externally to Internet clients through a hosted application. In both models the threat of confidential data falling into the wrong hands is real. When data is transmitted over a public network such as the Internet, additional care should be taken to make sure that the three components are properly configured and thoroughly tested. Internally, only employees who need access to confidential data should have it, and we ensured this by applying a special filter for a report deployment. As a software provider for healthcare organizations that stores confidential patient information, we are required to conform to the regulations imposed by HIPAA. However, in other industries, many similar regulations exist. Having security policies and procedures in place for any company is good practice, even when not working under stringent regulations. Fortunately, SRS is designed to use the core-level security mechanisms that may already exist in your organization.

CHAPTER 10

■ ■ ■

Business Intelligence and SRS

Most companies accumulate business data that, if analyzed correctly, could provide insights into what direction the company might take to achieve ultimate success. The aim of BI is to provide data in such a way that it can be immediately utilized to make important decisions. Microsoft's Business Intelligence platform comprises many services and applications that work together to facilitate the analysis and delivery of critical business data. SQL Server is at the heart of the BI model, providing data storage, data transformation, notification, scheduling, analysis, and now reporting services.

Having the right data available is just the first part of the challenge in building an effective BI system. The second part is to ensure that this data is delivered in an effective and accessible way to all of the people who need to see it so that the right decisions get made. This is where SRS comes into play. In our company, we found that by integrating SRS with many of the other components of the BI platform, we were able to dramatically improve our overall business strategy by having necessary information available for our employees wherever they were and whenever they needed it.

In this chapter, we will examine the following five projects that we have extended to include the SRS reports for our software development company:

- **Microsoft CRM:** We had been using CRM to track sales leads, correspondence, and marketing efforts. However, we found that the basic reports delivered with Microsoft CRM were too limited in the information they provided to assist us in making business decisions. Using SRS, we were able to extend the functionality of CRM.

- **Help Desk:** Almost every software development company provides technical support to its customers. Being able to report on the performance metrics of a support department is critical to maintaining satisfied customers. Using a SQL Server–based help desk application, we will show how we use SRS to provide analysis of support incidents.

- **SharePoint Portal Server:** Part of the Microsoft Office System, SharePoint Portal Server provides our company with an intranet portal that we have departmentalized. Any information relevant to the company as a whole or to the individual departments is indexed and searchable. Integrating SRS reports with SharePoint let our employees easily find the data they required to do their jobs. We will show how to add SRS reports to SharePoint. Since SRS builds on Windows SharePoint Services, the work that we do here will also work on WSS included with Windows Server 2003.

- **Project Management:** Developing software is an ongoing process of adding new functionality, assessing the risk of migrating to new technologies, and testing. In order to make this process efficient, our development team uses Microsoft Project 2003 to track every milestone along the way. Falling behind schedule at any point in the project affects release dates, which has a cascading effect on all other departments. When we made the decision to migrate all of our existing reports to SRS, I decided to use SRS itself as a project management tool to track each report as it was migrated. I will show how I built the report to track the progress of the migration so that it could be used both in conjunction with Microsoft Project 2003 and as a stand-alone report to show delivery time frames.

- **Analysis Services:** Having the ability to "slice" through the dimensions of data often renders unexpected and meaningful results. When OLAP Services was introduced with SQL Server 7.0, I was tasked with building a data warehouse, transforming our OLTP data into an OLAP cube. That project was maintained through Analysis Services that shipped with SQL Server 2000 with new functionality added, such as Data Mining models. In this section, we will demonstrate the basic steps of building and populating an OLAP cube for Analysis Services, based on the data from our healthcare application, and show how to use SRS and multidimensional expressions (MDX) to build reports.

Most companies have similar applications to the ones we are using here. We are providing these examples to give you some ideas of how, with a modicum of effort, SRS can easily enhance these types of business applications. Our purpose is not necessarily to provide a step-by-step guide, but more to show how a company might use SRS. If you use any of the applications mentioned in this chapter, such as CRM or SharePoint Portal Server, you can easily integrate the ideas here into your own environment. We will make the CRM reports used here available on the Apress website.

Extending Microsoft CRM with SRS

Customer Relation Management (CRM) applications have been around for many years. These products facilitate communication with customers, both before and after the sale. A successful business understands its market segment and maintains a good relationship with its customers by delivering products that meet customers' changing needs. This is especially true for a software development company, such as ours, that develops a specialized application. Our customers must meet strict governmental guidelines imposed by the Healthcare Insurance Portability and Accountability Act (HIPAA), which means that we must modify our software to accommodate those guidelines. If we did not, we would have many fewer customers. But aside from required modifications, we also value customer feedback on how to make our software better. Often, a sale is dependent on one or two key features. Knowing what a potential customer needs— and, even more importantly, why a customer decided to purchase other software—is the type of information that, if tracked and analyzed, can assist in making business decisions about the direction of the company.

We began using Microsoft CRM almost immediately after it was released. It falls under the Microsoft Business Solutions platform and holds the distinction of being the first Microsoft business solution that was designed and built internally. It is a .NET application and uses SQL

Server for database storage. It provides much of the functionality we needed for tracking our sales goals as well as communicating with our customers and contacts through integration with Microsoft Exchange Server.

However, it does have a few shortcomings, and one of those is with its reporting capabilities. CRM uses a Crystal-based reporting engine (bear in mind, CRM was released before SRS). The real issue is that the standard reports just do not provide enough of the kinds of information we needed to track, such as which customers had subscribed to the industry newsletters that we provide, or how the company learned about our software. This is important information to us, as it dictates how our advertising money is allocated. If we know that a large percentage of our sales in the last 12 months were generated from web searches, for example, we would want to improve our web presence.

We will show two of the CRM reports that we deployed with SRS: the Sales Projections Chart and the Lead Conversion report. Both of these reports are available for download at the Apress site and can be used directly with any Microsoft CRM version 1.2 database.

Though CRM is not the easiest database to work with, once you understand where to retrieve description information that relates to CRM entities, such as opportunities, leads, lead sources, and industry codes, the battle is half won. The values related to these entities are stored in the StringMap table. Both reports are based on the same basic query shown in Listing 10-1, where you can see that StringMap.Value is used to return the Lead Source and is joined to the LeadBase table.

Listing 10-1. *CRM Query for Projected Sales Chart*

```
SELECT
     OpportunityBase.EstimatedCloseDate,
     OpportunityBase.Name,
     OpportunityBase.StatusCode,
     OpportunityBase.EstimatedValue,
     RTRIM(CAST(DATEPART
       (yyyy, OpportunityBase.EstimatedCloseDate) AS char(5)) +
        DATENAME(m, OpportunityBase.EstimatedCloseDate)) AS Estimate_Close,
     OpportunityBase.CreatedOn,
     StringMap.Value AS [Lead Source],
     LeadBase.NumberOfEmployees,
     LeadBase.SIC,
     LeadBase.FullName AS [Lead Contact],
     LeadBase.IndustryCode.
     CAST(OpportunityBase.OpportunityId AS nvarchar(80)) AS
        OpportunityID
FROM
     OpportunityBase INNER JOIN
     LeadBase ON
     OpportunityBase.OriginatingLeadId = LeadBase.LeadId LEFT OUTER JOIN
     StringMap ON LeadBase.LeadSourceCode = StringMap.AttributeValue
     AND StringMap.AttributeName = 'leadsourcecode'
WHERE
     (OpportunityBase.StatusCode NOT IN (4, 5)) AND
(OpportunityBase.EstimatedCloseDate BETWEEN GETDATE() AND @SixMonthDate)
ORDER BY OpportunityBase.Name
```

■**Caution** Before we begin, I should point out that accessing the CRM database directly for reports is not supported by Microsoft.

The CRM Sales Projections Chart

This is a fairly simple and compact chart that shows at a glance the projected sales for the next six months. There are several reports available within CRM, called pipeline reports, that deliver good sales forecasting information. However, if any key information is not included on Crystal CRM reports, modifying the reports is no easy feat. There was one piece of information that we needed that the CRM pipeline reports did not seem to have, and that was a chart of sales projections based on the lead source, such as through web search or partner.

I created the Sales Projections Chart with SRS to add the lead source information using steps similar to the ones used in Chapter 3, adding 3-D effects and a nondefault color scheme. In Figure 10-1, you can see that the layout of the chart has the Lead Source field applied to the series of the chart while the Estimated Close Date is defined for the category. The Estimated Value field makes up the Data section of the chart. This report has a parameter called SixMonthDate that is used as a query parameter in the WHERE clause of the query to provide a date range for the EstimatedCloseDate field between the current date and six months in the future. Any CRM leads or opportunities that are expected to close the sale within that date range will show in the chart. You will also notice that the report's title section contains a parameter value expression for the SixMonthDate parameter. The default value for the SixMonthDate is six months, but because the default parameter can be changed by the user to be, say, three months into the future, the report title would need to change to reflect the user's date range. Adding the parameter value to the report title will dynamically change when the parameter value changes.

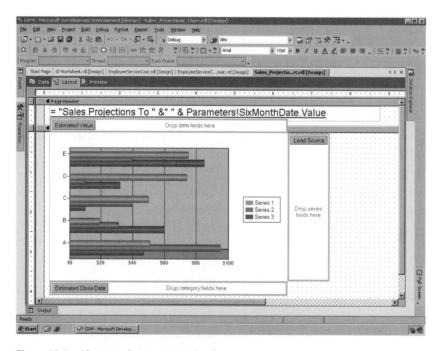

Figure 10-1. *Chart to show projected sales*

In order to set the default parameter value for the date range of six months out, I used an expression that takes the current date and adds six months to it.

```
=FormatDateTime(DateAdd(DateInterval.Month,6,Date.Today),DateFormat.ShortDate)
```

By combining several functions and .NET class library property values into a single expression, I was able to create a date range with desired formatting. In the preceding expression, the FormatDateTime function sets the output of the DateAdd function to a short date, which does not include the neutral time of 00:00:00 that would have been returned from DateAdd function. Finally, the DateInterval.Month enumeration uses the value of 6 to add six months to the current date.

CRM Lead Conversions to Opportunities

When a lead is converted to opportunity, which in CRM means that there is a potential interest in the purchase of a product, it is important to be able to report on that information to ensure that someone regularly follows up with this potential customer and sends important product information.

To this end, we decided to create the Lead Conversion report that a marketing employee could easily view that showed only opportunities. Further, by having a link within the report to the actual CRM Opportunity form, the employee could then open the form without having to open the CRM application and navigate to the form manually to update the information related to opportunities. This is made possible by adding a URL link to the navigation sections of the report.

In this case I designed the report, which is a listing of all of the companies that make up the projected sales from the chart, with the intention of having the report essentially be an extension of CRM itself. The report contains detail information for each opportunity including the opportunity name. I added a `Jump To URL` link to the report on the navigation tab for the text box that holds the opportunity name. The link will use the URL-addressable syntax for CRM so that when the opportunity name is clicked in the report, the CRM form associated with that opportunity is displayed. The expression to add to the `Jump To URL` field is

```
="http://hwcs03/SFA/opps/edit.aspx?id={"& Fields!OpportunityId.Value &"}"
```

The link will open the opportunities form and pass in the field value of the `OpportunityID` when the opportunity name is clicked in the report. One note of interest here is that the `OpportunityID` field value is a Global Unique Identifier (GUID) data type and SRS does not work well with GUIDs. In the SQL query, I used the `CAST` function to convert the field to be a data type of `NVARCHAR`, as follows:

```
CAST(OpportunityBase.OpportunityId AS nvarchar(80)) AS OpportunityID
```

Then I passed in the braces in the expression for the URL link. Figure 10-2 shows the report and the hyperlink to the CRM form at the bottom left of the browser. Notice also the pointing finger icon, indicating a hyperlink.

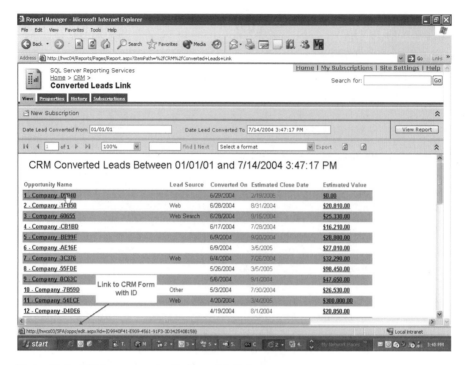

Figure 10-2. *CRM opportunity listing with link*

Using SRS with Custom Help Desk Applications

Almost any company that makes software will be faced with providing technical support for its customers. The ability to quickly address a customer's issue is crucial to maintaining their satisfaction with both the product and with your company as a whole. Having been a support technician and manager of a support department in the past, I know the importance of help desk applications. They need to be automated in the sense that customers can enter and track their own support cases, and they also need to be engineered so that support technicians can quickly enter case information and troubleshoot problems.

Since we are a software development company, we utilized our own internal resources to build a help desk or incident-tracking system. This type of—call it "home grown"—application makes perfect sense, because who better to build a system tailored precisely to our needs than us?

Our help desk application, called PTS for Problem Tracking System, has grown substantially over the years from a meager start as a Microsoft Access application to a full-blown SQL Server–based .NET Web service. Even so, reporting has typically been an afterthought or back-burner project. When SRS came along, offering a web-enabled and flexible reporting environment that integrated directly with SQL Server, we could not help but take immediate advantage of it to give our support engineers and managers reports that they could use to assist them with supporting our customers.

Report Requirements and Design

We really wanted to be able to deliver one or two reports that could be used by both managers and technicians to see all open cases at once and with time frames, so that they could immediately see which cases to work on next. In addition, we needed to have some level of analysis with the report so that other important decisions could be made as to the root cause of many of the issues being reported. For example:

- Were they predominantly training issues or legitimate issues with the code?

- Should department managers add more resources to train customers?

- Could online help have resolved the issues with a support case being opened?

- Which clients had the most cases in a time frame?

These are some of the questions that the report should be able to address. The report would therefore need to be rendered in a format that supports this level of analysis, and we have found, as we have mentioned previously, that Office Web Components suited our overall analysis needs. When the report is complete we could deploy it either within the help desk application itself or through our intranet portal site for the support department, which we will step through in the next section.

Building the Report

Fortunately, having built the help desk application ourselves, the database was already familiar and queries of the nature I have described had already been built for the most part. What SRS allowed us to do was centrally deploy and maintain the PTS report, as well as be able to pass parameter values to it in the report URL if we needed to without developing an ASP reporting solution to provide the same functionality.

The following list is representative of the type of information stored in most help desk applications, including our custom-designed PTS database. We developed a simple SQL query to retrieve this information from the database.

- Priority: Critical, High, Medium, Low

- Call Date and Time

- Customer Name

- Incident Type: Support, Training, Implementation

- Elapsed Time of Incident

- Tier Level

- Status: Open, Closed, In Progress

- Support Technician

- Product

- Version

- Problem Category

- Billable

The report layout contains two sections. The first section shows the status of the cases that are currently open and provides an excessive caseload threshold indicator by way of a color-coded legend. The threshold region of the report uses business logic to generate the color-coded indicators: if more than five cases are open and there has not been a follow-up within 45 minutes, the text will be red. Typically, there are always at least one or two open cases at any given time.

The second section of the report contains a matrix data region that will be rendered in OWC when deployed and that aggregates the caseload count returned from our query for groupings such as service type, customer name, and product version.

With a matrix report that is intended to be viewed with OWC, you need to make sure that you have all of the groupings defined for both columns and rows. In layout form, the matrix does not necessarily look appealing, but when it is rendered within OWC it will take on an entirely different look and feel.

There is one caveat when rendering a report for OWC format: the value in the Data section of the matrix must be a SUM aggregate to successfully render. What we really need here is a count of all of the incidents, not a sum. To work around this, I added a field to my SQL query called CountExpr that returned the value of 1 as in

```
Select 1 AS CountExpr,...
```

I was then able to use the SUM function for the Data section and render the deployed report successfully with OWC. The report layout that includes the table that counts the current open cases and the matrix data region can be seen in Figure 10-3.

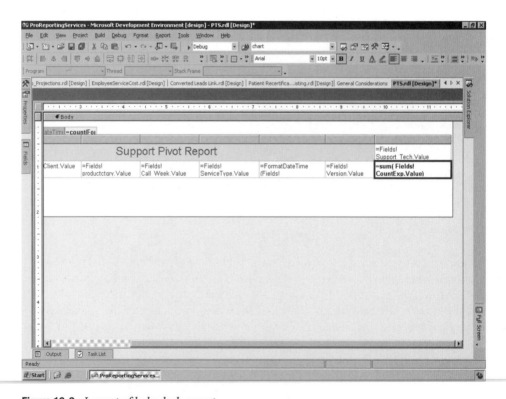

Figure 10-3. *Layout of help desk report*

For the first small table in the report I used a filter to limit the data to count only the open cases for the current day, and added a grouping to the detail row for the same expression I used for the filter value, which is

`=FormatDateTime(DateTime.Today,DateFormat.ShortDate)`

Rendering in OWC

There are two important considerations when designing reports for OWC rendering. First, by default, the grouping names for each column will be of the form `matrix1_fieldname` (for example, `matrix1_calltime`) and the OWC rendered report will automatically be assigned these grouping names. Therefore, it's important that you assign appropriate names to these grouped columns. You can do this in the Groups tab of the Properties dialog box for the matrix data region. As shown in Figure 10-4, both columns and rows for all groups can be edited from the Groups tab for the matrix data region. I have already changed several of the group names but left some unchanged for reference.

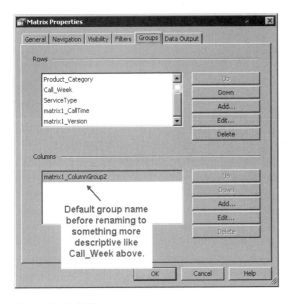

Figure 10-4. *Editing group names*

The second other important design challenge to bear in mind is that OWC rendering is currently—at least in SRS SP1—limited to displaying data from a single page. In my testing, I have determined that the single page it renders is only the first page; all data beyond the first page does not survive the export and is truncated from the report like a failed Klingon teleportation. To overcome this, you will need to extend the page height settings to the maximum setting of 85 inches in Report Properties, and also select the option to "Fit this matrix on one page if possible" on the General property tab of the matrix data region itself.

Incorporating SRS with SharePoint Portal Server

SharePoint Portal Server, which is a component of the Microsoft Office System, is an important addition to the BI platform, as it serves as an intranet portal site, providing document management, collaboration, subscription services, and extensibility through custom web parts. Web parts encapsulate web content and services, such as news feeds or shared documents or even other websites. In this section, we will use a SharePoint web part to embed a link to an SRS report that will be deployed on a portal site.

In our company, we use SharePoint Portal Server to enable interdepartmental collaboration for sales, development, support, engineering, and marketing. Each department maintains their own SharePoint site and employees use the portal to access information related to their specific job functions. The support department, for example, needs customer contact information and support-incident information in a single location to make their jobs easier. In this section, we will demonstrate how an SRS report can be easily incorporated into SharePoint. We will use the report from the previous help desk sample to deploy to the support portal; however, any SRS report could be added in the same way. If you use SharePoint in your organization and would like to add your own custom SRS report to your portal, the concept is the same.

Preparing the SRS URL

A typical SharePoint portal site is made up of many different web parts, each competing for space. Though their size can be adjusted to fit the content to which they are linked, it is a good idea to limit the size of the content, in this case the SRS report, to only the essential elements. This will save space for other web parts on the page and make the report visually more appealing.

The first step is to create the URL that will make the report compact enough to fit within a webpart. We can do this by using commands in the URL string that will hide the report toolbar and any parameters, if we have defined them. We can also set the default zoom percentage for the report, though for an OWC rendered report, 100 percent is the recommended and default percentage. Our URL to the support department's PTS report that will be incorporated into a web part on our SharePoint portal site will be

```
http://hwc04/ReportServer?/ProRS/PTS&rs:Command=Render&rs:Format=HTMLOWC➡
&rc:toolbar=false
```

The second step is to navigate to our support site on the SharePoint portal and select Create. As you can see in Figure 10-5, there are many types of content items that can be added to a SharePoint page: document libraries, lists, discussion boards, surveys, and web pages. For our example, we will add a web page that will be the SRS report in the link given in the previous paragraph, and of the three predefined types of web pages—basic, web part, or workspaces—we will add a web part page.

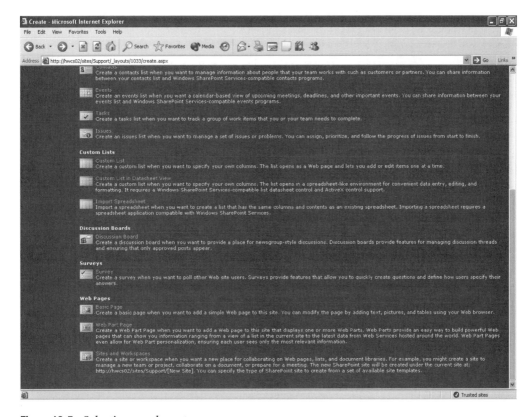

Figure 10-5. *Selecting a web part page*

Once we select the web part page we can choose a layout defined by a template, or create a full blank page. Because we are not exactly sure how large the rendered report will need to be when combined with the web part, we will select the Full Page, Vertical layout template and then select Create, as shown in Figure 10-6. We will name the new page Help Desk Reports.

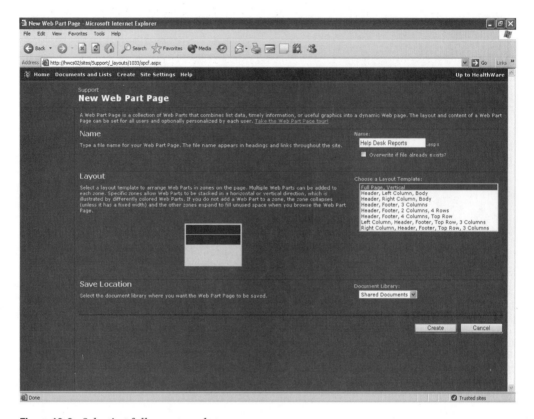

Figure 10-6. *Selecting full page template*

When the page is finished creating, it will open in design mode. From here we will select the Page Viewer Web Part from the web part list and drag it to the empty page. Now all we need to do to link our report to the web part is assign the URL that we have already put together in the web part's tool pane, as shown in Figure 10-7. We can see that the default size is not going to be large enough to contain the report. We will need to change the height and width of the web part to be 12 inches by 10 inches.

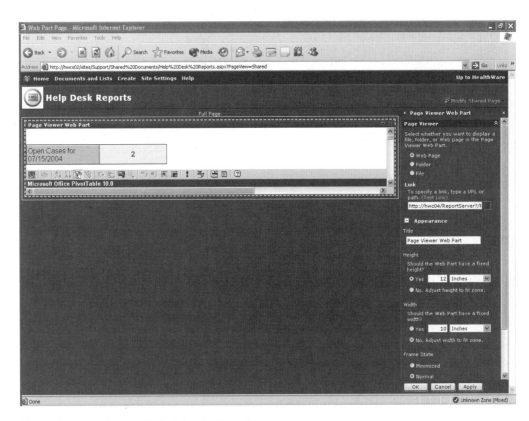

Figure 10-7. *Adding the URL string to the web part*

Finally, when the report is rendered in the portal, as shown in Figure 10-8, it has all of the properties associated with OWC, so you can dynamically change the layout of the report to home in on exactly what you are looking for. In this case, I can see the two open incidents and the technicians who are assigned the cases. I can also see the call time and the version number of the product that is being supported. Although I cannot save the layout of the report because all of the fields added to the SRS report will be expanded automatically, I could export this report to Excel and save the layout there. OWC is really the best tool for analyzing large amounts of data, and when it is fully supported as a customizable extension to SRS, it can truly extend the value of any BI solution.

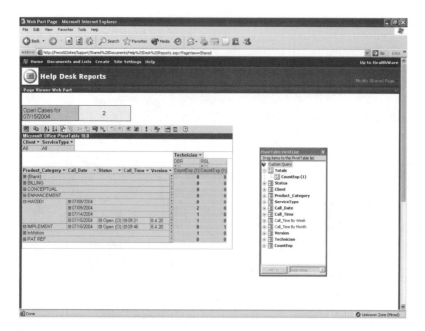

Figure 10-8. *Final report rendering in SharePoint*

■**Tip** Of course, this section shows a way of adding an SRS report to SharePoint, but I felt it worthwhile to mention here that if you are using SharePoint Portal Server, Microsoft has several web parts available that do allow the saving of layout information. One of these web parts is the Office PivotTable that we have been looking at in this chapter. With the Office PivotTable web part, you can connect to the same data source that an SRS report can connect to and gain the added benefit of saving your layout. The Office 2003 web parts for SharePoint are available at http://www.microsoft.com/downloads/ details.aspx?familyid=38BE67A5-2056-46A1-84B1-337FFB549C5C&displaylang=en.

In addition, Microsoft will be offering web parts for SRS in the coming months. These web parts will allow you to take advantage of SRS without having to roll your own web parts using URL addressability.

Project Management and SRS

There is one final example of integrating SRS within a Business Intelligence model before we move on to Analysis Services and SRS. When SRS was first announced as an add-in product to SQL Server 2000, we knew, as I said previously, that we would incorporate it into our base application, primarily to standardize our reporting on a single platform and move away from Crystal Reports and other applications that we had used over the years. When I was tasked with migrating nearly 200 reports from our current system to SRS, I was a little overwhelmed. On the one hand, I needed a period of time to learn the new product, and on the other hand, risk assessment had to be implemented for the new technology because SRS is not simply a report designer, it is a full-blown report delivery system.

Coincidentally, at the same time we decided to move to SRS, our development team had just begun to design an enhancement to our application. We felt that the two projects could be developed in parallel, with me migrating the reports and with them delivering the new .NET enhancements. As a software development company, keeping on schedule through every aspect of a project is important for several reasons, mainly to stay on track with other departmental goals such as product testing, marketing, and documentation.

The development department uses Microsoft Project 2003 to record their project and task milestones throughout each phase of a project, whereas my work as an engineer and data analyst does not always require this degree of granular detail and planning.

I proposed a compromise solution (and this was probably because I really did not want to have to use Project): I would develop a project management report using SRS. In the report, I would track every report that was slated for migration to SRS. My project report would provide timelines and status information similar to those provided by Project (though on a much more limited basis than what Project can deliver). As I migrated the reports from other reporting solutions, I would update a SQL database table that contained the project information, which would then be reflected in my SRS report. Developers could use my report to incorporate the report project information into their own projects so that they could account for my development time.

In hindsight, developing this report of reports, as it were, was probably the best first SRS project that I could have undertaken because it forced me to design a report that was flexible enough for everyone in the company to use for different purposes: My supervisor needed to know how much time I was devoting to the task of writing reports per week, the support and testing departments could use the list in their jobs as they worked with the application and answered customer questions, and finally the development department could see where I was in relation to their projects.

The first step was to extract the listing of reports from the current SQL Server database that our application used. We store each report's name, base query, description, filename, and format in a table within the healthcare database. I used DTS to pull this information into a single table, along with other crucial pieces of information for which I would have to create custom fields. I categorized and subcategorized each report according to its location within the application (for example, financial or clinical), and added several tracking fields that were in line with a project management application, such as status, in_ progress, completion date, estimated time, and the date last updated.

It would be important to know which reports would be new, which would be replacements, and which would be removed entirely. By using a combination of filters and parameters I was able to deliver the report so that it would show only the reports that were being completed in SRS, and I used color formatting to distinguish them from the previous report formats. One of the features that I wanted was the ability to link to each of the reports themselves so that they could then, from one location, be printed as samples to include in product literature and customer newsletters. I added a JumpTo hyperlink for each report name as well as a document map for easy navigation. Because I was new to SRS at the time, many of these tasks were completed via trial and error and I encountered lots of syntax errors, or other errors, that all needed to be debugged. Many of the features that I added to this report are demonstrated in Chapter 4. Figure 10-9 shows the reports with the document map, parameters, color coding, and estimated completion time used to track deliverable dates. The single table with the project data used to create this report is included in the PRO_RS database, and the RDL report file itself, HW_Reports, is in the code download on the Apress site.

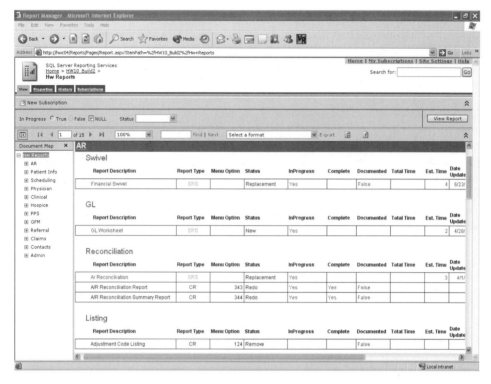

Figure 10-9. *Report to track SRS report development*

Building SRS Reports for SQL Analysis Services

When I began the journey of building an OLAP solution for our healthcare application with SQL Server 2000 Analysis Services, I was really eager to jump right in and start analyzing data the very first morning. I had become the resident expert at developing SQL queries to interrogate our OLTP database, and since this was the source database from which I was going to build the warehouse I thought it would be a simple case of adding a few queries and processing the cube. It did not turn out to be quite that easy. In retrospect, however, going through the process of creating an OLAP data cube from a known source of data was worthwhile because I was able to apply the same skills that I learned there to many other projects.

In this section, I will briefly walk through the steps I went through to build and browse the OLAP cube, Financial, that we will use to build an SRS report using MDX. I will also cover several of the challenges faced with building SRS reports from OLAP sources. The good news is that with Analysis Services and SRS for SQL Server 2005, many of these challenges are addressed. The steps I took to build a working OLAP data cube are as follows:

1. Define measures and dimensions for data mart database.

2. Transform OLTP data into OLAP data via Data Transformation Services.

3. Design cube based on transformed data.

4. Process cube according to storage and performance requirements.

The Financial cube as well as the prepopulated data mart database, HWOLAP, used to build the SRS report with MDX are included in the code download from the Apress site. The steps we will walk through to get us to the point of building the report are included to demonstrate the steps required to deploy an OLAP solution with SQL Server 2000 Analysis Services.

Defining Measures and Dimensions

Before you can design an OLAP cube, you need to know what it is that you will want to analyze. *Measures* are data elements that contain a value, typically numeric, that can be preaggregated with dimensions, which are data groupings. In our case we have several measures defined: charge, payment, adjustment, cost, and quantity. You may recall from previous chapters that this is the same kind of data we have been analyzing all along, pulled straight from the OLTP source database. *Dimensions* are data groupings that define a specific point for a measure value. Patients, Employees, Diagnoses, and Visit Types, such as home health aide or skilled nurse, are all examples of dimensions. In an OLAP cube, all of the aggregations, which are sums or counts of the measures as they relate to the dimensions, are preprocessed so that when queried, all that is required is to return the data values to the client application and not waste CPU cycles calculating the measures. This is one of the main benefits of Analysis Services: all of the processing is performed ahead of time.

Once the dimensions are defined and measures are pinpointed in the OLTP database, they will need to be transformed and migrated to an intermediate database, often referred to as a data warehouse or data mart. A data warehouse holds consolidated data from multiple data stores, whereas a data mart is composed of transformed data from a single source. This step is necessary. The dimensions used for our data mart database are given in the list that follows.

- **Physician:** The patient's attending or referring physician

- **Service Type:** Type of visits and supplies associated with a patient visit

- **Age:** Patient's age

- **Payor:** Payor source for the patient—e.g., Medicare or commercial insurance

- **Diagnosis:** Patient's diagnosis

- **Charge Time:** The dates on which the patient received medical service

- **Patient:** Patient's name and identification number

- **Program:** Patient's admission history into a specific program of care—e.g., Hospice or Home Health

Having defined the dimensions and measures for our data mart, we will next set up a DTS package to migrate the data from the OLTP data source to the OLAP database.

Transforming OLTP Data with DTS

DTS is a very useful tool for both administrators and data analysts who work with and transform data from many different data sources. In addition to providing a extensive library of functions with ActiveX scripting, it can be used to automate tasks and convert data from any number of platforms. Building a DTS package is the ideal way to transform OLTP to OLAP data structures.

When I first designed the DTS package that we will be using in this section, I did not have a destination database or tables defined. I let DTS create these objects for me. For this example, the OLTP database is the one that our clients use with our healthcare application. For reference, the OLAP or data mart database is called HWOLAP.

The DTS package used to populate the healthcare data mart consists of only three task types:

- Execute SQL task

- Data Transform task

- OLAP Services Processing task

Purging Existing Data: The Execute SQL Task

The initial workflow consists of purging the data that exists in the data mart database. Because data will be moved to the data mart database on a regular schedule—once per day, for example—I decided that it would be best to purge the data that existed in the data mart and repopulate with current data.

I chose to purge the data as opposed to maintaining a log of the last record moved since the previous execution of the DTS package and using the log value to initiate the data transfer from that point. This was just easier and the time it took to purge the data and repopulate it was negligible. The Execute SQL Task issues a simple DELETE FROM statement for each of the destination tables in the data mart database, then moves to the Data Transform task when complete, as shown in Figure 10-10.

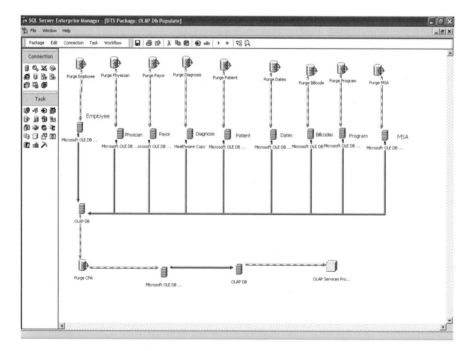

Figure 10-10. *DTS package to transform OLTP data*

Data Transform Task

In the DTS package, the Data Transform tasks execute when the purge tasks are completed. The Data Transform tasks consist of a source table or query, a destination table, and any defined transformations. As you can see in Figure 10-11, the Patient Transform task (called, humorously enough, Patient Pump) uses a SQL query to pull information from the source OLTP database, to be moved or pumped into the destination table in the data mart or OLAP database.

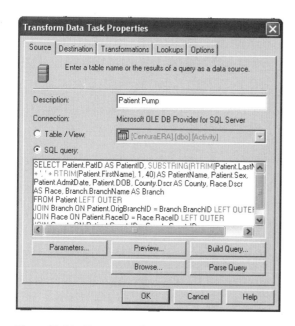

Figure 10-11. *Data transform source query*

Because DTS can create new destination tables from source tables or queries, the task of designing the new OLAP database that will house the dimensions and measures was far less time consuming than it would have been to manually create the destination tables. In Figure 10-12 you can see that by clicking on the Create button on the Destination tab, DTS will automatically produce a script that will create a table based on the values from the source query.

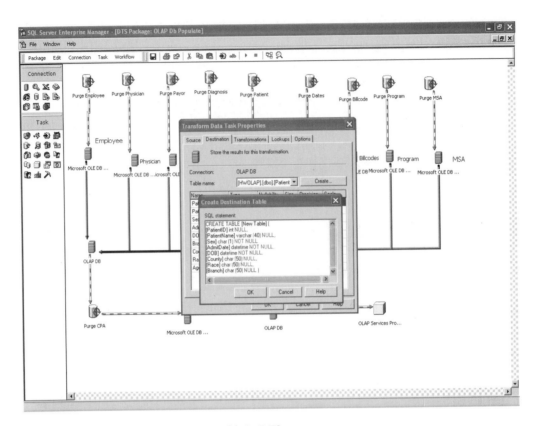

Figure 10-12. *Auto-created destination table in DTS*

If any transformations of data are required, they can be done on the Transformations tab. For the Patient Pump task, we have one ActiveX script transformation that derives the patient's age, which is not a field that is stored in the source database but is a very important metric when looking at cost of care for patients. Figure 10-13 shows the script to determine the age and load it into the destination field Age.

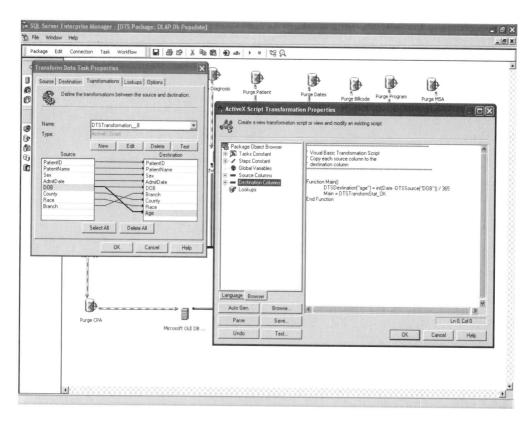

Figure 10-13. *Scripted transformation in DTS*

OLAP Services Processing Task

The final step in the DTS package is to process the OLAP cube itself. After we build the cube from the new database, the step can be scheduled to process every night to refresh the cube data just as we are refreshing the data mart data. We will now execute the DTS package to purge and load in the new data that we will use to build the cube itself. Figure 10-14 shows the individual steps of the package executing.

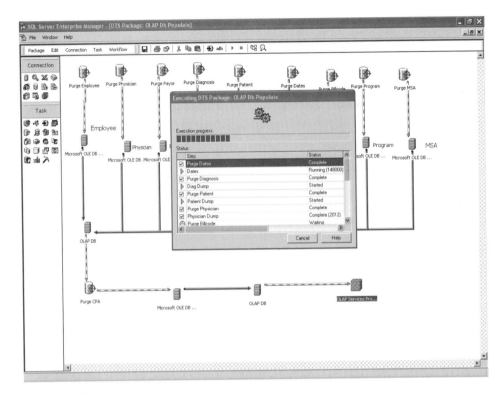

Figure 10-14. *Executing the OLAP DTS package*

OLAP Cube Design

Now that the OLAP source database is populated with the values that will make up the measures and dimensions, we can turn to the tools of Analysis Services to design and build the cube.

In the Analysis Manager application, the first step is to create an OLAP database that will store the cube. This is not the same as the relational database that we will use as the data source. We will call the database AS_DB, for Analysis Services DB, to distinguish it from our OLAP source database called HWOLAP.

Designing the Cube

When the database is created, it is a blank working environment where cubes must be created. We will create and process a cube called Finance, which will serve as the source for the MDX query that we will use to build an SRS report. We can simply right-click the Cubes folder under the new database and select Wizard.

The first step is to create a new data source to connect to the HWOLAP source database. We do this by using the OLE DB Provider for SQL Server and supplying the appropriate credentials.

Next we must select the fact table from the data mart that holds our measures. In this case, it is the CPA table. We have called our fact table CPA, for charges, payments, and adjustments. A fact table holds both measures as well as fields to link to the dimension tables. Our measures, again, are charges, payments, adjustments, cost, and quantity. We can drag each of these available fields over to the Cube Measures section, as shown in Figure 10-15, and then continue to build each dimension.

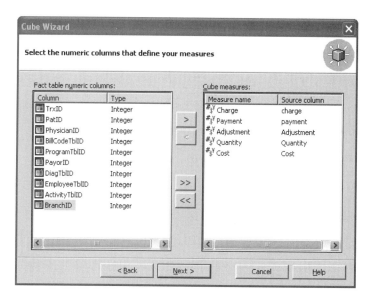

Figure 10-15. *Adding measures to the cube*

Dimensions are based on sets and subsets of data forming a parent-child relationship. One simple example in our case is the relationship that exists in the Service Type dimension. A service is categorized by its type: an "S" for a medical supply or a "V" for a visit. Below this categorization is the actual service or code description that makes up a charge for a patient, such as a "2 X 2 Gauze Strip" as a Supply or "Home Health Aide" for Visit. In the healthcare industry, these services or codes need to be tracked and reported separately.

We will set up the dimensions with this parent-child relationship in mind. Dimensions can be defined through the wizard or through the dimension editor. The wizard lets you select what fields make up the members of the dimension and whether it is a time-based dimension or a standard dimension. Time-based dimensions are automatically grouped by year, quarter, month, and day through the wizard. Once all of the dimensions that we have defined have been created through the wizard, we can continue on with the initial Cube Wizard by selecting the newly created dimensions. When the wizard is complete, the new Finance cube is available for editing in the Cube Editor, as shown in Figure 10-16.

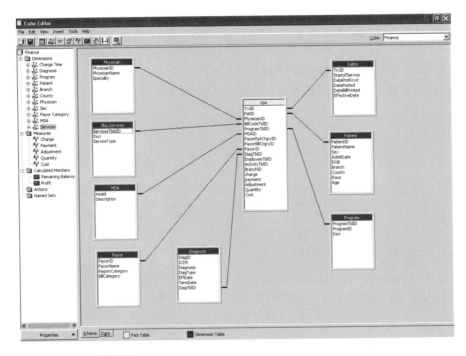

Figure 10-16. *Cube Editor*

Processing the Cube

The cube, at this point, has not been processed. Processing is a crucial step because you will need to define the storage method for the cube:

- **MOLAP:** Multidimensional OLAP stores the source data in the Analysis Services partition, which can be queried without the need for the source database. MOLAP delivers the fastest response times for queries.

- **ROLAP:** Relational OLAP requires the intermediate or data mart database to store the relational data. Queries with ROLAP are typically slower.

- **HOLAP:** Hybrid OLAP uses a combination of both MOLAP and ROLAP to deliver fast response time with queries but requires access to the source data in the relational database or data mart.

Each storage method has its benefits, but the bottom line is that there is a trade-off of space for performance with each method. The number of aggregations that are preprocessed is directly proportional to the amount of space required for the cube data; more aggregations means better performance but more disk space required. I typically choose the option, as shown in Figure 10-17, to execute Until I Click Stop. You can see that for this cube there are 222 aggregations with approximately 50MB space required.

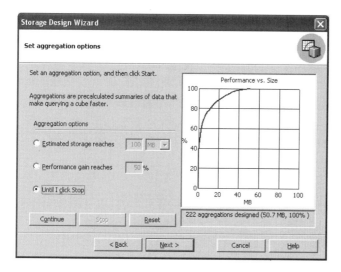

Figure 10-17. *Aggregations versus space*

The final step in the wizard is to process the cube. Processing time varies depending on the number of rows and aggregations defined for the cube. You only need to process the entire cube once and then AS will incrementally update the cube based on your settings. Figure 10-18 shows a successful processing of our Finance cube in the AS_DB database. Now that the processing is complete, we could attach to it via the Analysis Services Cube Editor's Data tab or through another OLAP-enabled client, such as Microsoft Excel's PivotTable service. OLAP browsers that are available through such applications as Excel or from other third-party sources provide an interactive environment for organizing the dimensions and measures that make up the cube, allowing for multiple points of view and data analysis.

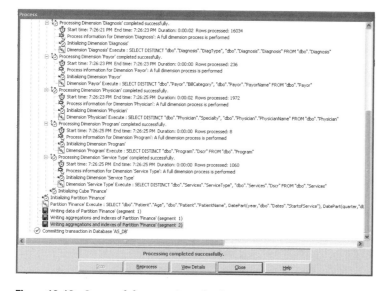

Figure 10-18. *Successful processing of cube*

Building SRS Reports with MDX

Multidimensional expressions (MDX) are used to query OLAP data cubes in much the same way that SQL interrogates SQL Server databases. Though MDX shares some of the same attributes as SQL, it can be used to answer questions that would take much more logic and coding to answer with SQL. When designing OLAP reports for SRS, just as when writing SQL statements for relational databases, you will need to be able to write MDX to be able to utilize cube data.

Let's look at a fairly simple MDX statement that we can use with the Finance cube. Listing 10-2 shows an MDX statement that lists the quantity of services for a period of time, by service type. It is a single dimension result.

Listing 10-2. *Simple MDX for Finance Cube*

```
SELECT{[Measures].[measureslevel].[Quantity]} on columns,
{[Service Type].[Service Type].members} on rows
From Finance
```

The output of the query can be seen in Figure 10-19. The MDX designer is called MDX Sample Application, which ships with SQL Server Analysis Server. I have used other MDX designer applications in the past but there are few that provide a graphical design environment. Fortunately Microsoft will include one in the SQL Server 2005 that will eliminate many of the syntactical types of errors that I find common with MDX.

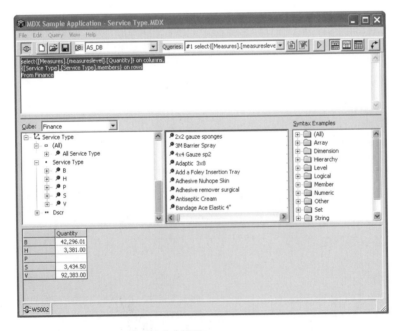

Figure 10-19. *Output of simple MDX query*

Let's add a little more to the basic MDX query before moving to SRS. Listing 10-3 shows a slightly more advanced query that we will use for our SRS report. In this query we use a calculated member to derive an average cost per service type. Calculated members can be defined when the cube is designed or in the MDX query by specifying With Member in the query and then defining what values the calculated member will be derived from. In our query we will use the cost per visit divided by quantity of visits as the calculated member value. Calculated members can be very useful in MDX to ascertain values that might otherwise be unavailable in the defined measures. This query joins two dimensions, the Service Type and the Charge-Time. In this case we specify a year, 2002, and all of the levels beneath it.

Listing 10-3. *MDX with Calculated Member*

```
With Member [Measures].[Average Cost Per Service]
as '([Measures].[cost]) / ( [Measures].[quantity])'
SELECT {AddCalculatedMembers([Measures].members)} on columns,
NON EMPTY CROSSJOIN({DESCENDANTS([Service Type].[All Service Type],
[Service Type].[Service Type], SELF_AND_AFTER)},
{DESCENDANTS( [Charge Time].[2002],[Year],Self_And_After)}) on rows
FROM Finance
```

As you can see in Figure 10-20, the results now have levels associated with them, first the Service Type and then the ChargeTime.

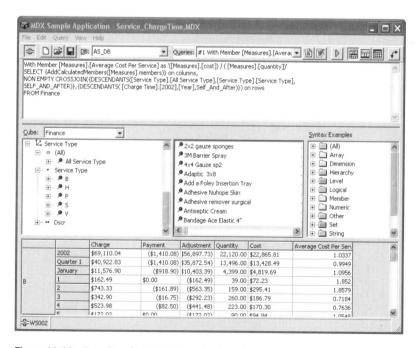

Figure 10-20. *Results of MDX with calculated measure*

Now let's go to SRS and add the MDX query that we just created to a report. We will create a new report and data source for the purpose. The new data source provider will be Microsoft OLE DB Provider for OLAP Services 8.0. We will enter the Data Source on the second tab of the data source Properties box as the name of the OLAP server we are connecting to, called WS002 in our case. We will leave Windows Authentication selected and choose our OLAP database, AS_DB.

Next, add a blank report to our project and create the data set. Like SQL, MDX can be pasted as text and the field names will automatically be generated for you to use in the report. You will, however, have to use the generic query designer, since SRS 2000 does not have an OLAP query designer. (You'll be happy to know that SRS 2005 does.) However, you will notice in Figure 10-21 that the results displayed in the query designer within SRS are very different from the output in the MDX Sample Application. The results in SRS are flattened, showing a record for each aggregate or grouping. SRS was forced to render the dataset two-dimensionally, with many NULL values where the values would have been otherwise aggregated.

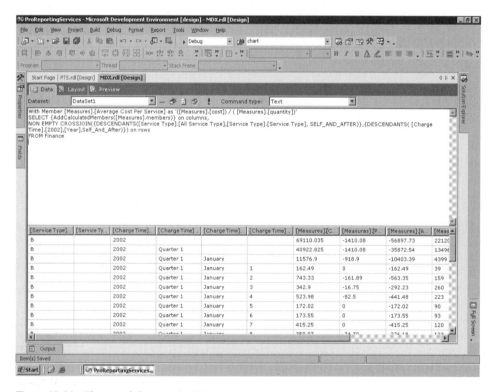

Figure 10-21. *Flattened data set in SRS*

With the data set defined, we can create a matrix report like the ones we have already created, adding all of the formatting, filters, parameters, and interactive functionality such as drilldown and drill-through. As you can see in Figure 10-22, the rendered matrix report example looks and feels similar to a standard SQL report. The added benefit of using MDX and OLAP for SRS reports is performance. Because the data in an OLAP cube is preaggregated, the report is processed in far less time than it would take for a standard SQL query to derive the same information.

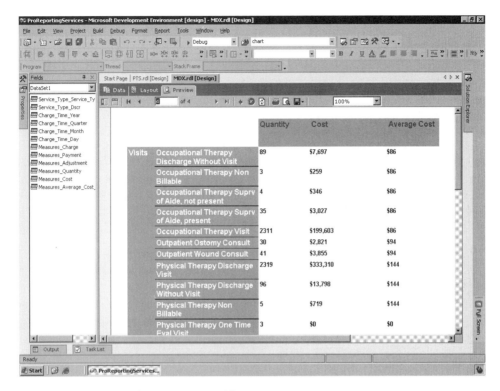

Figure 10-22. *Output of matrix report with MDX*

In SQL Server 2005, Microsoft will add enhanced functionality to both SRS and Analysis Services that will make building and reporting on OLAP data much easier. There will, for example, be a graphical MDX query designer that will lessen the time to build custom MDX queries. In addition, Analysis Services itself will make building entire OLAP solutions, from design to transformation to processing, a step-by-step procedure that can be accomplished in minutes, not hours or days.

While SRS and OLAP are complementary technologies for an overall BI solution, it is important to remember that they serve different purposes. SRS, at least in its current incarnation, is a reporting platform, not a cube browser, but can still be used to effectively deliver reports from OLAP sources. The BI platform consists of many clients and technologies, as we have seen, and SRS is but one tool of many. In the future we may see it take a lead role by being able to accommodate controls that will populate on the delivered reports, so that a basic SRS report can become a central point of delivery for the kinds of tools that can successfully analyze and mine analytical data.

Summary

In this chapter, we explored how to incorporate SRS into a Business Intelligence model, specifically looking at the business model of a software development company. From lead to customer support, understanding how to transform and analyze the data that drives your business will help you make important business decisions. Delivering that data to decision makers is a pivotal link in the BI chain. With SRS, Microsoft has provided organizations with another tool that can easily tap into and extend the reach of crucial data. Working with other applications and products in the Microsoft BI platform—such as SharePoint Portal Server, Analysis Services, and Office—SRS will prove to be an invaluable BI tool now and in the future. With the release of SQL Server 2005 looming on the horizon, let's now take a look at what enhancements we can expect to see in SRS in the coming months. Chapter 11 focuses on the future of SRS.

CHAPTER 11

■ ■ ■

Future SRS

In this book, we have examined many aspects of Microsoft SQL Server 2000 Reporting Services—but this is the just the beginning. Microsoft SQL Server 2000 Reporting Services (SRS 2000) is the first edition of the reporting application to be a strategic part of the Microsoft Business Intelligence platform. While SRS 2000 has many great features and is very impressive for a version "1.0" product, Microsoft has a lot of plans for the long-term future of SRS. In the near term, we can all look forward to the next version of SQL Reporting Services (SRS 2005) that will ship with SQL Server 2005. In this chapter, we are going to provide a broad overview of a number of the features that are planned for SRS 2005:

- Tighter integration with SQL Server

- Improved integration with SQL Analysis Services

- More options for developers

- End user ad hoc Report Writer

Tighter Integration with SQL Server

While SRS 2000 was essentially released as an add-on to SQL Server 2000, SRS 2005 is baked right into SQL Server 2005. This gives you a richer and more integrated experience. With SQL Server 2005, all of the management of SRS can be handled directly from within SQL 2005's new SQL Server Management Studio. This is a replacement for the Enterprise Manager and other tools, and can manage all SQL Server 2005 features including Reporting Services, Analysis Services, and, of course, SQL Server itself. You can even manage remote instances of SQL Mobile Edition.

There is also the new Business Intelligence Development Studio, which provides you with a Visual Studio–like environment for creating, editing, and deploying reports. Whereas before you had to have Visual Studio to create and debug reports, with SQL 2005 and SRS 2005 you can do it out of the box without purchasing an additional product.

The New Management Studio

As many of you know already, the management tools for SRS 2005 and the new SQL Server 2005 Management Studio (MS) will be tightly integrated. Figure 11-1 shows how the report server can be browsed from within Management Studio.

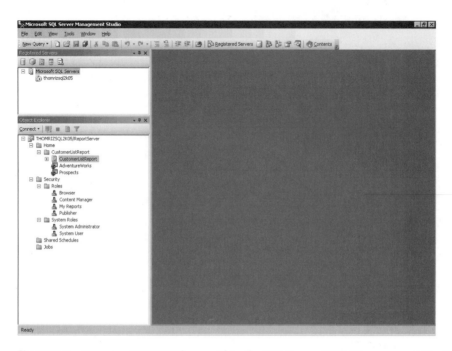

Figure 11-1. *Browsing SRS 2005 from within the SQL Server 2005 Management Studio*

You can also perform many actions from within MS that previously required you to browse to the report server with a web browser, such as setting report properties, maintaining shared schedules, and so on. This makes SRS 2005 features accessible directly within the IDE. Figure 11-2 shows a report's properties being accessed from within the IDE. Of course, with SQL 2005 you can still use the web-based Report Manager from any system with an appropriate browser.

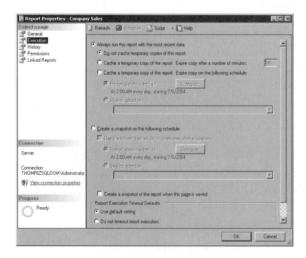

Figure 11-2. *Setting report properties from within the Management Studio IDE*

The New Business Intelligence Development Studio

SQL Server 2005 includes a new feature specifically for working with the SQL 2005 Business Intelligence features. Of course, this includes SRS 2005. This feature is built on the Visual Studio IDE, so anyone familiar with Visual Studio will feel right at home. Figure 11-3 shows the IDE available in SRS 2005.

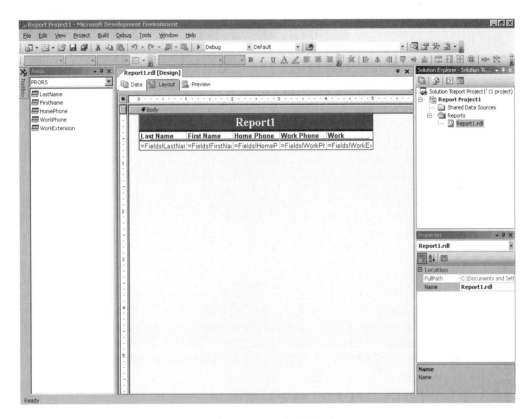

Figure 11-3. *Business Intelligence Development Studio in SRS 2005*

Because the BI Development Studio is based on the Visual Studio IDE, it will provide a common user experience for developers, database administrators, query builders, report writers, and others involved in the process of the reporting life cycle. Many of the features available in the BI Development Studio are the same as those that Visual Studio delivers with Visual Studio 2005. Another benefit of the BI Development Studio being included in SQL Server 2005 is that it provides you with a report development IDE, so you no longer need to purchase any version of Visual Studio in order to build reports using a graphical interface.

Tight Integration with SQL Analysis Services

One of the features that we missed the most in writing this book was an MDX query builder that would work with SRS 2000. While some third-party tools existed, the query builder included with SRS 2000 is just a simple text editor. There is no graphic design interface for building MDX queries, making it cumbersome and time consuming to use Analysis Services as a data source for SRS 2000. For more details on what you can do with SRS 2000 and Analysis Services, take a look at Chapter 10. For information about how the experience improves in SQL 2005, read on.

With SRS 2005 all of this changes; it has a query designer built right in. Now you can easily query data stored in cubes and use them as a source of data for your reports. Start out by adding your Analysis Services data sources to your project in the new Business Intelligence Development Studio and then view them graphically in the designer, as shown in Figure 11-4.

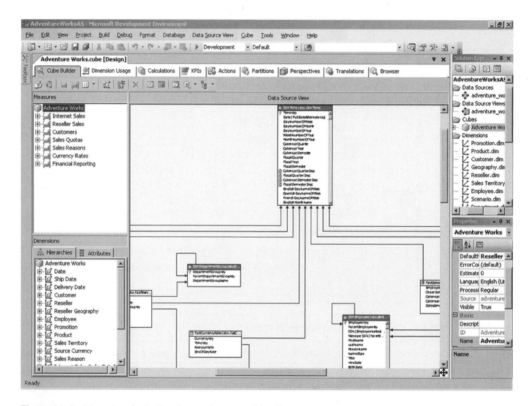

Figure 11-4. *View Analysis Services cubes graphically*

With SRS 2005 you can build your queries graphically and then immediately see the results, in a way very similar to how you would use the SQL query-building tools in SQL 2000 Enterprise Manager or SRS 2000.

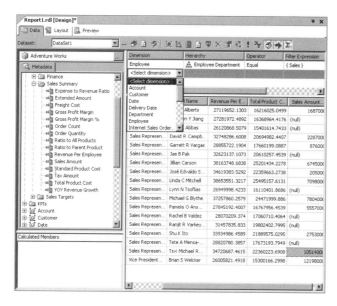

Figure 11-5. *Create MDX queries and view the results*

This tight integration with Analysis Services gives you the option to use the powerful capabilities of Analysis Services to structure and analyze your data and then use SRS 2005 to present it to your users. Using Analysis Services can allow you to put data into a format that has more meaning to the user without creating extremely complicated and often long-running queries.

Remember that not only can you have a report that is based solely on data from Analysis Services, you can also have a report that combines data from a relational database and from an Analysis Services cube all in the same report. With SRS 2005 you will be able to add data from both to your reports, using a graphical query designer.

More Options for Developers

In this book you saw some of the ways in which you can integrate reporting into your custom solutions. With SRS 2000, you were primarily limited to interacting with SRS through the Web services–based APIs and to rendering your reports through URLs. With SRS 2005 and VS.NET 2005, there are a number of new options available to you.

Report Viewer Controls

One welcome change for developers is the inclusion of new viewer controls for both Windows and the Web. These new viewer controls give you a much easier way to quickly embed reporting capabilities into your application without the need to create your own custom viewer. With SRS 2000, it was simple enough to embed a web browser control into a Windows Form and then navigate to the report URL to render the report. This is what we did in Chapter 6 when developing a viewer for our custom application.

However, the new Windows Form control that ships with SRS 2005 simplifies things even further by allowing you to just drop the viewer control on a form and set a few properties. This new control also means that there is no more dependency on Internet Explorer to render a report. You can see an example of this in Figure 11-6.

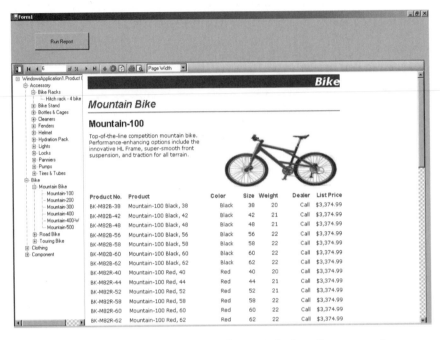

Figure 11-6. *Viewing an SRS report using the new Windows Form control*

Rendering Reports Without a Server

For many software projects, one of the main limitations of SRS 2000 was that it required you to have a server running SRS. This made it difficult or impossible in some environments, and in certain scenarios, to utilize SRS as the reporting mechanism—for example, if you had a user with a laptop who needed to run reports while disconnected from the network where your SRS server was located. As a result, users often fell back on technologies such as Business Objects Crystal Reports or Data Dynamics Active Reports. With SRS 2005, this problem has been solved. The same new rendering controls that make it easier to render your reports with SRS 2005 make it possible to render them without a server at all.

These new controls can render reports without the need to have access to an SRS server. With SRS 2005, you now have a single technology reporting system that can provide a viable solution across a wide variety of applications and circumstances. No longer will you have to use one technology for applications without access to a server and an entirely different and incompatible technology for those applications with access to a server.

This implementation is well thought out and well implemented in SRS 2005. The controls use the same RDL as the SRS server and offer the option to render reports locally without the need for an SRS server. Local report rendering supports background processing and offline snapshots, thus providing a very powerful solution for a variety of needs. With local rendering you can distribute report generation to local systems, provide reporting capabilities to users while disconnected from the network, and more. You can also use the same control to view reports rendered by an SRS server. This gives you a great option to use the same user interface regardless of whether or not you have an SRS server.

The beauty of this is that the exact same report can be deployed two different ways depending on your need. You can deploy directly to a desktop system where connectivity to an SRS server is not desirable or possible, and to an SRS server when scalability and enterprise features such as report history, running reports on a schedule, and push delivery are important. This also offers some great options if you need to generate reports on applications running on a laptop.

Use DataSets as Data Sources

One feature that developers are going to love is that you can pass in DataSets, or any object that implements the IEnumerable interface, as a data source. The IEnumerable interface exposes an enumerator for your data, allowing SRS 2005 to iterate through the data in a way similar to how you would access it in a foreach loop.

With the embedded controls, you essentially set properties on the control (such as an array of data sources), the report RDL, and options (such as Show Toolbar and Show Print) and then call the Render method. Many of the optional properties are similar to the options for the URL rendering available in SRS 2000.

New End User Reporting Tool

SQL Server 2005 will include a new ad hoc query tool that will allow end users to select and filter information from a reporting solution, and then use this information to create and view their own reports. This new feature is called ActiveViews.

ActiveViews is arguably one of the most important new features of SQL 2005 because it enables end user ad hoc reporting for SRS customers "out of the box" for the very first time.

ActiveViews uses SRS 2005 to manage and render all of the reports created with the tool. It uses metadata to describe the data available to the end users and to put it into terms that most end users can more easily understand. It allows you to define fields, relationships, and aggregations that end users will use to create their reports. This metadata isolates users from all of the database-specific terminology and allows them to see how information is related without them needing to understand the technical details of the data and its structures and relationships.

This metadata can be initially created using a wizard that is included with SRS 2005, as shown in Figure 11-7, and then the results can be modified to suit your particular needs. You can edit auto-generated relationships, change auto-generated names, and more. This allows you to create a user experience where your users will see exactly what you want them to see, and it will work the way you have defined it to work.

Figure 11-7. *Creating metadata for a report*

Once the metadata has been created, users can begin to use it. If they have the ActiveViews server installed, a new button will appear in the Report Manager labeled New Report. If the end user has appropriate permission, they can use this to create a new report or to modify an existing one. In addition to needing the necessary permission in order to modify a report, the report must also have been created using the tool or converted to provide the metadata used by ActiveViews. The ActiveViews interface allows the user to select items to display on the report, as shown in Figure 11-8.

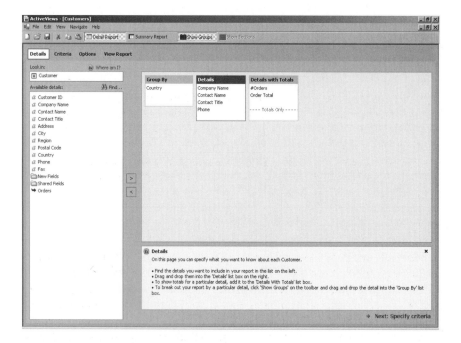

Figure 11-8. *Selecting report details using ActiveViews*

The user can also set up report criteria that limit the data displayed according to the criteria selected. In the following example, shown in Figure 11-9, the user is selecting information only for customers in Germany who have placed more than five orders, or have orders totaling more than $1000.

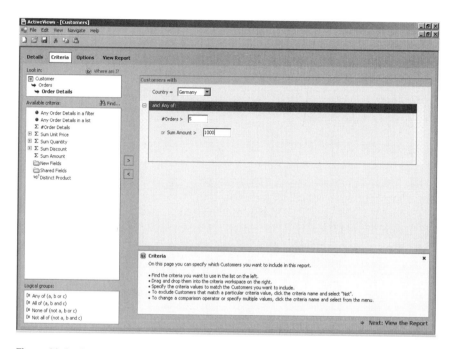

Figure 11-9. *Setting report criteria using ActiveViews*

As you can see, ActiveViews provides a powerful reporting tool that allows end users to create the reports that they need using a simple wizard-driven user interface. This hides most of the complexity normally associated with creating reports, such as building SQL queries and stored procedures, creating relationships between data, and dealing with often cryptic names and syntax. This new feature of SRS 2005 can go a long way toward allowing end users to directly create reports and reduce the burden on developers and IT staff in your enterprise.

Beyond SQL 2005

Microsoft will undoubtedly integrate SRS more tightly into other products in the future. Already there are rumors that many of its Business System applications, such as Microsoft CRM, will use SRS as its future reporting tool. Given SRS's use of metadata to drive the application, and Microsoft's inclusion of ActiveViews technologies, this seems highly likely. In addition, the Microsoft Operations Manager (MOM) team has demonstrated the use of SRS for their management reports in MOM 2005, and the SQL Server Best Practices Analyzer already uses SRS for its reports.

You have already seen in this book some ways to use SRS to integrate reports into SharePoint Portal Server and CRM. Additional integration with both products also seems highly likely given that they are both Microsoft products that can benefit from the reporting capabilities of SRS. CRM makes extensive use of reporting and SRS seems likely to replace its current reporting technology. For SharePoint one of its primary goals is to bring data together in one place, and what better data to include than that from SRS. Microsoft is hard at work building report web parts that SharePoint users can embed in their applications to create rich Business Intelligence portals.

Integration into other Microsoft products such as Office, Small Business Manager, Great Plains, and others can be expected as well. I would expect that many Microsoft products that currently feature Crystal Reports technology will have Microsoft Reporting Services in them in the future.

Summary

As you can see, Microsoft has a lot planned for SRS. With SQL 2005, SRS will provide features that address many of the requests that users had using SRS 2000: new viewer controls for Windows Forms and Web Forms, a new MDX query builder, and, one of the most requested, an end user ad hoc reporting tool.

With SRS 2005, Microsoft has given users a viable option for the reporting needs of a single desktop, a department, and an entire enterprise. Microsoft is clearly indicating that SRS is a part of their plans going forward, so I think we can safely say we will see even more exciting new features and deeper integration with other Microsoft products with each new release.

Index

Numbers

0–3 security levels, explanations of, 217
3D Visual Effect, applying to charts, 66–67

Symbols

##, significance of, 35
& parameter for URL access, description of, 125
/ (slash), using with ListChildren method in Report Publisher, 156
? parameter for URL access, description of, 125
@ (at) characters, using with parameterized stored procedures, 24–26, 43
= (equals sign), preceding expressions with, 46

A

AcctPeriodMonth parameter, adding functions to, 166–167
AcctPeriodYear parameter, adding functions to, 166–167
ACT (Application Center Test)
    testing performance with, 190–191
    viewing test results in, 193–194
Active Directory
    advisory about querying of, 42
    querying for report delivery, 203–204
    setting up junderling Windows account in, 221
ActiveViews ad hoc reporting tool in SQL Server 2005, features of, 273–275
Add Web Reference dialog box, displaying for Web services APIs, 135, 152
administrators, report properties available to, 227
Adobe Acrobat, viewing document mapping in, 82
advanced queries, creating, 19–20. *See also* queries
aggregations, setting for data cubes, 260–261
aliases, example of, 20
Analysis Manager, designing OLAP cubes with, 258–261
Analysis Services
    building SRS reports for, 252–265
    and tighter integration with SRS, 270–271

using for BI (business intelligence) reports, 238
AR Reconciliation report
    configuring History properties for, 167
    creating shared schedule for, 164–165
    with default parameters, 169
    executing and caching, 173–175
    in Report Manager, 167
    report parameters for, 166
assemblies, accessing from embedded code, 110–111. *See also* custom assemblies
assembly references, adding to reports, 115–116
at (@) characters, using with parameterized stored procedures, 24–26, 43
auditing reports
    with SRS auditing, 229–230
    with Windows auditing, 231
authentication, overview of, 220–221

B

Basic Authentication, using with SRS Viewer, 136
BI (business intelligence) applications
    comparing, 265
    creating with CRM, 238–242
    creating with SharePoint Portal Server, 246–250
    customizing with help desk, 242–245
    and MDX (multidimensional expressions), 262–265
    and OLAP cube design, 258–261
    for project management, 250–252
BI Development Studio SQL Server 2005, features of, 269
Blank values, using with data sets, 39–40
BLOBs (Binary Large Objects), significance of, 68
Block layout, choosing for reports, 76
bold formatting, applying to fields, 80
bookmark links, adding to reports, 88–89
BookmarkID, adding to Employee Name field, 88
bookmarks, description of, 86
borders, adding to reports, 79
Branch table, description of, 12–13
Branch_DS data set, creating, 96
Branch_URL parameter, creating, 90

forums.apress.com

FOR PROFESSIONALS BY PROFESSIONALS™

JOIN THE APRESS FORUMS AND BE PART OF OUR COMMUNITY. You'll find discussions that cover topics of interest to IT professionals, programmers, and enthusiasts just like you. If you post a query to one of our forums, you can expect that some of the best minds in the business—especially Apress authors, who all write with *The Expert's Voice*™—will chime in to help you. Why not aim to become one of our most valuable participants (MVPs) and win cool stuff? Here's a sampling of what you'll find:

DATABASES
Data drives everything.

Share information, exchange ideas, and discuss any database programming or administration issues.

INTERNET TECHNOLOGIES AND NETWORKING
Try living without plumbing (and eventually IPv6).

Talk about networking topics including protocols, design, administration, wireless, wired, storage, backup, certifications, trends, and new technologies.

JAVA
We've come a long way from the old Oak tree.

Hang out and discuss Java in whatever flavor you choose: J2SE, J2EE, J2ME, Jakarta, and so on.

MAC OS X
All about the Zen of OS X.

OS X is both the present and the future for Mac apps. Make suggestions, offer up ideas, or boast about your new hardware.

OPEN SOURCE
Source code is good; understanding (open) source is better.

Discuss open source technologies and related topics such as PHP, MySQL, Linux, Perl, Apache, Python, and more.

PROGRAMMING/BUSINESS
Unfortunately, it is.

Talk about the Apress line of books that cover software methodology, best practices, and how programmers interact with the "suits."

WEB DEVELOPMENT/DESIGN
Ugly doesn't cut it anymore, and CGI is absurd.

Help is in sight for your site. Find design solutions for your projects and get ideas for building an interactive Web site.

SECURITY
Lots of bad guys out there—the good guys need help.

Discuss computer and network security issues here. Just don't let anyone else know the answers!

TECHNOLOGY IN ACTION
Cool things. Fun things.

It's after hours. It's time to play. Whether you're into LEGO® MINDSTORMS™ or turning an old PC into a DVR, this is where technology turns into fun.

WINDOWS
No defenestration here.

Ask questions about all aspects of Windows programming, get help on Microsoft technologies covered in Apress books, or provide feedback on any Apress Windows book.

HOW TO PARTICIPATE:
Go to the Apress Forums site at **http://forums.apress.com/**.
Click the New User link.